THE SURVIVOR

THE
SURVIVOR

JIMMY EVANS
& MARTIN SHORT

MAINSTREAM
PUBLISHING
EDINBURGH AND LONDON

First published in Great Britain in 2001 by
MAINSTREAM PUBLISHING COMPANY (EDINBURGH) LTD
7 Albany Street
Edinburgh EH1 3UG

ISBN 1 84018 674 7

This edition, 2002
Reprinted 2003

A catalogue record for this book is available from the British Library

Typeset in Van Djick

Printed in Great Britain by
Creative Print and Design Wales, Ebbw Vale

Contents

PROLOGUE

Taking on the Liberty-Takers

NOTHING'S going to stop me. George Foreman has blown my life apart so I'm going to blow his apart. I've got a beautiful home, a beautiful life and a beautiful wife . . . but I've just found out that this creep has been lurking around in the background whenever he's had the chance. And I'm very active. I'm often away on business. And he's wormed his way into my wife's affections. He's broken the underworld code. Everybody's warned him. Even she's warned him. He knows he's guilty and he's got no excuse. Now I'm going to blow his bollocks off.

Tonight he knows I'll be coming round to his poxy little council flat, so he's lined up his brother, Freddie Foreman, and all his other pals to defend him, but so what? This mob has a fearsome reputation for wiping people out but I don't care. I don't really give a fuck who they are. Whoever invades my private life, my home life, my marriage, I'll do the same thing to them as I'm going to do to George.

It's 17 December 1964. We've got there at eight so it's already dark. Just me and Dave Norman. The only reason I've brought Dave along is because I've been told that scumbag George has a little boy and I don't want him to rush to the door and stick his head under his old man's arm as soon as I ring the bell. I'm going up there with the sole intention of blowing Foreman's bollocks off, so I know I'll be aiming low, level with a kid's head. That's why I have to make sure I don't shoot his kid as well. Later I'll experience no such compassion when this mob chucks a petrol bomb right through my little girl's bedroom window.

But now I send Dave on ahead, to draw Foreman out and report back to me. Then I'm going to tell him to leave. Only one man's going to do this job. Me.

So up Dave goes and, keeping to my script, he tells Foreman, 'I'm Mary's brother. She's down in the car. She wants to see you. She's hurt.' But Foreman doesn't come down. Even if she's hurt, he isn't going to show his face.

Then Dave comes straight back down and says, 'I didn't see any kid but please don't go up there, Jimmy. Forget it. The lights are out, the landing light too, and they're all there. They're waiting for you mob-handed.'

'How do you know?' I say, and Dave says, 'When he came to the door, he called out, 'Fred! Fred! They're here! They're here!'

That makes me feel a lot better. If it's not just George up there but brother Fred and all his familiars, I might be able to do a lot more damage. I've calculated that George isn't going to be on his own because I've seen him with his pals earlier this day in Cable Street. They've seen me too, raging like a volcano, so they know I'm in no mood for a quiet chat.

Now I'm thinking about all the people they are supposed to have killed and shot and 'disappeared'. That's their reputation in criminal circles. They're called the 'Underworld Undertakers'. More like the Underworld Liberty-Takers, I'm thinking.

So I say, 'Go home, Dave, and forget about it, I'll be OK.' I leave him in his car, and up I go. I'm wearing an Aquascutum raincoat, with only one button done up, and carrying the double-barrelled sawn-off shotgun underneath. On this raincoat the pockets have open flaps going through to your clothing underneath, so I'm holding the gun through the right-hand flap. No mask, no hat. They'll know it's me.

Later Hungarian George, the printer, tells me that he's there that night inside the flat with the Foremans: 'I didn't know that was you coming up, Jimmy. I just went up to do some business and they were all running all over the place, about eight of them, messing around with their guns.'

As I walk up these grubby, urine-stinking tenement stairs, I'm thinking of all the crap I've heard about this little mob – 'They kill . . . They do this . . . They do that . . .' Everybody's been telling me what monsters they are – and I'm saying to myself, if there's going to be any monsters around here tonight, they're gonna be me. That's why I don't just only have the shotgun. I also have a Cobra .38 down my belt, but if you hit someone in the bollocks with a .38, it ain't going to have the same repercussions. This little Cobra's just my back-up piece.

So as I approach this flat, I can see they've left the door open. How fucking Mickey Mouse must they be to think that I'm going to creep inside, when I know they'll be waiting there for me? Do they think I'm fucking stupid? They're acting like amateurs. They know I'm coming so they should have people waiting downstairs in a little van or something. Then when they see me on my way up they can slip out and follow, so I won't be able to get out again. But instead they're all sitting huddled upstairs, waiting to hear my footfall on the stairs. Real Mickey Mouse gangsters.

But I'm not that stupid and as I approach I knock a couple of times. Then I call through the door, 'Are you coming out, you fucking jellybaby?', because I know he can't back down in front of his pals. And, according to Hungarian George, this really does put George Foreman on the spot. Now he has to go to the door, otherwise his so-called gangster friends will brand him a coward. He'll lose face as well as bollocks.

Sure enough, it's George Foreman himself who comes to the door and he says, 'Yes?' And he's putting on a pretence: he has a serviette in his hand as though he's halfway through his evening meal.

So I say, 'What about my fucking wife?'

And he takes a bow, wipes his mouth, gives me a ceremonial underarm wave into the flat and says, 'Come in and let's talk about it.'

As he stands up to his full height, I say, 'The only thing that's going to do any talking around here is this', and I lift out this sawn-off shotgun and I add, 'Happy Christmas, you cunt!'

When he sees the rusty old chopped-down barrel, he goes up on his toes. And though the main lights are out, he's opened his door so wide that there's a bit of light coming from the passage behind. So just when he goes up on his toes, I can see his eyes popping out like organ stops. He knows it's pay-day.

Now I'm standing with the end of the barrels just three feet from his tackle. A foot further away and those long-reach cartridges in the breech would cut him in half. But that's not what I want.

Then I fire.

His feet leave the ground and he hits the wall at the end of the passage. The shot has carried him right back and, as he's flying, it spins him round and his foot bangs the door shut just as I'm about to kick it in and have a pop at the rest of them. I don't know what stops me but straight after the shooting, there's a silence, then screams from adjoining flats and windows going up and lights going on. So I keep my collar up and walk calmly down the stairs. I get to the bottom and out into the yard, then I look up expecting to see a row of heads with guns all pointing at me. But there's none of that. It seems like they're keeping well out of the way.

Mission accomplished. George won't be ruining any more marriages.

I had decided to use that particular shotgun only at very short notice. It had Damascus barrels and I was using number five cartridges, partly because five is my lucky number (which over the years has made it very unlucky for some). And I was lucky because once I'd sawn most of these barrels off the shotgun could have blown up in my hands. These number fives contained about 280 little shot. Later, when this thing came to court, they stuck 279 in a jar and used them as evidence. They couldn't find the last one but they'd dug all the rest out of his groin and the wall behind him.

A few days later Charlie Kray telephoned me to say that this single cartridge had done George Foreman plenty of damage: 'It went through his groin like a tennis ball. Blew away his prostrate, half his arse and half his cock. He's had two operations and he's got a few more to come.' Then Charlie went on, 'It was only a matter of time. If you hadn't done it someone else would have done. That's the type of person he is. People can't leave him in their wives' company for two minutes.' Imagine. Charlie Kray was Freddie Foreman's business partner at the time and he's saying all this to me. Then he added, 'Ronnie sends you a message. He says: tell Jimmy Evans he did well. That will show those South London mugs what the East End is all about.' Funny, Ronnie Kray just hated South Londoners.

There's been lots of times when a villain's been fucking about with another villain's wife and there's been arguments, but I don't think there's been another time, ever, when someone has taken a weapon and blown that person's bollocks off. In Sicily maybe but not in London. Here people say it but don't do it.

After this, nobody could come up to me and say, 'You never did anything about him fucking about with your old woman, did you, Jimmy?' No one could ever say that to me but, if they dared, they could always go up to Freddie Foreman and say, 'Oh, what about the fellow who blew your brother's bollocks off, Fred? You've never done anything about that, have you?'

But now – more than 35 years on – Freddie Foreman claims he did all sorts of things to avenge the family honour, like murdering Tommy 'Ginger' Marks two weeks later, on 2 January 1965. That's another story – Fred and his crowd turn up in a car in Bethnal Green just when Ginger, me and a couple of other pals are going to oblige a jeweller's. Only they don't kill me, or any of the others, because they're not looking for us that night. They don't even recognise me. Instead they shoot Ginger, drag him into their car and he's never seen again. Body-snatchers as well as undertakers.

Today Freddie Foreman has belatedly confessed to killing Ginger Marks on the grounds that Ginger had been my accomplice the night I shot off brother George's manhood. But Ginger wasn't with me that night – only Dave Norman who didn't look a bit like Ginger. And Freddie Foreman never did anything to Dave, even though both Foremans knew exactly who he was.

No. The only reason why Fred Foreman would have wanted to kill Ginger Marks and get him out of the way was because of a conversation that had taken place a few days prior to Ginger's murder. Ginger repeated this conversation to me and another pal just an hour or so before he was shot and his body snatched. He told us that, a couple of days earlier, an old pal of ours named Colin 'Dukey' Osbourne, who was at this point on Freddie's firm, had come over to the East End and met up with Ginger. And according to Ginger, Dukey said, 'Tell Jimmy not to pay too much attention to the Foremans. It's only a matter of time before the little mob who were on the train job put two and two together about what's been going on between Freddie Foreman and his pal, Tommy Butler.'

' The little mob who were on the train job' were the notorious Great Train Robbers, who had got away with £2,500,000 in cash 17 months earlier, on 8 August 1963. And Tommy Butler was the detective leading the hunt for all the robbers who had avoided arrest in the first weeks after the robbery – the likes of John Daly, Roy James and, much later, Jimmy White, Buster Edwards, Charlie Wilson and Bruce Reynolds. Butler was getting the glory for nabbing them all.

But while all this was going on, Butler used to frequent Freddie Foreman's pub, as did another detective on the trail of the train robbers, Frank Williams. Both Butler and Williams were mates of Fred's. Later he claimed he used these connections only to help the robbers – by being the middleman for the return of some of the stolen cash – but, according to Dukey, that was only his cover story. The truth, said Dukey, was that while Fred Foreman was pretending to help the robbers, he was helping the very detective who, with a horde of press photographers in tow, was rounding them up one by one. So was Foreman marking Butler's card as to their whereabouts? Was Freddie telling Tommy Butler where they all were?

See, Dukey Osbourne had sussed that Foreman wasn't the staunch fellow he was claiming to be. That's why he told Ginger it was 'only a matter of time' before the train mob 'put two and two together' about Foreman and his 'pal' Butler.

And as Ginger – whom I always called by his real name, Tommy – said to me, 'If Fred Foreman is such a good pal of the mob who were on the train, and at the same time he's Tommy Butler's pal, how come they've got 30 fucking years?'

OK. So why didn't Freddie shoot Dukey, the source of the story? Well, Dukey wasn't shouting it from the rooftops – he knew that Foreman and Co might kill him if he did that – but Dukey trusted and liked Ginger Marks. Dukey also used to work with me. He even stayed at my home a couple of times. So Dukey felt he could confide in Ginger and told him all about Foreman's relationship with Butler. So, of course, a few days later Ginger repeated the whole story to me, because we were very close and he knew I'd shot George Foreman only days before. But though he told me, I don't think he ever told anyone else that Dukey Osbourne was the source. Instead he was just telling all and sundry that Foreman and Butler were hand-in-glove. And Ginger was indiscreet. He used to talk to everyone in the East End. He knew everybody – he worked with different teams – including lots of people who may have reported straight back to Fred Foreman.

So today when Fred says he shot Ginger to avenge me castrating George, that's 'bollocks' – if you'll excuse the term. Now he claims he killed Ginger for being with me the night I shot his creepy brother George when he knows that's a load of crap. But he has to give that excuse, otherwise all his cronies will realise he was nothing but a coward with police friends in high places.

And that's the mistake I made. When I shot George Foreman I had no idea what clout those brothers had with Scotland Yard. None of us straight faces in the underworld had the slightest notion. At that time we did not realise Freddie Foreman's strength inside the Metropolitan Police. We did not know scumbags like this could exist. That's why for the next ten years and more I was the victim of a constant bombardment of fit-ups. The Foremans I could not give a fuck about, but try dodging the bent Yard when they are conspiring to put you away.

I could have had a nice little war with Freddie Foreman if his allies had been nothing more than a few other so-called gangsters, but instead they were the crooked cream of the Yard CID. Yes, I had plenty of guns but they had plenty of guns. And they could easily make petrol bombs. Worse still, so Reggie Kray later told me, they also had access to a crematorium: Freddie Foreman's standard means of getting rid of bodies. And on top of all this, they had the full artillery of a crooked legal system where police would engineer fit-ups by giving perjured evidence to suit not just Scotland Yard's own notions of rough justice and retribution, but also to do favours for their own special pals in the underworld.

So what was it that could turn a man like Freddie Foreman – now a self-declared murderer – into someone far deadlier with the police than he ever was with a gun? You have to ask what hold, what leverage for blackmail, did this man have on the Yard that so many top cops would feel compelled to comply with his wishes? What secrets did he know? What bodies (other than gangsters' bodies) had he disposed of? What sordid crimes had he helped cover up, so that men of the rank of Detective Chief Superintendent Tommy Butler would collude with his vendetta against me?

This book tells every detail of that vendetta, a vendetta which I survived in better nick than all those slags put together.

But that's the story of my life. I am the survivor.

THE SURVIVOR

ONE

'Mrs Bridger, Your Jimmy's
Lying Under the Trains Again'

WHEN I was nine we were living in Gainsborough Road, Hackney Wick: me, my mother and my father – or as we East End kids used to call our parents, my old lady and my old man. We were the Bridger family. Right opposite us – between the public baths on one side and a factory on the other – was what we called the Red Path. It led up to the goods yard which us kids considered ripe for plunder but, while the others went there to rob the freight trains, I used to enjoy lying down between the tracks under the trains while they were being shunted along, grinding and clanking, above me.

I used to have more fun lying under the trains than seeing what was in the freight boxes. The older boys would be busting open the wagon doors and seeing what they could nick but I preferred the sense of security that I found between those rails. Right above me I could see flames and flashes as firemen stoked furnaces while the engines roared over me. This would excite me. I loved it.

Yes, it might have been dangerous but this was 1940, the Blitz was on and I was probably safer under those moving trains than I would have been running about in the yard. While we were there, nine times out of ten there'd be an air raid. The siren would go but sometimes you wouldn't even see the planes before they dropped their bombs. No worry for me. I was already sheltering under the trains.

The other kids couldn't understand me. They'd go running home and tell my mother, 'Mrs Bridger, Mrs Bridger, your Jimmy's lying under the trains again.' Every time this happened, I would get another hiding. See! Only nine and I was already being grassed by my mates.

I must admit that during the war I led my mother a terrible dance. I got in scrape after scrape but this had been going on ever since I was a tot. I seem to have been programmed from birth to get into trouble.

We had been living in Gainsborough Road since the 1930s in a big, four-storey house that my old man had picked up. It was close to an old coal-yard where two carts had been abandoned, on end with the shafts upwards, each facing the other. These were perfect for brick fights. There'd be one gang from Homerton at one end and us Wick kids at this end, both gangs sheltering behind the carts. This was when I was no more than five or six – around 1936-37 – but I was heaving bricks as good as the next man. We'd get our ammunition and then, when we'd run out, the older boys would shout, 'Jimmy! Get some more ammunition.' Then I've scampered out to get more bricks. I had an ideal container: a jumper my old lady had knitted me. It had a funny colour but it was very useful because I'd hold it out and fill it up with half-bricks and stones to take back and tip behind my gang's cart. Then I'd go and get another lot.

On one of these days, in the heat of battle, something made me look up. I could hear this swishing – I was mesmerised – and suddenly this thing's hit me. It's gone right down in the top of my head. It turned out to be half a slate. Someone had aimed it perfectly and it hit me right on the fucking head. And I can feel it. I don't want to try and pull it out but I don't know what to do. So I've gone running out of the gate into the main road and the milkman, who knew me and my old lady – he would deliver milk with a horse and cart – he's picked me up, taken me to her and she's screamed and gone mad: 'Look at that jumper! I've just made that for you.'

There's me smothered in claret and bits of fluff off the jumper stuck on it, and she's worried about the jumper. And I'm in shock. So the milkman says, 'I'll take him to Homerton Hospital. You'd better come with us.' And there's my old mum and me on this horse and cart. And every time the cart swayed this slate was wobbling about. Eventually they got me to the hospital and somehow the doctors managed to get the slate out. It must have gone in deep or else it would have fallen out. It was sharp like an axe. I felt like a fucking Mohican. I must have looked like one too.

I survived, as I would survive time and again. The fact that I had lived till I was nine was a miracle because I had revealed a capacity for getting into lethal scrapes ever since I was a tot.

My first memories are of the place where I lived with my old lady and a man who (as I later found out) was my first stepfather. The house was called Forty Acres and it was near the Tarpots Inn in Thundersley, not far from Southend. Thundersley was a little village but it had its own coal-yard where they kept huge cart-horses. When they weren't out on the road, they'd be in the yard munching away on oats. To me they looked colossal. They were also a challenge. I was about three and a half and I can just remember reaching up and swinging on one of these horse's back legs, just where the kneecap bends backwards. I'm hanging on to that bit of flesh and I'm swinging underneath.

One day I was doing this and a woman we knew – Mrs Richards – said to my old lady, 'Hetty, don't look now – don't scream – but he's swinging on the horse's back legs.' So of course my mother ignored Mrs Richards' warning and she's looked. And as she's looked the horse has pissed – it must have been a female – and it's pissed all over me. So now I was screaming because it's boiling hot piss and it's pouring all over me. So I fell off and I threw a lump of coal at it.

I never did that again, but a few years later I did something to another lad who was even more accident-prone than me. In those days, on the back end of every fire engine was a ladder with a great big wheel at one end that the firemen used to turn the ladder. When it wasn't in use you could spin this wheel freely, like a catherine wheel, as I found out in a moment of mischief. One day one of these fire engines was parked in Percy Street, outside my pal Patsy Roberts' house. Now Patsy's old lady was a great big woman – like a washerwoman – but, as I was talking to Patsy, I looked at that great big wheel and I had an idea. 'Let me tie you to it,' I said, and the mug stood for it. He let me do it.

Poor old Patsy was always falling off things and hurting himself, and I knew he'd be mug enough to let me bind him with string to this wheel. I then swung the wheel round so he was doing rapid 360-degree turns, like the girl in a knife-throwing act. He was screaming, 'Stop! Stop!', but I kept swinging the wheel faster and faster until I heard Patsy's old lady shouting, 'You fucking Jimmy Bridger!', and I ran off. A few minutes later my old woman had to face Patsy's mother fuming on our doorstep while I hid upstairs. Another beating for that.

Then there was the time I took a new carpet from our house. It was a runner, about 12 feet long, and I used it to make a tent when I went camping by the canal cut from the river Lea. It rained so the carpet got wet but, instead of lugging it back home, I just chucked it in the river. When my old lady realised what I'd done, she went potty. I told her I'd chucked it in the cut. She said, 'Why?', so I said, 'Well, it was wet anyway.' That made her even pottier because she had only just bought it and was still paying a penny a week to Perkins, the local furnishings store. You can be sure I got another whack for that.

I did a lot of other things that sent my old lady's head spinning. I was in trouble most days. Sometimes I wanted to say sorry to her, especially when I was hiding under the bed covers waiting for her to whack me, but I could never bring myself to do it. This was a shame because she had endured a terrible time even before I came along.

As she later told me, she was the 13th and last child of a family of Irish extraction. Her father had a very, very violent temper. I remember seeing photographs of him. He was a biggish man – well, he looked big in those old sepia pictures – with a big moustache. From what my mother told me, I understand that her mother and father's bed was an old brass one, decorated at each corner with balls topped off with sharp points. And one day when she was very young, she heard her mother screaming. She opened the bedroom door and there he was, smashing her mother, stark naked, against these sharp points. She had holes all over her back.

Such a violent temper showed he had something wrong with him but it was my grandmother who suffered. One day my mother was coming home from work – she was only 13 but already 'in service' as a domestic – when she heard bells ringing. In those days this could mean a fire engine or an ambulance – both horse-drawn with bells. It turned out to be an ambulance which galloped past her, went way ahead and then seemed to pull up outside her parents' house. They were living not far from Kings Cross at the time. By the time she got there, the ambulance staff were carrying her mother out on a stretcher. She had committed suicide in the outside toilet, all because of the pain and strain of living with this violent old bastard.

Some days later my mother was coming home again and found that he too had been taken away – alive but to a mental institution. He never came out.

So that wasn't a very promising start to my old lady's life, but it got worse. Put in service as a child, she was working in one of those huge houses in Portland Place next to Regent's Park. As she described it to me, it was just like that TV series *Upstairs, Downstairs*: emptying piss pots, cleaning out ovens and running errands. Then somehow, somewhere – going for a walk in Regent's Park, I guess – she met a man called Marky Mendoza. He was living

THE SURVIVOR

in Kentish Town at the time and he came from a very, very big Italian family.

Later this Marky Mendoza would turn into a kind of villain. During the late 1940s and early '50s, he was involved with the notorious Messina brothers when they were running all the prostitutes in Soho, among other rackets. That was more than 15 years after he'd met my mother. Back in 1930 she was only 15 herself but that didn't stop him humping, pumping and dumping her.

I can't blame him, I suppose. My mum was a little skinny, dark-headed bird and she must have been quite attractive but when she told him, 'Mark, I'm pregnant', he didn't show her any sympathy. He said, 'Don't worry. It happens to girls every day of the week. It makes no difference to me.'

So now she's all on her own in St Bartholomew's Hospital. It's in the early hours of Monday, 5 January 1931 – a right nasty, rainy thundery night – and she's giving birth to me. I was two months premature and I weighed less than 3lb. She told me, I could have fitted into a milk bottle. The nurses didn't beat about the bush. They went to her and they said, 'Don't bother to ask to see him, he's not going to survive.' Their very words, so my old lady told me when I got old enough to understand.

When I was 14 years old she took me back to St Bartholomew's and she said to the staff, 'I want you to see that kid you said weren't going to survive.' Mind you, she hadn't been doing me any favours when I was born. She had been trying to get rid of me. She had been drinking gallons of vinegar – some old wives' tale, I suppose. That was why I was born premature, and I think that's probably why, even today, every time I walk past a fish and chip shop, I get withdrawal symptoms.

So again, I was a survivor. Against all the odds and even the wishes of the nurses, perhaps, who may have thought I'd have a rotten life anyhow: born a bastard to a slip of a girl who had tried to abort me anyhow. They had no idea I would have a charmed life.

After that start, it isn't surprising that my mother never regarded my survival as an unmixed blessing. For the rest of my life she would blame me for things I hadn't done and which certainly weren't my fault. She used to stare at me and say, 'Every time I look at you I see your father. If the pair of you were in a bar, and he was at one end and you were at the other, you'd recognise each other immediately, because you resemble him down to a tee.'

Like they say, you can't help what's in you.

So there she is: 15 years old, with a baby, no husband and no hope of a job. I don't suppose they would have let her keep her job at Portland Place with a kid hanging on her arms. But somehow she managed to get a husband straightaway. I think this had been arranged for her, even before she gave birth. The 'bridegroom' – if that doesn't dignify him too much – was a very old man called Evans. To him at his age she was probably a blinding little sort. I suppose she knocked him over. She soon did anyway.

It was this Evans who owned Forty Acres, the house at Thundersley near Southend where I spent my earliest years. He had plenty of money. He had a building firm in England and in America, but what I remember most is his guns. The house was only a bungalow but it was full of shotguns.

One of my earliest memories is of standing on a chair, leaning back against the wall, and knocking down nine or ten shotguns that were all leaning up against the wall. I can still hear my mother screaming at me. Many years later she told me that, at that very moment, old Evans told her, 'Oh, that's all right. They're all for him later when he grows up. They'll be his anyway.' And, funny thing, I've always had a fascination for guns.

Evans himself was a gun fanatic. He used to shoot rabbits in the mornings, even from his bed. He gave my mother the job of weighing the shot, loading the cartridges and priming them, but he also took what strikes me now as a sadistic delight in making her fire the guns herself. She was a tiny thing, only small, and sometimes he would load a cartridge up extra strong himself, then he would say to her, 'Here! Try this, Hetty. Try this!' and then, 'No, don't pull the butt tight to your shoulder. Hold it away a bit.' Of course, if even a big man does this, a shotgun will recoil with a kick but when she did it, it smashed her right across the yard. Obviously, you should never tell anyone to hold a shotgun away from the shoulder. You have to hold it close to your shoulder.

So old man Evans was a bit of a crackpot and a bit sadistic. Then suddenly he died. They had been married for three years so she should have got his money, but she never got a penny. It all went to his two ugly sisters. So now she had to go back to work, carrying me under her arm, three miles there and three miles back. She was destitute all over again but once again she displayed the strong instinct for survival which I would inherit. She did what she probably thought was the sensible thing and married the man who lived next door, Bill Bridger. When I was four he moved us up to London, first to Tottenham, then to Hackney Wick and the house in Gainsborough Road.

It was this man, Bill Bridger, whom I always regarded as my real dad. I thought the world of him. I idolised him because of all the blinding, marvellous things he did for me. He used to work south of the river at the Woolwich Arsenal, but instead of catching the bus to the north end of the Woolwich foot tunnel, he would sometimes walk all those miles and give me his fare money, so I could go to the pictures or buy a knife or something. Or he'd go without his little bit of tobacco for a week, for me to buy this or that.

So there was I, thinking the world of this bloke as my dad, when the time comes for me to leave school. In those days most kids would leave elementary school at 14 when you would get a school leaving certificate. So I was sitting in the hall and larking about with another kid when I realised that I was the only one still waiting to be called up to collect this certificate from the dog of a headmaster, whose name – perversely – was Mr Pretty.

Now this bastard did not like me because he could never make me conform, so while I was waiting for him to call out 'Bridger!', which I thought was my name because it was the name of my old man, instead he calls out, 'Evans. Evans. You! You're Evans! Come here. You're leaving school today.' And he thrust this certificate bearing the name Evans into my hand.

This was a surprise to say the least. I always knew there was something funny – because of remarks I had picked up when my mother was talking to female friends and relations – but I had never put two and two together. I had never cared about the fact that I could remember living in another house, Forty Acres, with another 'father'. When you're a little kid these contradictions don't always strike you with the force they should, but now this headmaster does this to me and suddenly I've got to sort it out.

So I go straight home and find my old lady acting as if she was expecting trouble. She must have known what was going to happen that day. When I came in she was on her hands and knees, scrubbing the floor, and she wouldn't look up at me. So I kicked the fucking bucket over, got her by the hair and said, 'Who the fuck am I? What's going on?'

She still wouldn't look up at me, which made me even more annoyed, so I repeated, 'Who the fucking hell am I?' So she got up and said, 'Wait till your dad comes home.' Funny thing. She always called Bill Bridger my dad – even at that moment.

So then I waited for him to come in and he told me the truth. He explained how he was only my stepfather. Then somehow it dawned on me that my mother must have married that man called Evans, with all the shotguns, only to give me a name because if there was no name on your birth certificate in the space marked 'father', it was effectively branding you a 'bastard': in those days a disgrace on you and your mother for the rest of your lives – though not today, I've noticed. Now nobody seems to care.

So in due course Bridger told me the rest of the story. He said, 'I'm not your dad but nor was Evans. Your real dad's name is Marky Mendoza.' And then he filled in as much of the detail as he knew. He said, 'The Mendozas are a big family, and they've got cafés in Kentish Town.'

And then little things started coming back to me, like I remembered sitting on Bill Bridger's lap one day when I was very little, about four years old, when he said to me, 'I always wanted a little boy to call me dad.' And I thought, I am your boy, you are my dad. I didn't realise.

He was a terrific fellow and, you know, it's a very, very funny thing, but the whole affair only brought me closer to Bill Bridger. It made me think even more of him. He had told me who my real father was but I never looked at it that way. As far as I was concerned, this was just a technical cock-up: I only had the one father. I didn't know the first one, I scarcely knew the second one, I only knew this one – Bill Bridger – and he would always be my old boy.

It's a pity but my mother wasn't as loyal to him as I was. She had a girl by him – she's my half-sister – but when I was 23 she left Bridger and moved in with a fellow who lived a few doors away. He was Albert Harrington and, as it happened, he wasn't a bad bloke: it was she who had bad ways. She also had bad timing because she made this move just when Bridger found out he had terminal cancer. I said, 'You shouldn't leave him.' She said, 'Well I've got someone else.' I said, 'Well, you can fuck off with someone else. If you can't be with him when he needs you now, then don't be around at all.' And off she went with Albert and the six-year-old girl.

By now Bill Bridger was in Homerton Hospital but I brought him back home with me. I wanted to take care of him like he had taken care of me. They said his feet had got to be massaged with alcohol and things, because they get bed sores. I said, 'Don't worry, I'll do all that crap.'

It took over a year for the cancer to finish Bill Bridger. During all this time he had absolutely nothing to do with my mother. When they finally took him in, he didn't have any energy left. I sat on the edge of the bed, got him in my arms and he was just a little bag of bones. Things get reversed in life: one day you're in his arms, then it comes round, that's what it's all about. I said to him, 'I ain't half going to miss you, you know.' I was 24.

One day, towards the end of his life, he had brought the conversation back round to my real father, Marky Mendoza. He had first told me about him when I was 14 and the man had never been mentioned again. I had put the thing out my head, I didn't want to know. Ten years went by, then suddenly he said, 'You've got to go and see your real dad, you know.' I said, 'What are you on about? As far as I'm concerned, you are my real dad.' He said, 'No I'm not, you go and see your father.'

And then he told me something he had never said before. He said, 'After your mother told me what happened, I went round there with a big chopper down my belt. I was going to smash Mendoza over the head for deserting her. But when I got to where he and his crowd were hanging out, they were about twenty-handed and I thought, oh fuck it, it ain't my business anyway' – he wasn't stupid – 'I felt like killing him but at the same time I was thinking, he is your real father, so I didn't do anything. Anyway, it was a long time before I came along.' Then he said, 'But now I want you to go and see him. I think you should.'

Then poor old Bridger dies.

By now I knew a face called Tony Mella – big Tony Mella – a well-known underworld character who crops up later on in my life, in tragic circumstances. Tony came out of Clapton where I spent most of my teen years. So I used to see Tony and he let me know that he was very friendly with Marky Mendoza, who had something to do with the racing tracks which Tony would frequent. And Tony would say to me, 'I saw your old man the other day having a drink. He said he wants to see you. He'd like to see you.'

Well, somehow, between Tony Mella and another man named Tommy Hall, a meeting was arranged at a pub called the Stag opposite the Roundhouse at Chalk Farm, just up from Camden Town. It was a summer evening, I got all dressed up and arrived at eight o'clock, as agreed. But as I went to push the door to go in, I felt something was holding me back. I thought, all these years I've never been interested in seeing this man, so why should I bother now. I thought, fuck it, I don't need him.

See, no matter what Bill Bridger had said, I felt disloyal to the old boy by even agreeing to this meeting. I also felt that, after all these years Marky Mendoza had probably got a load of kids of his own, and they probably wouldn't want me intruding in his family. And so I never pushed the door open. Maybe I should've done, sometimes I regret it, but I never regretted it enough to fix up another meeting.

Not that I ever got the hump with Marky Mendoza, I've never felt he let me down. I've had a terrific life. If it wasn't for him I wouldn't have enjoyed that life. And the same for any kids about that might look the same as me. They're lucky to be here. The chances are, you ain't going to make it. It's a miracle just to be born. You've won the lottery already. Make the most of it. That's what I've done.

THE SURVIVOR

TWO

Growing Pains

MARKY Mendoza probably supplied one key element of my character. Let's describe that as an inclination to break the law. My mother's father may have given me another one: a ferocious temper.

When I was little, a lot of the kids in school used to call me 'Jimmy Stromboli'. I took no notice. Much later in life I met a bloke called Georgie who had been at school with me. My old man (Bill Bridger) used to like him and he would give me money so we could go to the pictures together because this kid had no parents, just grandparents. So one day I was reminiscing with this fellow and I said, 'Georgie, why did you and the other kids used to call me Stromboli?' And he said, 'You used to have such a bad temper. When you got angry, you were like a volcano erupting.'

To show how bad this temper was, I'll tell a story against myself which involves an old couple who were friends of my old man. I called this couple 'aunt' and 'uncle' though they weren't related to us. At weekends we'd go to visit them in their little house in Lea Bridge Road, Leytonstone, where this Aunt Edie's father was also living, but stuck in a wheelchair.

During these visits we would be sitting around the table and the adults would start playing brag, a card game. Well, although I was very small, I insisted on playing brag too. The aim of the game is to get three threes. If you get three threes you've won the game. So my old man, every time he got a three, would slip it to me under the table, because he knew that I had to win. If I couldn't win – if someone else won – I would get in such a temper that I used to run up to this old fellow in the wheelchair and kick shit out of the wheelchair. Worse still, because I was only little and I'd completely lost my rag, my aim wasn't good and I'd be kicking his legs too. Stromboli, Etna, Vesuvius, call me what you like, as a kid I was volcanic.

I learned nothing from the example of Bill Bridger's meek, conciliatory nature. Instead I took my cue from my mother, who also had a terrible temper. She beat the crap out of me so often that the school board officer would come to the house to check she wasn't taking parental discipline to the point of cruelty. These days her actions would be called child abuse and I would probably be placed in care for my own safety but in those days it was common for kids to get a good strapping – not just from parents but from teachers and policemen. Yet even this violence helped shape a third feature of my character. Call it resilience, endurance, guts or, as Americans say, the ability to 'tough it out' – whatever 'it' might be. When I was very young I resolved, consciously or unconsciously, never to submit. If there was a fight going on, I wouldn't run away. I'd be in the thick of it.

I was only eight years old and we were still living down Hackney Wick in Gainsborough Road when some kid called Nicky Gargano who was a terrific boxer, bashed me up in school. But rather than hide away, I decide to go looking for him. On this particular day I tied a lump of rope round my waist and attached my old lady's flat iron to it. Then I went to school, all tooled up and bent on swinging the iron around and whacking him with it. I couldn't do it there but later some kids told me that he had gone fishing along the cut (the Lea Canal) at Bow. So I tracked him down, walked up behind and whacked him with the iron. After that there was no more trouble from Nicky, at school or anywhere else.

Not that there was any point in going to school. We learned nothing, not even at primary level. All we got was abuse, especially from the caretaker who smacked a pal of mine, Jimmy Sims, round the earhole. Jimmy really got the hump and he told me he wanted to get in this school at the weekend and do mischief. So we broke into the school, in Berkshire Road, one of those five-storey monstrosities that scarred the lives of so many kids 'educated' by the London County Council. And when we got up to the top floor we came across some big gallon tins of malt in the teachers' cupboard. Me and Jimmy both loved malt and we were eating as much of this stash as we could, till it made us sick. All of a sudden, 'Miaaow!', and in comes the caretaker's cat. So, as Jimmy had the hump with the caretaker, he's grabbed the cat, dumped it in a tin of malt and slung the whole lot out the fifth-storey window. Despite the racket, there was no sign of the caretaker. We ran off, and for the first time we appreciated the meaning of the phrase, 'revenge is sweet', especially if it's malt-flavoured.

A year or two later, when I was about ten, I performed my first semi-professional act of theft, and again it involved something sweet — in fact, tins of sweets. It started with this kid Peter Swinburn coming round one weekend and he's said to me, 'Let's go and get some sweets.' What he meant was for us to break into the Clarnico's Sweet Factory which was near my house in Gainsborough Road but on the other side of the canal. They used to make big round tins with Clarnico's name on them, filled with lovely, quality sweets, and we knew that there were warehouses full of these tins. We also knew that they were guarded by a couple of watchmen, so we dreamed up a scheme to nick a wooden sleeper from the railway yard, dump it on our side of the canal then strip down to our underpants, push the sleeper into the canal, and swim with it across to the warehouse. We managed to do all this, then we secured the sleeper on the other bank and crept into the warehouse. In those days there were no alarms to worry about, only those watchmen who were nowhere in sight.

Till now we had intended only to get a few boxes of sweets for ourselves but once we're inside this massive factory, and we find these hundreds of lovely big tins and boxes of sweets, we decided we're going to make a 'birdy' of it, a commercial job. We've seen all the goodies, now we're going to have a pay-day. We sneaked dozens of these tins out of the warehouse and stacked them alongside the canal, with the intention of balancing them on the sleeper and swimming across with the entire load. But when we went upstairs to bring down our last load up all of a sudden, 'Gotcha, you little bastards!' It's the two watchmen.

Well, we're just skinny little ten-year-olds in our pants. And while I was still holding these tins of sweets in my arms, my pal Peter has managed to shoot beneath the grasp of one watchman, out the door, down the stone stairs and away. So while that watchman went after him, the other one said, 'I've got you now', at which I've jumped out of a window, a long way down on to gravel and broken glass. I've done my ankle and it was killing me but this great big burly bloke wasn't going to jump out. He's gone down the stairs and by the time he's reached where I had been, I've jumped through a window and run into the ground floor of this huge warehouse, where they stored the large empty jars in which shopkeepers would store sweets on their shelves. They had no lids on them and they were lying on top of each other. Some were broken and smashed with jagged glass sticking up, but others were solid and still in one piece. So as he's chased me, I've run through this warehouse on top of all these jars, missing every single jagged, broken one, until eventually I come out on the other side, run out back on to the canal side and jump in.

But my troubles aren't over because there's all this barbed wire in the water. During the war the authorities have laid barbed wire the length of obstacles like canals to slow the advance of an invading enemy, but I don't know that. All I know is that here and now it's stopping a little thief like me escaping. And I feel myself being sucked in. As a child you have no idea how shallow these canals are – you think they're bottomless – but now my feet were trapped in all this slime and broken glass and my body is trapped in the barbed wire. I'm still underwater and I can't hold my breath any more, but all of a sudden I have this burst of strength and manage to pull myself through the barbed wire coils and come up. It fucking hurts me, I'm cut to pieces and my ankle's swollen, but I've popped up and got a deep gulp of fresh air. And as I turn my head, I see the watchman who's chased me and his mate with his hat off, scratching his head, both looking in wonderment – I assume – at the fact that I've survived the jump out of the first floor window, completed the assault course over all those big jars of smashed glass barefooted when I could have been cut to pieces and, if I'd slipped, I could have severed an artery and bled to death – and then dived into the barbed wire and managed to struggle free. And they can still see me swimming across the canal. By now Peter's dressed and he pulls me out of the water. So I've quickly grabbed my clothes, stuck them under my arm and I've climbed on his back, and we're running along laughing, even though my ankle's killing me. When we get under the canal bridge, I manage to dress and he takes me home, cut to pieces by the barbed wire but otherwise OK.

Talk about a survivor. Not that my mother or even my old man seemed to notice I'd been in the wars again.

When the real war broke out in 1939, for East End kids like me life became a kind of paradise where all the normal rules of law and order were turned on their head. With all the able-bodied and generally law-abiding men between 18 and 40 away doing military service – or captured or killed in action – there were only old fellows around to keep kids like me in order. As for our mothers, they were so down-trodden, over-worked and skint, they couldn't keep us in line either. So we were free to run wild.

My biggest joy was the amount of unexploded weaponry which Hitler was dropping out of the sky for me to play with. We used to collect all sorts of bombs and anti-tank shells and bury them all round the garden. How my old man never set one off digging up the garden with a shovel, I'll never know.

I was a dedicated collector so one day, when I was over the Hackney Marshes with a pal of mine, I spotted one: about three foot six high and the fins still on it. Perfect, I thought, I must have this (because the ammunition field where they used to explode the bombs was only quarter of a mile up the road from where I lived). So we pinched the newspaper delivery man's home-made trolley – wooden, with pram wheels and a handle – and we trudged down to the marshes and we rolled this bomb on it. Then up and down we went, carrying the bomb across this pock-marked terrain, so that by the time we turned into my street the trolley had collapsed. When we got to the front door I pulled the string hanging through the letterbox with the key on it and got the door open. We managed to get the bomb over the step, which was about twelve inches high, and we toppled it over into the passage. Then it got wedged in the door. Now we couldn't get it out and we couldn't get it in. So I said, 'Fuck it, leave it.' And we stuck the remains of the trolley in the gutter and ran off.

I don't know what we did while we were away but in the meantime it gets dark, my old man's come home and as he's come in, he's tripped over the bomb and smashed his leg. He didn't even know how it got in the doorway, it could have bounced from a plane for all he knew. Anyway he's struggled round to the ARP (Air Raid Precautions) post and the next thing the army bomb disposal unit has turned up, with big red flags and sirens going. They unwedged the bomb and took it back where I got it from and blew it up.

That was the sort of thing we did as kids during the war, living in the Wick on top of the Hackney Marshes. We didn't have any computers. We just had bombs and shells and buckets of shrapnel to collect each morning. It's a miracle we weren't blown to pieces. And of course there was always the chance that we would have been killed by a direct hit on our homes. We were bombed out twice in Hackney Wick, so I was given one short spell of evacuation. I was sent to a place called New Duston outside Northampton, where I'm afraid that I rapidly revolutionised the only crime the local kids got up to, which was scrumping. Most kids would just grab a sackful of apples, but I used to saw the apple tree down. Then I would tie a tow rope on it and haul it back up the street to where I was lodged. I was such a pain in the fucking neck that in no time I was back in the Wick.

Talk about being a survivor. I even survived landmines. These weren't like bombs. Landmines came down on parachutes and they made a terrifying noise. You would be in your little metal shelter and you would hear one coming. It swished, it went sshhhhw, sshhhw. And the swishes got louder and louder, and the reason it was swishing was because this huge mine was suspended on the parachute, and it's coming down and down until it lands and explodes. Well, one afternoon a pal and I found a landmine over Hackney Marshes. And I had always wanted one of the little clocks that came out the side of the landmines. I loved any little gadgets and right there in front of me was a mint specimen.

When I went on these expeditions I always had a little hammer and a chisel down my belt, so to prize off this clock my pal and I get astride and we're both sitting on this landmine as if it was a tandem bike, with the fins and everything behind us. The parachute's not there any more, but I've got the chisel and I'm thrusting and banging away trying to get this clock out.

All of a sudden something's grabbed my collar, and simultaneously my pal and I had been picked up by this great big burly park warden. In those days park wardens looked like mounted police. They had these terrific hats and all the tackle you don't see today. We were right beside the River Lea so he's grabbed us, run us across the road and thrown us down the river bank. And as we went down, it went off.

Through that instant act of bravery this man had saved our lives, when he could so nearly have got killed himself. Imagine: two kids sitting on a landmine, banging away and only seconds to go off. He had guts. I don't think I even thanked him. But I was a survivor once again.

And I'm not done yet, because I hear something go clunk on the ground beside me. It was a big lump of shrapnel from the landmine. Marvellous, I thought, because I was collecting shrapnel, but when I picked it up it burnt my hand. I pissed on it to cool it down and it went all the different colours of the rainbow, so it must have had oil in it.

But I got my revenge on the Germans, and in a way which gave a hint of my future career.

I had developed a taste for guns when I was a tot in the house of my first stepfather, that gun fanatic Evans. Remember, he had promised me all his shotguns but I never got them so I had to wait until the war before I got a gun of my own. This came out of a German plane that had crashed and must have been supplied to the pilot in the event that he could evade capture. I don't know what happened to him – killed on impact, I expect – but now I had his Luger. The handle had been burned off a bit so I'd go to the woodwork room at school and carve out my own handle for it. This was about the only reason I could find for going to school.

As it turned out, my second stepfather also liked guns. When I was still a kid he bought me an air rifle and taught me how to shoot it. This was called a Diana airgun which I soon put to use in what amounted to armed robbery. I stole a boy's bike and when his 14-year-old sister tried to stop me, I hit her over the head with the air-gun and got away, as if it was my right to defend myself in an act of theft. From then on it was all sorts of different guns, until I had my big break – or rather, break-in.

It was near the end of 1942 and I was still 11. Not far from where we lived there was a big building in Riseholme Terrace, off Victoria Park, which belonged to a Mr Villiers. He was the local millionaire and he used to run clubs there for boy scouts and other youth groups, so it was an obvious place for the Territorial Army to set up a barracks. Only I latched on to the fact that the guns weren't in a secure armoury, they were just left lying around. This was too much of a temptation for me so I used to climb through the window with a pal of mine, and one time we found a .22 rifle with some boxes of .22 ammunition.

This set my mind working because for some time I had been brooding on a thing which I had witnessed several times over the Hackney Marshes where we used to spend most of our time. Right on the marshes there was a prisoner-of-war camp which housed German POWs. Now, believe it or not, in the evenings these POWs would be let out for a bit of a stroll without any supervision whatever. They had to wear a uniform with a diamond marked 'POW' on the back of their jackets, which should have made them pariahs in the eyes of the locals. But no! To my astonishment, I would see all the little tarts from the Kingsmead estate block of flats hanging around outside the gates waiting for them.

This annoyed me because my old man was always telling me little stories of when he was in the Navy during World War I over 20 years earlier. And I used to pay attention to all these things and I had a sense of loyalty for my country, especially at that time when the Germans were bombing our fish and chip shops. I had even witnessed people being killed by them. I used to know a French lady who ran the local toy shop, and as I walked round the corner during an air raid I was just in time to see a bomb hitting her house, and she and her family going up in the air while they were still sitting at the table having their evening meal. It all seemed like slow motion and I couldr' believe it. Oh yes, this was war — or as close as I could get to it at my age then.

So when we got hold of this .22 rifle, we walked back to the marshes with it on my shoulder, with my pocket full of .22 ammo. When we got to the River Lea we hid amongst big dock leaves and bushes right opposite the camp gates, and waited for them to come out for their evening break. Sure enough, as we're watching them come out, we see this little fat blonde bird sneaking off with a German POW and down the river bank. By this time I have jacked a cartridge into the rifle and boom! From across the river I shoot him up his bare arse. There's a fucking scream and, next thing we see, he's rolling down the bank into the mud.

Strange to say, I got a little 'hard-on': this was the first time I had ever shot anyone. We took the gun back to the TA unit, but later on I nicked it back again and kept it indoors, for safe-keeping or until I saw another German screwing one of our women. Otherwise I kept in training by sticking German shells — which had primers on them — into brick walls, standing back with the .22 rifle, then shooting the primers to send the shell flying and blowing down half the brick wall. I don't know where the shells ended up. Left alone, I would have done more damage to the East End than Adolf Hitler.

My partner in these patriotic enterprises was Eddie Thorne. For a short while I had been evacuated with Eddie to New Duston, near Northampton, along with his brothers, Ernie and Ron, so I knew them all well. Eddie was car crazy and when I was about 13 he taught me to drive. Not long afterwards he moved from Hackney Wick to Poplar, near enough opposite the Blackwall Tunnel. We also moved to a prefab in Morning Lane, opposite the Hackney Empire, so now Eddie and I lived quite a long way apart. As I had no money I couldn't take a bus to see him, so I really did take one. I used to walk round to the bus depot in Mare Street where I'd find the big diesel buses fired up and the engines running, and I'd just get in one of these double-deckers and drive it into Mare Street. I'd go straight down Mare Street, across Mile End Road into Commercial Road, right up Sidney Street and park it outside his house in Poplar. And Eddie would say, 'Is that our bus?' And I'd say, 'Yeah, I just got here.' So we'd both get in it and we'd go for a ride, until it ran out of diesel, then we'd nick something else and come back. It wasn't like today, they never had radio controls, so we could nick buses or any other form of transport and never get caught.

Meanwhile my schooling was going the traditional way of the lower working class: down the shoot. I never had any real education. Every time I went to school the sirens were going, and I'd end up in the basement in what we called the air raid shelter. That's if I went to school at all. If I did, my main reason for going was to use the woodwork centre so I could make a pair of handles for that old Luger. Suddenly one Thursday the headmaster Mr Pretty said, 'You only come to school to do woodwork, now you're not going to have any more woodwork.' And he stopped me doing woodwork. So that Friday evening I went back into the school with a pal of mine whose name happened to be Georgie Foreman. He wasn't the other slag from South London. This one had guts and together we carted all the tools out. We put most of them in his Anderson shelter and the rest in an empty house next to my house. See, the way I was thinking was, if I can't do any more woodwork, no one's gonna do any!

I was feeling pretty good with myself when this CID officer came round and accused me of doing the job. It turned out that Peter Swinburn, the kid who had been my partner in the raid on the sweet factory, had grassed me up. He knew I had done it because the day after the woodwork centre had been broken into, he'd come to my home to moan that they couldn't do any woodwork because there weren't any tools (just as I had planned, of course). Then Peter noticed there were wood shavings on my trousers that must have fallen from the jack-planes that I had stolen. So the bastard stuck my name up.

This left me with no way out, but one 'fair cop' wasn't enough for the CID man who said, 'We suspect that the caretaker must have been involved because he was the only one who had a Yale key for the door.' He had no idea how I could have got in except through the door. He also had no idea that, although I was only a kid, I had a criminal mind. What I'd done was tell my pal to lift me up so I could get on the flat roof which had one of those skylights. If you were inside the workshop, you could open this skylight by pulling a bit of string on a pulley with teeth on it. So I figured that all I had to do was force the skylight open just enough to get my hand in and turn the wheel so that it opened a bit more. Then I could get my arm in and turn it all the way, open it up fully, get in the workshop that way, and then wind the skylight close again. Then I would open the Yale lock on the door from the inside, let my pal in and start performing. We were loading up sacks of lovely big jack-planes and chisels and the entire Aladdin's Cave of really good tools.

At first I wasn't going to admit anything, but when the CID said that the caretaker was involved, my old man said to me, 'Look, he's got three kids, and he's gonna get nicked for something he ain't done', and he persuaded me to own up. So then the CID man said, 'Well, in that case, how did you get in?' I told him. He was surprised because till then they could not work out how anyone could have got in except through the front door.

Then we agreed to give all the tools back, and my old boy did some sort of plea-bargaining. He told the cop, 'Look, I don't want this lad to be in trouble at his time of life, he's only young yet.' And now my old lady and the other boy's mother had spent a week carting all this gear back to the school. So all I got was a caution. After all, there was a war on.

The one person who wasn't happy was that stinking headmaster, Mr Pretty. He still wouldn't let me in the woodwork centre so I never went back to school, except to collect my school-leaving certificate a few months later. Maybe that's why he spitefully revealed my real name in front of the entire school, when he could have taken me discreetly to one side. Maybe he had already written me off not just as an educational lost cause but as a social menace.

And maybe he was right. Over the years he had dealt with enough little tearaways to know that, while I was hopeless at learning anything at his school, I was still an exceptional student. If Fagin had been my teacher I would have come top of the class. In the years to come I would be taught by many Fagins. I would learn my lessons not in the classroom but on the streets, on roofs and in the vaults.

THREE

A Criminal Apprenticeship

THEY say, don't look for it in the stars, it's in the genes. That's true. I was born with a criminal mind from day one. But there's nurture as well as nature, and whatever 'bent' I inherited (from Mendoza or whomever) it conspired with my upbringing to create the perfect thief.

Very early on in life I learned that, if I wanted anything, I had to go and get it. No one ever gave me anything. No one ever smashed me over the head with a bag of diamonds. I never got any legacies (for all that my first stepfather Evans had promised). I've had two weddings and neither time were we given even a single spoon. And I have never had any 'help' in my life. I don't say this with self-pity, I hope, I am only trying to explain what drives someone from the 'lower depths' to become a professional criminal.

One incident may help make the point. When I was nine years old I used to go past a parade of little lock-up shops opposite the Bank of England, in the heart of the City of London. They were on the outside of the Royal Exchange – they are still there – and one shop in particular fascinated me. It sold cutlery.

One morning my old boy and I went by this place on a number 30 bus, just when the staff were opening up and they were putting out this long showcase. It was about six foot long, four inches wide and four inches deep and it had a glass top. Inside were all beautiful little penknives with bone handles and little snippers. All it had to secure it were two hooks, like little door hooks, and two screw-eyes on the wall, and they'd hook this showcase on the wall every morning. Nothing more.

Now I couldn't get this thing out of my mind – I had to have it – so I thought and thought: if I grab it, how am I going to get it back home? I can't stand there, in the middle of the City of London, smashing the glass off and taking all the goodies out. No, I've got to get it somewhere where I can take my time and enjoy it. Then I thought to myself: if I'm walking along, these big City gents with their top hats and their briefcases will be looking down at me and they'll see all my plunder. So I thought, I know how to do it: turn it upside down, so the glass is facing downwards and it will look like a big block of wood.

One day I ran all the way there on my own. It must have been three miles from the Wick to the Bank of England but that was nothing: I used to run everywhere. When I got there I walked straight up, unhooked this six foot long showcase, put it on my shoulder – upside down – and walked off. No cries of 'Stop, thief!', no hot pursuit, I had got clean away. So now I marched all the way back to the Wick and got the showcase up to my little hide-out, among the dock bushes by the railway arch (near where I used to lie under the trains). At the bottom of a factory wall I had found an air brick which I could take out. In the cavity behind I could store things of value before putting the brick back in place. Here I broke open this showcase and started handling these lovely little penknives and other goodies. I told myself, I'm going to have a pay-day: some I'll flog, some I'll keep, some I'll swap for other goods.

Many, many years later I'm sitting with my legitimate business partner, an old pal called Martin Stockman who ran a clothing factory with me. We were talking about little things we got up to when we were kids and I told him about when I nicked this showcase full of fancy knives opposite the Bank of England. Suddenly he said, 'So it was you, you bastard! I had my eye on that! I wanted that – I was going to do the same thing!' And he named every knife in the box. So, after all those years it turned out that he'd had the same thoughts but I beat him to it. It was mine from day one.

Who was it who said everyone has a little bit of larceny in their soul? Well, in time the little bit in my soul turned my attention from what was outside the Bank of England to what was inside. And one of the causes of this conversion was a man called Tommy Smithson. Later Tommy would become a famous underworld figure – 'infamous' might be a better way of putting it – but at this time I knew him because his old lady ran the Gem Café in Graham Road, Hackney. She was a Scouser, from Liverpool, but he was a real East Ender.

I got on very well with Tommy Smithson. He was Hackney's resident gangster, he could have a tremendous fight and, to top it up, he had a big, black straight-eight Buick sedan like they had in Chicago in Al Capone's days, so all the local teenagers liked Tommy.

All the little mob with him were older than I was but they took a shine to me because of the things I used to get up to. Tommy used to like me and he would tell me stories about when he was in the merchant navy, like how he used to dive off the funnel, his head missing the handrail by about two inches. He didn't have any nerves in his body. There were lots of stories around about Tommy Smithson, especially around how eventually he died, shot in the head in Maida Vale.

One evening I was sitting in his old lady's café with Tommy when in walk two other gangland figures who would also meet sorry ends: big Tony Mella and his sidekick, Alf Malvin. They sit down at our table and Alf Malvin, a big tough-looking bastard, turns round to Tommy and says, 'I tell you what, Tom, let's play smashing each other over the head with plates!' He wasn't referring to the joyous custom associated with Greek festivities – none of these fellows was Greek – he was hinting at the friction which had always existed between his pal Tony Mella and Tommy. Well of course this idea would have annoyed Tommy because it was his old lady's café but Tommy had another scheme in mind and he said, 'Yeah, all right, Alf. You go first.' So big Alf picks up a plate and smashes Tommy over the head with the flat side of it. Then Tommy says, 'My turn now, Alf', and he gets a plate and holds it sideways and goes bosh! And it's split Alf Malvin's head right open.

A couple of months later Tommy encountered a few police outside the coffee stall in Narrow Way, Hackney. He took a truncheon off one and knocked some of them out. In the battle that followed, they busted his jaw. So I was sitting in the Gem Café at the same table with Tommy and all this wire sticking out from his wired-up jaw. And he said, 'I can't drink this fucking coffee', and he yanked the wire out of his jaw and put the wire on the table, just so he could get the coffee into his mouth. These sorts of things may sound ridiculous but they would impress people, especially kids of my age then.

Anyway, Smithson liked me and one day he said, 'What are you doing?', and I said, 'I'm working for Fitzpatrick, the roadworkers, on the pneumatic drills.' This was true but my old stepdad had predicted, 'You won't last a week. That firm's not called Catch'em and Kill'em for nothing. It'll kill ya.' I shocked him by staying for six months, wrestling with these big pneumatic drills and coming home with my eyes all blind because the tar and the hot weather used to swell your eyes up, so the old boy had to guide me in the door. At least this showed him I had done a good, honest day's work. I did it partly to earn his respect but also for the money.

But Smithson said, 'Why don't you change your job and get a few quid?' I asked how. 'Look, there's something I want to show you,' and he took me in his big Buick up to the City of London, just off Old Broad Street, and he pointed to a shop with the shutters down. He said, 'See that. That's a jeweller's shop. They're looking for staff to train. Go and get a job there and I'll talk to you later.'

The following Monday I went up there and they gave me a job in the workshop. This was up a stairway in a room which had a big window through which you could look down into the retail shop itself. It was a bit like being in a prison except that – to my amusement – it had the same kind of fanlight as I had used to slip through into the school woodwork centre and nick all the tools. You just drew steadily on a cord on a pulley and the fanlight opened. But, of course, this wasn't a school toolshop, it was a jeweller's with a big safe downstairs. So you can imagine how my mind was working – and Tommy's too.

This was the start of my first big love affair – with safes. In those days you didn't blow safes open, because they all had square backs which you just had to rip off. For the moment that was no concern of mine. I was still only 14 and my job was limited to telling Tommy how to get from an empty office block next door into the jeweller's – through the fanlight window which I would leave open – and down to the room containing the safe.

One morning, after a long bank holiday weekend, I go into work and it's all been done: the safe's been ripped open and everything's gone. All the jewellery and the money. Tommy had got a result. I don't think I got anything out of it. I just liked him so I did him a favour.

Inevitably the police questioned everybody, with the usual 'Did you see anything?' routine. Yes, I did happen to leave the window open that evening, but anyone could have done that and, as far as I know, no suspicion fell on me. For Tommy and his crew it was a lovely bit of business. For me, it was probably the beginning of a serious criminal career.

I wasn't out of it yet. I had to stay working at the jeweller's in case anybody put two and two together. I just carried on doing my normal duties, which included winding up wall clocks which this firm maintained in offices all over the City. Every Monday morning I would set off with a big winder

THE SURVIVOR

key to visit maybe 20 firms. I would wind up each clock, make sure it was properly balanced by listening to the beat – tick tock, tick tock – and then move it a bit, to line up with markings I had pencilled on the walls.

To do this job I had to walk through the Fenchurch Street area where the big shipping companies had their headquarters. In their windows firms like P&O, the Savill Line and Cunard had huge models of lovely ocean-going boats in glass cases. I had always wanted to have one but – don't worry – I wasn't going to steal it. What I really wanted was to go to sea on the boats themselves and when I went in some of these premises to wind up their clocks, I'd get a smell, a flavour, for the seafaring life. In those days working-class kids never went abroad – at least, not on holiday. They were only sent abroad to fight and die for their country. On the other hand, for years my old man had filled my ears with stories of life in the Royal Navy during World War I and now Tommy Smithson was telling me about his own days at sea.

All this stoked my imagination to the point that I applied to do the two-month training course that would qualify me to get a job on board one of these ships. Then I told the jeweller's I was quitting. No one there linked my departure to the raid a few months before. All the staff must have been thinking, what healthy young lad wouldn't leave a menial job in smoggy London for the romance of the open sea?

Before I could do the training course I got into a bit of trouble with Eddie Thorne, the pal who had taught me to drive at 13 and whom I used to go joy-riding with in double-decker buses. One weekend I was with him and his two brothers when we all got arrested for nicking a car. I ended up on remand in Wormwood Scrubs prison. I was just 15 and I was the youngest person in the entire jail. When the case came up at a magistrates' court we were acquitted. That was lucky because, if I'd had a criminal record, I would probably have been thrown off the training course.

So I'd survived again but, if ever I was to go to sea, I now had to survive the course itself. It was held on the *Vindicatrix*, a ship that was stuck in the mud of the River Severn in Gloucestershire. Or rather she had been a sailing ship a long time ago, but the mast had been cut down and now she was just an old hulk.

On the entry form I had applied to do catering so they started me off in the kitchens. First we were told to carry empty buckets down the stairs to get the porridge oats. The instructor pointed to a line of big clean dustbins containing the oats and I walked over to one. I didn't spot that the lid was moving about but I did notice that all the old hands were standing well back. I thought, what's the matter with this mob? Then I took the lid off. The bin was 12 inches deep with cockroaches. They were living on these oats. They scampered all over me and everyone laughed. That was my introduction to the merchant navy.

I completed the course early in 1947. I had just turned 16 and I had a little bit of time before I joined my first ship. With time to kill, I teamed up again with Eddie Thorne. He was several years older than me and he was now in the army, but when he was on home leave we did all sorts of minor villainy: more car theft, muggings, small-time robberies, whatever came up.

We were having such a good time and making a nice bit of money that he said, 'I don't want to go back to that army camp but my leave's up and if I abscond I'm in trouble. I'll get nicked. They'll put me back in Shepton Mallet military prison, but I'd do anything for a couple more days mucking about with you.' He said, 'I've got to have a cast-iron excuse, something natural, physical.'

I said, 'Can't you sprain your ankle or something?'

He said, 'No, but have you still got that .22 rifle?'

I said, 'Yeah.'

He said, 'Would you shoot me in the leg with it?'

I said, 'Of course I will.'

In fact I was pleased to oblige because I love guns. So we go back to my prefab, I get out the gun and there in the kitchen with the back door open he pulls up his trousers (so no cloth can enter his body and cause the wound to fester) and he says, 'About there.' So down I go and bosh! The .22 goes through the top part of his leg. It's in a terrible state. And Eddie? He's in agony.

I look at the mess and say, 'Before we go down the hospital, you've got to make a hole in the trousers where it's meant to have gone through, but how are you going to explain the shooting?'

He clutches his leg and gasps, 'All I'm going to say is I was cleaning the rifle, and it fell over and went off.'

Eddie was in agony. He couldn't walk. And it worked: he was allowed more home leave because of it. And I'll never forget him saying, 'But wasn't it worth it!' So that was the second time I shot someone (the first was the German POW) and I'd done such a clean job that Eddie had no complications.

Unlike Eddie Thorne, I didn't have to go in the army. Now the war was over, if you spent long enough in the merchant navy you didn't have to do national service. And I spent more than enough. I was on the ships for ten years – less time off for bad behaviour. It was one of the best periods of my life.

My first spell lasted 18 months. First I worked on Black Diamond boats that ran up the coast to Newcastle and brought coal back down to London Docks, off Frog Island. This good coal was for export to America, while we were importing rubbish American 'nutty slack' for our home fires. That's what they call the 'special relationship'.

I did trips to the Baltic in winter. We used to get stuck in the ice, frozen in, and the boat would be forced out of the water lop-sided as the cargo drifted to one side. I had to chip the ice off the rails to help the boat right itself. As we neared Stockholm, before we could see land we would see kids on bikes riding around on the ice. And when we got close to Russian ports, Leningrad and Riga, their icebreakers had to come out and break a way in for us.

Then I did two trips on the *Stratheden* to Australia and back, six months each time. In Sydney I visited my old lady's brother, who had emigrated there, and all his kids. They made a great fuss of me. At a time when working-class people could not afford foreign holidays, these travels were priceless experiences for an East End kid. And I was still only 16.

But my experiences had scarcely begun. I now took a job on board the *Hellesina*, the biggest oil tanker of the day. We set sail for Curaçao in the Caribbean to load up with Venezuelan crude oil and return to Shellhaven, near Dagenham, where Shell Oil had its own docks and refinery. I was just a deck boy and on the way out one of my duties was to climb down into the empty tanks and clean them with a wooden spade and bucket. The fumes are terrible and you think you are going to die. As you look back up, the hole that you climbed through is so far away that it is as small as a pinprick. Then you climb back up this long metal ladder into the Caribbean sun, to be rewarded with a drink. I was still just 17 so I was only allowed a lime-juice but my ship-mates would all get rum. I kicked up a stink, the crew demanded rum for me too and there was nearly a mutiny until the officers gave way. That drink was like an initiation ceremony, a rite of passage. I was now a full member of the crew. Soon I was allowed to take turns at the helm on the bridge.

Life on the *Hellesina* was luxurious compared to any other boat. It was such a big tanker that every crewman had his own cabin, even a deck boy like myself. On other boats you had no privacy – six, eight, even 12 to a cabin – but on the *Hellesina* privacy had its drawbacks.

THE SURVIVOR

In my cabin next to the bunk there was a big water bottle, held in a wooden frame so it wouldn't tumble off when the ship was rolling. This bottle was eight inches across at the base and when it was full of drinking water it would be quite heavy. One evening at the end of our return crossing I was on my bunk reading when in came one of the 'donkey-men', who worked down in the engine room. He was a big Welshman, with shoulders like Babylonian boulders all covered in hair. He sat down next to my bunk and started talking. I thought nothing of it until he put his hand underneath my sheet and tried to touch me. Now he's got his head down, so I leaned across and got hold of this big water bottle and bosh! I brought it down on the top of his skull. I split his head wide open.

I jumped straight out of my bunk. There was blood all over it and right across the floor. I ran into the companionway and shouted. Some of the crew gathered and I told an officer what had happened. All this time the donkey-man was sprawled on the floor unconscious. There's always a medic on board – someone who can stitch you up – so now our medic saw to him. Then he said, 'It's a good job we're so close to port because this fellow could have died.'

Very early next morning we docked in Shellhaven where an ambulance took the Welshman straight to hospital, but the same day the police came on board and arrested me, even though I was the juvenile victim of a homosexual assault by this big mug. It was obvious that when he went to hospital he blamed the incident all on me. Now I had to appear at a magistrates' court to be charged with something like grievous bodily harm. One of the officers came with me and he also took me to my trial a few days later. In the taxi he said, 'I'm glad you did that. It's about time. We've had bad reports before about the fellow. We're going to make sure that the magistrate puts this right for you.' So I was cleared. The captain must have thought I was in the right because I went straight back on the *Hellesina* for another trip to Curaçao.

By the time I returned I had done 18 months on the boats. It was time for a little break, I thought, especially as some of my older friends were becoming active thieves. I was tempted to join them but because I had been away for so long and I was still green, I wasn't clued up to the snares and pitfalls of the villain's profession. I had no way of judging the risks involved in hitting certain targets and I didn't know the people who were suggesting them. Otherwise I would have known better than to go on one escapade which had 'set-up' written all over it.

FOUR

Jimmy Evans, PhD

IT began with me sitting in the Gem Café one day, when in came Billy Cotterell and Dodger Seabrook. Dodger was a bit of a crank, always stabbing and cutting people. He lived in an undertakers in Chapel Street and, for a laugh, we would sometimes go and sleep in the coffins which were made there. At 20 or 21 Dodger and Billy were both older than me but they knew I was game so they said, 'We've got a job, would you like to come? There's a metal dealer called Woods with a big house in Loughton, there's lots of money and we're going to get it all.'

'OK,' I said and, as I had a Colt .45 back home in the prefab, I added, 'Shall I bring my gun?'

They said, 'No, don't bring that. You don't need that, it's only an old woman.' A good job I didn't.

They explained that the job had been put up by someone else: George 'Frogs Eyes' Fox. He was known as Frogs Eyes because he looked as if he had a thyroid condition, like the film star Eddie Cantor. If I had known Frogs Eyes myself I would have turned this scheme down flat but, being away on the ships so much, I had never heard of him.

Of course, we had no car so Dodger and Billy had arranged to meet Frogs Eyes at Buckhurst Hill station. When we got there he took us into a pub where everyone except me was drinking pints of beer. Suddenly George said, 'It's all right now – this is the time to do it – but I can't go with you, 'cos the people know me. I've got to go back to London. I'll just show you the house.'

If I had been more experienced, I would have smelled a rat at this point – why is this bloke walking out on us now? – but the others believed George was OK and off we went to the house owned by this metal dealer.

When we get there the Dodger and Billy bottle out – they haven't got the guts to front up the robbery – so it's me who has to knock on the door. Mrs Woods opens up and I ask, 'Is your husband in?' 'No.' I say, 'You'll do.' But – contrary to what Frogs Eyes had told us – Mrs Woods is not alone: she's with another woman. I start tying them both up but the the other woman flaps, 'The gardener's here, you know! The gardener's here!'

So in he comes, except he's not a gardener. He's a detective and he says, 'I'm the police.' And I say, 'No you're not, you're the gardener!' and I kick him in the bollocks. He tries to grab me but I get away, out the front door, only to find myself confronted by a gauntlet of police. Before I reach the garden gate, one of them throws a stick, it hits bang on and out I go. Then they all jump on me and smash me to pieces. They throw me in one of their Humbers and take me to Woodford police station, bleeding all over the place as if I've been hit by a lorry in broad daylight with everyone looking at me. They call a police doctor who puts 14 stitches in the back of my head. Later he makes a statement saying, 'If this boy's skull had not been so thick, he would have died.' Once again I had survived.

But I was still nicked. Dodger and Billy had got away and were hiding in a cornfield. They spent the rest of the day sunbathing. This must have upset the police because, as we found out later, they had arranged the robbery for the sole purpose of nicking that pair. I was a surprise bonus. I was put in a cell where I looked up and saw a big metal grill in the ceiling. Ah ha, I thought, if I can undo that, I can climb through. I had managed to undo one screw when bang! Down came the entire framework including the metal grill which smashed on my head. With my eyes bleary from the beating, I hadn't noticed the grill was cracked and removing that one screw was bound to bring the whole thing down on top of me.

I had no hope of bail because I faced charges of aggravated robbery, or robbery with violence. The police soon caught up with Dodger Seabrook and Billy Cotterell. When they were brought in I said, 'I never mentioned your names.' They said, 'Don't worry, Jimmy, we know who did. Frogs Eyes. Because Frogs Eyes had set us up.'

They were carted off to Brixton prison on remand. I was taken to Wormwood Scrubs. When I got to trial, I was still covered in bandages like an Egyptian mummy, so the magistrate asked one of the detectives, 'How did he get in this condition?'

The copper replied, 'His head got in the way of the truncheon.'

So I said, 'Yeh, 14 times!'

The magistrate did not like that. Dodger and Billy got six months, but I was given 'nine to 36 months' in borstal, the juvenile alternative to jail.

Later I found out exactly what Dodger and Billy meant when they said that Frogs Eyes had set us up. It turned out that he wasn't just a police informer, he was an agent provocateur. He was working for a local detective who had a fixation about Dodger Seabrook and had made him a target. That's why Frogs Eyes had set this whole thing up. While we were in the pub with him, the detective and his crew were up at the house, hiding one police car in the garage and parking two more just out of sight. Trust my luck, the fake gardener was this detective, so with me kicking him in the bollocks and initially escaping his clutches, it's no wonder that his underlings could give me a good beating and get away with it.

I had been doubly unlucky. Not only was this a set-up, but the set-up wasn't even aimed at me. Dodger Seabrook was the target. I was just there to make up the numbers. But I did have one piece of luck: I had not taken the gun. If I had, I would certainly have used it. I would probably have killed a copper (if not Mrs Woods) and I would have been locked up for life. This was only 1948 and we still had the death penalty. I was too young to be hanged but Dodger and Billy could have swung instead. It would have been just like Craig and Bentley.

They should have seen right through Frogs Eyes. To be a hard-core villain you must see things coming and they weren't up to it, but the experience taught me several lessons. Never work with people you do not know. Never trust someone who makes an excuse and leaves just before you're going into action. Don't ever think it's too late to pull out of a job if your instincts tell you something's wrong. Never under-estimate the deviousness of the police. And never think it's easy to beat an alliance of cops and villains.

There should never be alliances of this kind in the first place, but there always have been and there always will be some slimey bastards who want to run with the hares and hunt with the hounds. I call them Siamese Vipers: a smile for the chaps on one head and a copper's helmet on the other – and you know who I'm talking about.

The Loughton job had been a disaster but I turned it to my advantage. It was a fiasco but it taught me lessons to last me all my life. In fact, everything that's ever happened to me has happened for the best.

Not that it felt like that for the next six months, while I was back in Wormwood Scrubs until they could find me a place in a borstal. I was still only 17 and once again I was the youngest kid in there. A couple of the Messina brothers were in there too, for violence and bribery. It's likely that my real father came in to visit them but he wouldn't have known that, just a few cells from the Messinas, there was a kid named Evans who was his son.

There were a few diversions. From our cell windows we could see barrage balloons still soaring over Scrubs Common and girls in the WACS jumping out of the baskets doing parachute practice. But most of the time being in there was fucking hard. There was a poxy screw in there, known to all the prisoners as Tojo because he looked just like that Japanese general, complete with little brass-rimmed glasses. He was such a little bastard that one day he was slung from the top floor over the rails down into the well of the main jail. It was only then that the authorities stretched wire across the low levels, so no one could go splat on the floor any more.

In those days the prison wasn't overcrowded. We had individual cells. We also had metal pisspots. Every morning we used to slop out by grabbing a handful of sand from a big bin of sand on the landing and scouring our pisspot with it. Then we would sling the sand back in the bin. But that sand wasn't changed for days, if not weeks, so what we were doing was grabbing handfuls of other people's shit. We also had wooden floors, which we had to scrub with a big block of stone and a bucket of water. When the news came through that I was finally being shipped off to borstal, it was a pleasure to get out. Whatever lay ahead could not be worse than the Scrubs, I thought, especially as the borstal I was going to was at Portland on the Dorset coast.

Portland. It sounded OK, like the Portland stone that was used to face so many grand London townhouses and the British Museum. But Portland Borstal? I had heard that it was a right dodgy place: set up to break the will and smash the spirits of young thugs just like me. Years before, it had been a place of penal servitude for adults. Dartmoor may have been known as the toughest jail of all, but if you didn't tow the line there you'd get sent to Portland, which was even worse: England's Devil's Island. When Portland became a borstal, the only thing that changed was that the inmates were much younger. It was the toughest borstal of all, so the lags in the Scrubs were saying.

Although my sentence was 'nine to 36 months', I knew that no one ever got out in nine months and most people did the full term. When you're that age three years is an eternity, so I tried to escape before I even arrived. They were taking a load of us there in a coach and I was sitting next to a bloke called Lewis. I'd grabbed him to make sure he sat next to me because I knew we would be handcuffed together and he had skinny wrists. By the time we reached Winchester for a halfway stop and a leak, I had used the butter off the prison sandwiches we'd been given to grease Lewis's wrist. Then I told him, 'When we get down from the coach, you're going to slip your cuff off.' Sure enough, as we got out at Winchester, he eased his hand out of his cuff, I broke through the gauntlet of guards and I got away. Slipping off my shoes so as not to leave footprints, I ran through a stream, crossed into some woods and hid up in a tree, covering my white shirt with a blue overcoat, while the guards looked for me below. When they went off in another direction, I tried to smash off the cuffs with a piece of metal I found in a barn, but I smashed my wrist instead. Then I went back to look for my shoes. I was crossing the stream again when I felt something bite me. I looked down in the water and I saw that my bare feet were covered in crayfish. I couldn't get out of there quick enough. I ran out towards the dogs and got captured. I would rather be bitten by the dogs than by those little lobster things.

After this experience I was only too glad to be taken on to Portland where I was given a good meal and a hot bath and put straight in the punishment block for six months. Officially this was called 'A' Wing but we all called it Chokey because it was a prison within a prison. The mattresses were filled with coconut fibre and we had the job of pulling out the strands from the mattresses and undoing all the fibre that had been impacted by people sleeping on them. As this building was semi-underground – like a cellar – we shared the place with rats and cockroaches. At night you could hear them coming into the cell for a munch. And we were sleeping right on the floor, on flat bed-boards, so you could wake up to find them crawling over you.

There would be only four or six blokes in there at a time so, as the months passed, I became 'number one' and was given a little authority as 'party boy'. One of our daily punishments was getting up at 5.30 to wash outdoors. Now as party boy, I had to rise even earlier to get buckets of cold water out into the little exercise yard, and do a couple of other jobs, before the others even woke up. But in winter it was so cold on this desolate headland jutting out in the English Channel that the water froze as soon as I ran it into the buckets, so before any of us could wash, we had to break the ice. Then we had to do exercises in this freezing yard. And all we had on was a singlet, a pair of shorts and our boots.

For days on end Portland prison would be above the clouds. It was so damp that anyone with a sickly condition was lucky to survive, especially as all the screws there were nuts, and sadists too. During exercise periods they would give each of us blokes conflicting orders to make us run into each other. During one of these routines, one of the boys collapsed and had to be taken to hospital down in Weymouth. I never saw him again.

During my stay in Portland some evil bastards were there, including one 'Yorkie' Cooper. He had a head like an egg – no hair – and he wore tiny, steel-rimmed glasses. He was in Portland because he and his stepfather had killed a disabled person in a wheelchair. He thought he was a tough nut and he liked hurting people. But not everybody was like him and I made a good few pals who would become my partners-in-crime in later life.

One of the worst duties on Portland was being put on the Burma Road: digging rocks as big as tables out of the local quarry. There'd be 75 of us tying ropes round these rocks, digging around them with pickaxes and mattocks, and pulling them out. Then we'd smash them to pieces. We would be wearing just overalls, bibs and braces, even when it was snowing. It got so cold we used to piss on each other's hands to warm them up. Some people just couldn't take it. They would get other people to smash their legs with a shovel, just so they could get off the work party and be taken to Weymouth Hospital.

These conditions didn't really worry me because when I was in the merchant navy I had been to ports in the eastern Baltic, like Riga and Leningrad, in the real freezing cold. Also I decided to really get stuck into this task and I would get so hot when I was smashing the rocks that I used to strip down to the waist. The other blokes used to shout out above the roar of the blizzards, 'For fuck's sake, Evans, put something on! You're making us feel worse!'

I wasn't the only crackpot. Whenever we went to the quarry we had to walk along a farm lane, where cows would put their heads over the walls, so this bloke 'Curly' Whitfield used to take bets on whether he could knock out a cow by chinning it. Most times he would drop them with one hit.

But however freaky the inmates, the screws were even worse. There was a horrible little screw called Waters who was seething because a boy called Pannam never called him 'Sir'. So Waters decided to employ that bastard Yorkie to teach Pannam a lesson.

Yorkie was a 'trustie'. He had so impressed the screws with his capacity for violence against other boys that he was made the number one and party boy on the Burma Road. On days when we had to go out on the Burma Road, Yorkie had the job of running on ahead and opening up the huge toolshed. Then we would all walk up in file and collect our pick-axes and mattocks for our day's work in the quarry, until we would all be marched back for the evening meal.

This six-foot-two Yorkie was such an arse-licker that one day, at Waters's urging, he got two other blokes to hold Pannam down while he smashed him in the face. He broke Pannam's nose and the poor bastard had to crawl to the tap and break the ice off so he could get to the water to wash his face.

I decided that I'd had enough of this. I figured Yorkie had to go. I had to cut out any more bullying and give myself a bit more freedom. So a few days later, with Mickey Inglefield minding me, I did Yorkie myself with a pick-axe handle. I did him properly. They had to send the scumbag to Weymouth Hospital.

The funny thing is, I was never punished. Instead I took his job, like I'd planned. I was made party boy for the entire Burma Road. To the screws it was just like a game of conkers – winner takes all – only the conkers were not a bunch of chestnuts but us. We were like so many contenders for a boxing title. You're the champion only until someone else comes along and puts you into Weymouth.

Unlike Yorkie, I was never 'conkered'. I kept the party boy job till I left Portland but, just in case someone decided it was time for me to be deposed, I always had my own special weapon. This was a chain, carried by a pal called Ronny Bogellen, over his shoulder but concealed under his jacket. It was called a mortice chain and it had been nicked out of the woodwork shop by another pal, Terry Ward, the brother of Buller Ward who later fell out with the Krays. Bogellen just had to make sure he was always near me, so he could pass it to me if ever I had an argument with some of Yorkie Cooper's pals. See, fights – even battles – were always bubbling, with us Londoners on one side and everyone else – Yorkies, Scousers, Brummies, Scots – on the other.

But no one ever took me on. The chain was never needed. This may have been because each day we went out on the Burma Road I would make a show of strength to keep people's minds in line. As we walked to the quarry, we would pass a huge wagon wheel lying outside one of the workshops. It was six foot high, the metal band around it was eight or nine inches wide, its hub was two feet wide and it had massive spokes. So every morning I would lift up one side of the wheel, get underneath it on my knees (a bit like a weightlifter), tilt it towards me, stand up, duck and lift the entire wheel at arm's length above my head. That was tough enough – and I was the only one on the work party who could do this – but the tricky bit was getting the wheel down. I would have to tip it forward and then step back as it hit the ground, because the huge hub would spring the rim of the wheel back up.

But one morning I didn't move quick enough and as I stepped forward, boink! This rim's come up and chipped a fucking big lump out of my shinbone. I was in pure agony, the pain was excruciating, but I couldn't let the others see it. So I carry on to the Burma Road and I'm smashing these rocks all day long with this fucking pain. The pain went on for a week, but every morning I had to lift the wagon wheel as if nothing was wrong even if I now made sure that when I dropped the wheel I kept the rim well away from me.

Yes, it sounds nuts but sometimes there are things you feel you have to do to show force, so the others will think: if he can pick that up, he can pick us up – and throw us down. At least that's how it was on the Burma Road.

I often think back to Portland and I reckon that all the brutality of the borstal régime had the opposite effect from what the Home Office had in mind. Far from destroying the criminal tendencies of young offenders, this particular borstal only expanded them. Offering no education, no classes, it was the breeding ground for a new generation of serious villains who would spend the next 40 years working together on tens of thousands of major crimes.

I got no remission. I did the full three years. When I came out, I had spent the same length of time at Portland, and at the same age, as most students spend at university getting a degree. Portland was also a university of sorts and I had gone one better than my more academic contemporaries: I came out of there with a PhD – in crime.

FIVE

Family Man All at Sea

THROUGHOUT my time in Portland one special person was on my mind. In fact if it wasn't for that person, I might not even have been in Portland. I was only in there because I had gone on the Loughton robbery that turned out to be a 'ready-eye'. And I only went on that because I wanted to buy my girlfriend an engagement ring and get married with my share of the proceeds.

Her name was Mary. She wasn't bad to look at and she was one big reason why generally I behaved myself at Portland. After my failed escape attempt I had been in so little trouble that the governor gave me compassionate leave to get married. The girl had only two weeks to go before the baby was due, and I was trusted to go to London without an escort, attend my own wedding and then come back to Portland, which I did.

When she went into hospital I was so close to her mentally that, 150 miles away, I was having stomach pains too. That was how close we were. I was very attached to her then.

The baby was a girl and we called her Denise. I would love to have spent time with her as a baby but I never got any more home leave, so I only saw her and her mother when they were allowed to visit me. When I finally came home in 1953, I was no longer a bachelor but married with a wife and kid. By this time they had moved into the prefab with my old man Bill Bridger and my old lady. Then she moved out, leaving my old man in the prefab. With his cancer he needed plenty of looking after, so, with my wife and kid, I now had three generations of dependents.

In this situation many men would act 'responsibly'. They would get steady jobs and behave themselves. Others would desert the family and run a mile. Me? I did both. I took a steady job but I went back to sea. Now I had the best of both worlds: I was married but when I was away I was as free as a bird.

I could tell a lot of stories about the scrapes I got into at sea and on land, especially the dishonourable discharges. I was slung off boats in Russia, in Copenhagen, in Cape Town. In fact my whole time in the merchant navy was like being on a floating version of the East End because a lot of the characters that I met at sea were from the East End and a lot of them were semi-criminals. Not surprising when you think that the London Docks were really dug out of the East End and we grew up with ships almost moored in our back yards.

One East Ender I was on the boats with was the Krays' uncle, Limehouse Willie. He was tall and slim, and then he had a tight mop of curly hair. He had a nutty look in his eyes and he was always laughing. I liked him. We both sailed on the General Steam Navigation runs to Norway, Denmark and Sweden. All the boats were named after birds, like the *Tern* and the *Grebe* and I served on them for years as a steward. Alongside Limehouse Willie was another character who called himself Smuggler Bill. His real name was Billy Sully and later he became a small-time actor, on television and in Bond films. He looked like that TV detective character, Cannon. He tried to act like him as well, and he was a right character, a bit of a comic too.

On one of these ships my duties included getting the captain his daily breakfast. One morning I go into the galley and his silver tray isn't there, his silver coffee pot isn't there, and nor is his silver milk jug, silver sugar bowl or even his silver egg cup. Fuck me, I say to myself, I can't find these things, I'm running late and the captain's getting ready to get on the bridge. So I don't know why – maybe it was instinct – but I've run down to Smuggler Bill's cabin and he's sitting on his bunk, his feet up on his little table, and he's polishing the silver coffee pot and a little silver egg cup, and alongside are the other missing items, all with 'General Steam Navigation Co' engraved on them. So I say, 'What the fuck are you doing, Bill? That's the captain's', and Smuggler Bill replies, 'It's something for my old mum.' 'Something for your old mum!' I say, 'Fuck your old mum. What about the captain?'

I couldn't be bothered to have a row over this gear, and, as I liked Bill's old mum, I let him keep it. Then somehow I dug up another set without the old captain catching on.

Anyway, he was on this boat when we used to smuggle stuff out, mainly to Norway, then smuggle other stuff home. The Norwegians were desperate for real coffee so we'd take sacks of coffee beans out there. Then Smuggler Bill told me they liked rum and we had this idea to mix the rum essence you can use in cooking with a scarcely alcoholic drink called VP Wine. Bill said, 'Where can we get a load of Four Bells Rum labels? I know. We can soak them off the officers' bottles when they've finished the real stuff. Then we take the labels off those VP Wine bottles and replace them with Four Bells labels.'

So we used to take the seal and the foil top off the VP Wine bottles nice and carefully, then we'd remove the cork and pour in the bottles of rum essence. And these Norwegians were lapping it up. They used to go, 'Ahh, good rum!' We did this for a few times and we were making a bit of money. It was costing us about six bob (30 pence) and we were getting about six quid. Now we got carried away: we were bringing cases of VP Wine on board every time we came back to London Docks. We decided to speed up production by using a bath, but on these boats the only person with a bath was the captain. We had to wait for him to go ashore, then we'd enter his suite, tip all these wine bottles in his bath, add the rum essence and stir it all up. Then we'd funnel all the mixture back into the bottles. At first we thought we should fortify it with a bottle or two of real rum but soon we got greedy and dropped that idea. Just as we had perfected this process and made another bathful, I found that that all the white bath enamel was stained red. It was the colour of claret. It looked like someone had had his throat cut in it – but somehow I managed to bleach out the stain before the captain returned.

This little racket was just a sideline, of course. Most of the time we were more interested in getting to grips with any girl passengers. One Christmas the boat was going to Norway and there's nothing so beautiful, even in winter, as coming up the Fjords at dawn. On this occasion the only passenger was a beautiful little Norwegian girl of about 20. It turned out she was a nurse at St Bartholemew's Hospital where I was born and she was going back to spend Christmas with her family.

All the officers were firing after her, they all liked her, but for some reason she and I got on well. There was me, in my white jacket and blue strides (the steward's winter uniform), and during meals I'd be serving on the table and giving her a bit extra. And afterwards she would stay behind to talk to me. She spoke perfect English. She'd stay drinking and I'd be doing my job, wiping glasses and talking to her.

Early on in the voyage Smuggler Bill and Limehouse Willie said to me, 'Do you think that little bird would like to see the engine room?' So I said I'd ask her. They obviously fancied her but I wasn't interested. I already had a couple of girlfriends in Oslo and I couldn't wait to get there but on the last evening before we were due in I said to her after the meal, 'Have you ever been to the engine room on a ship and seen what it's like?'

'No.'

'Would you like to?' '

I'd love to.'

'OK. Meet me on the aft deck at about quarter past eight tonight.'

This engine room was manned by three donkey-men, each taking four-hour turns on watch: Smuggler Bill, Limehouse Willie and a third man we called Sonny the Welshman. So she turns up and it's windy and sleeting and cold, and she's only got on a white hat, a white dress, white gloves and white shoes, as if we were on a Caribbean cruise. So I say, 'You go first', but there's steam and oil everywhere and she's running her white gloves down the rail beside the steel steps down to the engine room. Unbeknown to me, hiding down in the engine room, behind the telegraph and some other instrument, there's Smuggler Bill with a pot of red paint and Limehouse Willie with a pot of green paint, like port and starboard. And while she's standing looking all round at this huge engine going 'chug, chug, chug', they are painting one of her toe-caps green and the other toe-cap red. Then she sees what's happened and goes, 'Oh no!', and they both get up laughing.

So now Limehouse Willie slid alongside her and put one hand round her bottom, leaving a big black greasy hand-mark on her dress, and his other hand on her breast with the same effect, and said, 'I've got some spirit in the cabin. That'll fix it.' She thought they meant cleaning spirit but he was on about the drinking kind. So we took her up to the cabin which all three of these donkey-men shared. It happened that Sonny the Welshman had just finished his watch, so he was already in the cabin when we walked in. He takes one look at her and begs us all to leave him alone with her. So we do the decent thing, we walk out and now he's got her all to himself. He's got her on his bunk and he's going to work on her.

Meantime we've gone up on the deck while this ship is chugging up the North Fjord in deep mid-winter. It's freezing cold, there's a blizzard, sleet, and it's blowing up a right storm, but we're going up there at full steam and lumps of ice bigger than a room are sweeping down with the current and crashing against the boat. But none of this is on our minds because we're thinking, what's going on in the donkey-men's cabin?

So I said, 'Willie, I want to see what they're up to.' And on the side of the boat there's a 'Jacob's ladder' tied to the rail. A good job it's tied to the rail because a Jacob's ladder consists of just a pair of ropes with wooden slats between, which can be rolled up, lifted and slung over the side of the boat. So I've gone over the side on this Jacob's ladder, still wearing my little white cotton steward's jacket and my navy blue trousers. I slide down and I'm looking in through the port-hole and there is the Welshman pumping away on this little Norwegian bird, giving it some stick. She's obviously enjoying herself too and I'm there looking through the porthole and thinking to myself, 'Blimey! no wonder they call them donkey-men.'

All of a sudden I feel this huge weight hanging round my neck. It's Willie! He's only come down the ladder behind me trying to see Sonny on the job as well. And he's hanging round my neck. And the wind's blowing and big lumps of ice as big as houses are smashing away just a foot beneath our feet. If that Jacob's ladder had collapsed under twice the weight it was meant to carry that would have been us gone.

But in the excitement of it all, you don't think of those things. Now I realise how mad we must have been but then it was just a laugh, especially when, all of a sudden, she's turned to one side and seen our faces looking in. And she's screamed and pushed Sonny off her. So we scampered back up the ladder and left it dangling. Limehouse Willie and I were just as nutty as each other. As for Sonny the Welshman, he did right by the Norwegian nurse. It was love at first sight, he made a big fuss of her and they ended up getting married. I've never seen Sonny again but if he's got a nice little family today, I'd like to think that I contributed to it by introducing them to each other in the first place.

I went on to work for the Castle Line, also as a steward, until I got slung off the *Bloemfontein Castle* in Cape Town for doing no work and larking around with my pal Smudge Smith. That boat was due to spend several more weeks on the South African coast but the company wanted to ship us straight back home so they put us on board the *Pretoria Castle*, which was a fast mail boat sailing for London the next day.

With just one night in Cape Town Smudge and I decided to go out on the rampage. We came across a gun shop and decided to break in. We spotted a little cavity between the shop window and the roof so Smudge lifted me up and over. I dropped down into the shop, looked along rows of rifles, picked up a pair and came out. We stuck them under our coats and made our way

THE SURVIVOR

back to the *Pretoria Castle*. We had been put in a cabin with ten other seamen that we didn't know from Adam, so we decided that we would give them a bright start to the voyage home. Next morning they were woken by cold metal touching their cheeks, and found themselves looking up the barrels of the rifles we had nicked that night in Cape Town. We were laughing but they didn't think it was funny.

Because we didn't have any duties on board the *Pretoria Castle*, Smudge and I still had the rest of the day to play around on shore, so we climbed a long way up Table Mountain. It was such a fantastic view, we could even see our ship in the docks below, as tiny as the models I used to drool over in Fenchurch Street. All of a sudden we heard the ship blowing its farewell blast and we realised it was about to sail away, leaving us stuck on shore. So we ran all the way back and, just as we arrived, the great big gangway was being pulled away from the side of the ship by a crane. Smudge was far behind me so he had no chance, but I ran right to the top of the gangway and jumped. I could hear women passengers, who were lining the rail, scream in horror. It was a leap of about ten feet but I made it. If I'd missed, I would have fallen 60 feet into the water and probably been crushed against the harbour wall by the liner. That far down, I would have had no chance against a structure the height and weight of a block of flats. A survivor yet again, I got no applause. Instead I was taken straight to the captain. 'You'll never sail on this line again!' he growled. As for Smudge, lucky bugger, he hitched a lift on the boat that collects the pilot when he's finished steering ships out of port. So as the pilot stepped off the *Pretoria Castle*, Smudge climbed aboard.

Now we were in even deeper trouble: thrown off one boat, bollocked on this one – and as soon as we got back to our cabin we found out we'd been grassed off over those stolen guns we'd waved around. No one had taken them away, they were still in our lockers, but we knew we'd have to get rid of them because they were identifiable from their numbers and we might go to jail if we were caught in possession. When we docked in Southampton and saw the customs men boarding, we knew for sure we'd be getting a spin. They gave our cabin a real going-over. It was clear they were looking for the guns but they found nothing. Moments beforehand we had thrown them out of the porthole into the harbour waters.

I was never allowed to work for the Castle Line again, as that captain had predicted, but I did pick up trips with Cunard. I sailed to Canada on the liner, *Samaria*. The crew cabins were so antiquated they had 12 or even 14 bunks in them. When I first checked in, I couldn't help seeing this strange character sitting on the bunk above mine, swinging his legs. As I laid my suitcase out on my bottom bunk and started putting my clothes in the narrow metal cabinet that I'd been allocated, I heard this character say out loud, 'I wonder what he's got in there.' The voice alone was weird enough to make you realise this fellow had problems. He drawled low and deep, just like Bernard Bresslaw in the TV series *The Army Game*, and he also had a slight stutter. To make things worse, he was thinking out loud. He couldn't help it. He didn't even realise he was doing it.

So I looked up at him and I said, 'You're wondering what I've got in there, ain't you?', and he put a twisted grin on his face and sort of laughed. Then I said, 'If anything's missing out of this, I know where to come to.' Nothing more was said. That was our introduction. That was how I first encountered Bobby Whitfield who later became known as 'Dodgy Bob', for reasons that will become obvious.

The ship gets under way and next morning we get up and all do our bits and pieces. By the following night we're right out in the Atlantic Ocean and everybody's asleep, except for Dodgy Bob. At two in the morning I hear him moving about above me. He puts his little bunk light on, then he slides off the bunk. Next he starts combing his hair, and over his pyjamas he's wearing a tie and a pullover, so I open one eye and say, 'Where do you think you're going?' and he says, 'Are you awake?' I say, 'Of course I'm awake! You've woken up everyone on the boat!' 'So then he drawls, 'I'm going out on the creep, going on a little creep around. You w . . . w . . . want to come with me?' And I say, 'Yeah, hang on.' Well, I was only young and game for anything.

He says, 'I've got these twirls (skeleton keys)', so we go up the companionway into the passengers' quarters, we get to the first door, he flops it open, we go in and he says, 'Keep your eyes and ears open while I have a rummage around.' There's the husband in one bunk and his wife snoring away in the other, and he's opened a drawer and he's rummaging away. He finds a few things, then he opens up the briefcase standing at the side and all the time I'm standing at the cabin door, keeping an eye out.

All those big liners used to have masters-at-arms to police the passenger areas, so I'm watching out to see if one of these blokes is coming along the companionway (unlikely because there's probably only one on duty at night for the whole of this huge boat). Out comes Dodgy Bob, he closes the door, he even locks it, and on he goes to the next cabin, and the next. Sooner or later a master-of-arms is bound to show up so I say to him, 'Fuck this. If it's on top, if a master-at-arms shows up, where are we going to run? We're in the middle of the Atlantic Ocean!' So he says, 'Well, wha . . . wha . . . what do you want to do?' I say, 'I want to go to my bunk and kip. I've got to get up early in the morning but I've got a better idea.'

As we went back down to the cabin, I explained my scheme. I said, 'When we dock in Quebec City, they'll put everybody's suitcases under an awning on the forward well deck. This'll be at night, and that's when we can slip in there and help ourselves to whatever we like.' 'Oh, all right then,' he said. So that night we docked. This was winter, when you can see icebergs at the entrance to the St Lawrence River, but my eyes were glued on Dodgy Bob as he set about all that luggage like a schoolkid digging into a jar of sweets. He was stealing watches, bits of jewellery and loads of cash. It was a nice little pay-day, especially as he hadn't had to work for it.

I called him Dodgy Bob because he just couldn't help doing dodgy things. In Quebec City he went straight ashore and had me minding him while he went in camera shops and other stores. He used to like me watching him in action. He'd say, 'W . . . w . . . watch me go in.' And I'd say, 'Yeah, Bob, I'll watch you go in. And I want to watch you come out again, with my presents!' And out he'd come, with rings, watches, everything.

Then he latched on to the fact that, along the St Lawrence River shore, people would still be sunbathing, even in winter. They'd undress and put all their clothing in their cars, and while they'd be lying there getting a bit of sunshine, he'd want me to mind him while he got in their cars and went through all their gear. He was just a crank, but I was young and, to me, it was fun.

The crew of the *Samaria* was packed with weird characters. Dodgy Bob wasn't the weirdest by a long way. There were two big homosexuals, and I mean big. One was called Cucumber Lil and the other was called Lulu. Just in case we were in any doubt, Lulu always wore a yellow woollen jumper—which he'd probably knitted himself – with red letters on the front spelling 'LULU'. As on most big liners, there was a recreational area for the crew, with a bar, which was always called the Pig and Whistle. And in each corner there'd be a lot of gambling going on: games like Over and Under, Find the Lady and the Crown and Anchor.

In this particular corner there was a fixed seating area, with slatted wooden benches, and gaps of as much as an inch and a half between the slats. I noticed that at the table where they ran the Crown and Anchor board,

Cucumber Lil would sit on one corner and Lulu on the other, while on the bench between they kept a biscuit tin to hold their takings and act as the bank. They would put all coins in the tin but they placed all the notes underneath it, directly on top of the slats with the inch and a half gaps. At any one time they'd be holding a lot of notes – £100 a night, sometimes a lot more, a fortune in those days. That was because the stewards used to get good tips and they'd gamble. But the area had very poor lighting so I thought up a feasible scheme.

There was another bloke on this trip whom I'd known since we were at school together. He was called 'Big' Charlie Reader and he got shot years later by Jacky Buggy outside the Pigalle when Shirley Bassey was appearing. So I told this Dodgy Bob that Lulu and Cucumber Lil would always turn up about nine in the evening to occupy their table, and I said, 'If you arrive about ten to nine and get underneath that seat and lie there before they arrive, when the notes start coming in you could pull some of them through the slats. It's so dark they won't notice.'

'Yeah, all right. Wa . . . wa . . . what happens if they suss me out?'

'Don't worry. Me and Big Charlie will mind you. We'll be there.'

'Oh, all right then.'

One night when we're a thousand miles out in the Atlantic, he does this. It's all going fine when, halfway through the session, one of these huge queens has caught a part of Dodgy Bob's body with his foot: 'Uh, what's going on here then? Some-fucking-one's underneath here, nicking our money!' Now these blokes were two big wrestlers. So as Dodgy Bob's scrambled out, they've chased him all round the ship and they've caught him, and battered shit out of him.

He's got no money out of it, he's got a black eye, and he's black and blue all over, but he just shrugged it off. 'Oh w . . . w . . . well,' he said, 'it was w . . . w . . . worth a try, w . . . w . . . wasn't it?,' That was Dodgy Bob.

Signing on for long-haul trips to the Americas, South Africa and Australia meant that I would be away for months at a time, but the pull of my real calling was becoming too great to resist. My old pals back home would always have work for me to do so every time I came off the boats it would be straight back to business, up to no good.

For this reason I picked up a useful cover job with a taxi valeting firm called the Barney Davies Cab Company. I used to wash black cabs at his depot in Three Colts Lane during the night and when the cabmen packed in work, I would drive them home in one of their own cabs. Each time I did this, I would have a cab for my own schemes until dawn. First I would earn a bit of pocket money, picking up people looking for a late cab home. Then in the early hours I would do smash-and-grabs. I would reverse into radio shops, or throw a jack through the window, load up and be off. Not that I had a driving licence, let alone a cabbie's permit.

Now I could roam all over London, not only because I had wheels but because I had plenty of pals everywhere. Before I went to borstal I only knew villains I'd grown up with, most of them in Hackney. Now I knew people right across London, bonded together because we had all done Portland together on the Burma Road. That Portland PhD served as a passport throughout my slice of the underworld.

Soon after my release I teamed up with some borstal mates. The authorities like to kid themselves – and the public – into thinking these places reform tearaways and make them better citizens, but they don't. They just propel you into joining a vast criminal network, not just the 'underworld', more like an underground resistance movement. It's the penal system itself that welds you together in a freemasonry of felons. And this is what it's designed for, to make sure there's enough crime around to keep hundreds of thousands of people employed in the criminal justice system: coppers, screws, judges, barristers, solicitors, probation officers, psychiatrists. Without us criminals, where would they all be? Out of fucking work, skint, is my guess. The system has no interest whatever in seeing thieves like I was becoming law-abiding supermarket shelf-stackers.

For instance, there was one bloke we knew from Portland called 'the Tortoise'. Much later on I was told that in 1963 he was paid 35 grand [£35,000] to burn down Leatherslade Farm, where the Great Train Robbers had mustered after they'd robbed the train. But the Tortoise never did burn the farm down. Instead he used his huge unearned fee to buy a big house and become a country squire. Thirty-five grand was a nice touch in those days. For that kind of money, in those days, I would have burned the whole of Aylesbury down.

Then there were all my new friends in South London. Before Portland I knew no one from there – it was a different world. Funny what a huge difference five miles and the River Thames made then. Till I was sent away I would only work with East End people whom I knew and trusted, but in Portland I met South Londoners like my pal Tony Samms and Mickey Inglefield whom I also liked. By doing time with them, I came to like them too.

By 1955 I was earning such a decent bit of money from crime that I hit it on the head with the ships. I quit the merchant navy and decided to become a full-time nuisance. I was an all-rounder. I was available for steam-ins (bank jobs), I was fast on my feet and normally I could think just as fast too. And I used to drive the cars. I was always nicking 3.8 Jaguars for getaways. Sometimes me and 'Ginger' Tommy Marks would take two or three Jaguars in one night until I was satisfied that we had just the right one for the job in hand. I became quite busy to the point that I could not drive through certain areas of London without someone from Portland popping up and asking if I needed anyone else on my firm.

I gave up the boats around when my old man Bill Bridger died. This was a bad time for me as I reflected back on his life, and mine. I was having a great life but I couldn't guarantee the same for any kids of mine. I had survived this far by the skin of my teeth. Would my offspring be just as lucky? Probably not, I decided, so I wouldn't let my wife have any more kids. See, I never knew where I was going to be next week, never mind next year. I didn't know what was just around the corner. It could be a good touch or it could be a chunk of bird. So one kid was enough.

On the domestic side of marriage, I never let her do a thing. In all our married life I never let her iron a shirt for me or anything. This was partly because of all my years at sea. If you've ever been on the ships you learn how to take care of yourself. Even today if I go upstairs and find any of my clothes ironed and pressed by my present wife, I get a little bit embarrassed. I'm always clearing up, doing my own things. I can't help it. I can't get out of the habit.

And back in the 1950s I couldn't get out of the habit of crime. There was so much villainy, I was out every night. I was out all the time. I had to be. For me it was an obsession. I loved it. I was nicking lorryloads, tying up drivers, doing ram-ups, looting jewellers': you name it, I did it. Then one evening for the first time I went to work with a safe-blower. I was sitting next to him while he did a box in a jeweller's. I've always been mechanically minded, that's one reason I've always liked guns. I also liked the smell of guns when they were fired. That lovely smell of oil and nitro, better than any aftershave lotion.

But when I was with this bloke, I took a liking to a new smell: the smell of gelignite. Once the box is blown and you're right up close to it, jelly gives you a right headache but it has a delirious smell. I loved it. Soon I got kinky for it. I even reached the state that I'd blow a box even if it was odds-on there was nothing in it. I just got the flavour and, you know what they say, practice makes perfect. So as I watched this bloke at work, I realised that opening a double-door safe is almost as thrilling as going to bed with a new woman. When you open those two doors you get almost the same pleasure as opening up a pair of lovely slender legs – especially when ahead of you, lying on the shelves, you see a few stacks of dough. Sheer pleasure.

SIX

The Making of a Master Safe-Blower

AFTER watching this safe-blower at work I thought: this is the game for me. I started making my own enquiries. Posing as a legitimate customer, I would go into safe sales showrooms, buy an old safe, bring it home and take it apart. Also jelly was easy to come by. We used to raid the quarries out in Kent and nick their supplies. It was so easy in those days: quarry bunkers only had an old padlock on the door.

But one day a fellow called Joey knocked at my prefab. I won't mention his surname but he will remember the incident. He said, 'Jim, do you want a sack of jelly and a load of detonators?'

I said, 'No, I've got loads of it', and it was true I had three or four lock-up garages with a bit here, a bit there: ringers, guns, even a machine-gun if one was needed.

So Joey said, ' Only we've done a terrific bit of work last night and I won't be needing any more jelly for a long while.' He went on, 'Well, anyway, will you do me a favour, Jim?'

I said, 'What's that?'

Now opposite my old prefab was a turning, Frampton Park Road, which I could see right up from my front room. So he went to my window, lifted the curtain and said, 'You see that Jag?' I looked out and 100 yards up this road there was a grey Jaguar. And he said, 'Will you keep your eye on that for me, Jim? Because there's a sack full of money in the boot and I can't move it for the moment. We just done a bank in Northamptonshire last night.'

I said, 'Yeah, all right. Don't worry about it. It'll be safe there.'

I later found out that there was £60,000 in that sack. This was the 1950s so today that £60,000 would be worth maybe two million. Joey and his little mob had made a hole in a brickwork wall under a waterside bridge which led them straight into this bank vault and also gave them a clean getaway. So for a couple of days I kept an eye on the Jag, looking to see if it was being watched by Old Bill, ready to ambush anyone who showed up to drive it away. There was no such activity, so Joey came and took it away. If I had been a different person, I might have gone over with a crowbar and stolen the money myself but Joey knew I was a man who could be trusted. I had enough money and jelly not to need any of his.

At that time safe-manufacturers were forever incorporating new devices in their products, but every single thing they brought out to counteract people like me, I'd get around. For instance, they decided to bring out drop-bolts. The idea was that the moment you blew the safe, two bolts would drop down through the safe door into the base of the frame, preventing you from opening it. They would also anchor the safes down with chains, then stick both the safe and the chains in a cement bedding. No problem for me because we would simply get them up with big railway crowbars. We used to have six-foot-six-inch crowbars, the kind that navvies used to prize up old rails before laying down new ones. We would use these 'canes' to lift the safe, then we'd snap the chains or burn them away with a little cutter. Then we'd turn the safe upside down because the drop-bolts couldn't drop upwards.

By this time I was getting better and better at safe-blowing. Because we were hitting only the most rewarding targets, I found myself blowing only the very best safes, makes like Chubb with stainless steel handles. Goodbye to the old manky ones with brass handles, I was now obliging some cream – the most advanced safes on the market.

Now the safe-manufacturers thought they could beat us by spring-loading the drop-bolts that we had just defeated. And for a while we found that even if we turned these new safes upside-down, springs would shoot the bolts upwards and shut us out. So to beat these spring-bolts, I invented a system where I had a bit of two-inch by two-inch wood with straps screwed on, so I could strap it to the handle of the safe and then tighten the straps. I would also attach a screw-eye or ring on to this piece of wood, so that when I was inside the room with the safe, I could screw in another screw-eye on to a door-frame or some other fitting nearby. Then I used a kind of chest-expander spring to clip into both these screw-eyes – one attached to the length of wood on the safe handle and the other attached to the office door-frame or whatever. Now I had a right good 100 pound or more pressure, far greater than the pressure of their bolts. This meant I could beat them and blow the safe because my spring was more powerful and quicker than theirs. Of course, the manufacturers would come back with some other idea but I would always come up with something else to beat it.

Then up came a bit of work in an office where a new Copeland-Chatterson safe had been installed, so I made use of a business card that I had picked up while visiting Charlie Richardson in his metal yard and called in on one of the leading safe showrooms in London. Keen as ever, the sales staff walked over to me and I said, 'Good morning, I've got a metal yard. Here's my card. We get some unsavoury characters wandering in and out and I'm a bit concerned, because we handle quite a lot of cash. So I'd like to inquire about a particular make of safe, a Copeland-Chatterson.' So they showed me various models, saying things like, 'This is good, that's good. That's very strong, it can't be cut.' So I said, 'How about gelignite? Couldn't criminals blow this one?' And they said, 'Well, yes, if they knew what they were doing, it could be blown.' See, these salesmen could not lie to a customer because if they claimed a safe was jelly-proof when it wasn't, and then it was blown, the sales firm and the makers could both be in trouble. Armed with this information, I went and blew the Copeland-Chatterson safe I had been tipped off about and relieved it of its load.

When I was preparing a job I would take the trouble to find out what other people didn't bother to find out. I'd be looking not for my way in but for my ways out. I would want to make sure that, if it goes wrong and the law turns up, I can escape from the place. I would reconnoitre every bit of business. Whereas other people would go and have a drink, I'd go in as a professional criminal, I'd check the job out in full. I'd find all the places where I could leave cars, especially back-up cars. And sometimes I would even tie an old bike in the back of a van so that, when we had done a job and each gang member went his own way, I would put on an old cap and an old brown tradesman's coat. Then if the hue and cry went up and the police set up roadblocks, I would peddle by them on an old push bike. More often than not, the police would leave cyclists alone. That's why I always came home. I never ever got caught – not on any business of my own. I only came to grief when the Foremans started arranging things for me with their police friends.

In the 1950s I did one type of bank with only one other pair of hands. They belonged to my pal Davey Norman. On one night alone we nicked nearly 50 grand in cash in wage packets but we had to leave another 180 grand in the safe because we couldn't carry it. We left 60 grand in a feeder safe as well because these wage packets contained a lot of coin as well as notes and the load was so heavy we couldn't drag it out to the motor. We didn't even open some safe drawers because we had run out of time. We just carried out a sack each and even that felt like a ton. By the way, all these amounts are the face value of the money in the mid '50s to mid '60s. To come up with an equivalent today they should be multiplied 30 times.

Anyhow, with what we did manage to get away with, on that job and many others, we funded a nice life for ourselves and our families. We always had plenty of money. We also had plenty of laughs, like the raid on the old pickle factory years before.

It all started when I had a visit from Curly King. He was a small fellow but with broad shoulders and a big ego. He said, 'Look, Jim, I've got a nice box in a big pickle factory in Bow. It may only make pickles but it's huge and they employ a lot of people. They've got this old safe and on the evening before pay-day there's going to be plenty of dough in wages – eight grand or ten grand.' This was a lot of money at a time when £5 paid for one family's groceries for a week, not the 150 or 200 quid you need today. With ten grand in those days you could have bought five nice little terraced houses.

So I went along with Curly, more for a laugh than anything, and because I liked him, and I had a look at this place. In those days it was common practice for offices and post offices to have an observation window on the street side of the building – a clear window where at night the copper on the beat could walk along, look through and check it out. So straightaway I spotted the observation window in the office and naturally I took it into account.

On the agreed night we got in the yard without any trouble. We just had to climb over a high wall. Then came the acrobatic bit: we had to balance on these huge six-foot-high barrels in which they would store these pickles. And all these barrels lined this wall leading into the back of the office where we would find the safe. So we made it tip-toeing across these barrels with no problem. When we got into the office I told Curly, 'While I'm working on the box, don't take your eyes off that observation window, and tell me if you see Old Bill coming.'

So I'm cracking away at the safe. I've reemed the hole open, I've got the jelly in, I've put in the detonator and I've just wound the wire round the handle. I was just about to get the battery out of my toolbag when I've looked over to Curly and I've seen that he's watching me with his arms folded in typical Curly style. But, all the while, up at the observation window there's this big helmet and a copper's face also watching me. So instead of Curly watching the window, spotting the copper and telling me, 'Nit Nit!', the copper must have been there for some time, probably not believing what he was seeing, and so mesmerised that he didn't have the presence of mind to blow his whistle to call for support. No walkie-talkies in those good old days.

I couldn't believe this. I said, 'You dopey bastard, Curly! There's Old Bill!' And I've yanked out the detonator, but I couldn't get the jelly out too so I had to leave it. This was a serious liability because if you get caught and you have left explosives in an unsafe condition where other people might unwittingly injure themselves, the prosecution could magnify that in court. They would slaughter you with that. You could easily get eight years for having just a trace of jelly on your clothing. But this time we just dived out the back of the office and, just like I had run barefoot across those glass sweet jars when I was a kid, so I'm now running along the top of these barrels, which have got no lids on, there's only the rims. So I'm running along there with my tool bag when, all of a sudden, I heard splash, and 'Help!'

I've looked round and I see that Curly, who was only short, has slipped into one of the barrels. He's drenched and he's holding his hands on the side of the barrel, just like Mr Chad (a famous cartoon character of the day). So I've run all the way back across the barrels and yanked him out of the barrel by his barnet. Now he's stinking of crappy vinegar and mouldy old pickles are sticking out of his clothes, but we ran off like crazy and both got away.

Christ knows how long that copper had been watching me – the self-styled master of forward planning – performing on this box. Perhaps he didn't want to challenge two safe-blowers. Maybe he was waiting for ten other coppers to walk round the block and help him. Maybe he was waiting till I'd finished, with the aim of panicking me to drop the bag so he could have a pay-day. Who knows what's going through a copper's mind? They don't know themselves. They're still looking for Jack the Ripper. In my opinion, the only requirements you need to be a copper are average height, an IQ of 15 and a passion for bullying.

Then there was the time that Dave Norman and I bought a lorry and made a ramp that hooked on the back, so we could strap on a big trolley, run it down to the exit point of an office block, load the safe on it and haul it back up the ramp into the lorry. So we had done this thing and we were just going to haul the trolley on to the lorry, and I was standing on the street, minding my pals, holding a two foot six inch crowbar behind my back, when all of a sudden a copper came running round the corner, whistle in mouth and truncheon in hand.

So he's running towards us and I've got this crowbar. As soon as I aimed it, I knew it was going to hit him. It was like pitching at a coconut shy and knowing you're going to hit the coconut as soon as the ball leaves your hand. The next day, there he was in the newspapers screaming it had broken both his legs. Anyway, we did get the trolley and the box on board and off we drove. So this was the rough justice of the game we were in. If I'd been nicked when I was doing my thing and gone to jail, those were the hazards of the business I was in. And if he got his legs broken that was the hazard of the business he was in. Just like they had smashed my head open on that ready-eye when I was a kid in Loughton and I got three years in borstal, for a crime which Frog Eyes had incited for the police.

This is equally true of the different fates that can befall different people working on the same crime. For instance, one day this guy Norman Hall told me, 'I've got something in Knightsbridge. I've looked it over and there's a load of bits and pieces.' So one night we got in there – Norman, my pal Tony Samms and me – and we loaded a big bag up with gear. I've got the bag on my shoulder but, as the three of us walked out around the corner towards our car, Old Bill came right round in front of us. And this copper said, 'Hold it there!', and I've said, 'No, you hold it!' I threw the bag at him, and we were gone. Norman's run one way, I've run another and Tony's chosen to follow me. And it happened that there was scaffolding up an alleyway, so as we went up the scaffolding on to the roof. We saw below us the police, already surrounding this small block. And no wonder, because all this territory was only yards from lots of embassies. So now the police had us surrounded on this little island and I knew that if I can't get off it there's no way out and I'm nicked. And I was in for a hiding too, because I've done the copper with that heavy bag so he's not going to be too happy. All of a sudden I said, 'Come on, Tony, jump! We've got to go', because we've got to get off this roof and on to another. 'Fuck that!' he said. 'That's not for me.' It was quite a jump from there to the other side. The poor bastard, he's hid behind a chimney stack and said, 'I'm staying here.' And within two minutes they were all over the place like flies round a cow's ass.

THE SURVIVOR

Meantime I've seen that the roof across the alleyway was a bit lower and the gap is about 14 feet. So I've run and leapt over the gap and I've done it, I'm over. Then I've gone down the drainpipe, I've found a window open on the first floor and I've gone in. I've closed the window again and I stay there. And I find that I'm in a café, and as I look out the front window, I'm going, 'Fuck me, they're everywhere. Hundreds of them.'

I'm waiting, I'm watching the time, because any minute now the café's going to be opening up and the staff are going to come in and they are bound to see me. I'm looking out of the window and there's one copper at one end of the alleyway and there's another copper at the other end, both looking away from where I'm standing. So I've gone downstairs and found a woman's change of clothes. I've put her scarf round my head, rolled up my trousers and I've put on a pair of woman's shoes with high heels. I've put my own shoes down my shirt to give me a bit of a chest, I've put this woman's smock coat on and stuck a shopping bag in my hand. Then I've come out the front door, closing it gently, and I've walked towards the copper at one end of the alley, swivelling my legs like Dick Emery or Kenny Everett. I've gone by this copper, I've squeaked a high-pitched 'Good morning' and then I've walked to my car.

I've never been so pleased in my life. Fuck going up in court before a magistrate on a Monday morning dressed like that. Only, of course, Tony was nicked. And they got him down that night, they dragged him off the roof and stuck him in a black maria. And this big, horrible Scots copper that I'd done with the big sack of gear growled at Tony, 'Where's your fucking mate?'

So Tony leaned across the seats in the black maria and said, 'I don't know who you're talking about.' Bosh! went the Scotsman. He smashed old Tony's nose and broke it straightaway. Tony said, 'Is that as hard as you can hit, you poof!'

So the Jock came back: 'I'll say it again, who's your fucking mate? Who is he? I want him!' And bosh! He's done him again. This hurt poor Tony – he's got a big scar across his nose to this day – but he was hurt far more by the 18-month jail sentence that hit him in court.

None of this was my fault. Tony owed it to himself. He could have done what I did. He was two years younger than me. He could have jumped too. It's happened time and time again with people I know. They would never put the last little bit of exertion into a thing but I did, and that's why I always came home. That's why I'm the survivor.

Mind, to be a survivor in this game you have to be very choosy about who you work with, and sometimes I was a bit too trusting. I didn't always spot the tell-tale signs of a weak character. For instance, there was a man called Ronnie Clare. Later on in life I found out he was a grass. I should have guessed. I knew he had no principles, because he used to try to get me together with his sister. He used to smoke the other stuff, cannabis, and I didn't like anything like that. It was Ronnie who stuck up a bit of business in a big place where we were to go in three-handed and tie up the night watchman. But the other face with us on this job, my old pal Davey Norman, tipped me off. He said, 'You know Ronnie's smoking the other gear. You can tell 'cos it smells like whiskey on his breath.' This was a revelation to me, I just thought it was whiskey. I was naïve where drugs were concerned. I knew all about jelly but I knew nothing about drugs. So now I thought, I'll teach him a little lesson.

So Dave, Ronnie, me and another pal got into this place and went straight to tie up the night watchman. He was about to get his head down for the night but he had a bit of a kink because we caught him with his trousers off and wearing stockings and suspenders. He begged us to let him get back into his trousers before we wrapped him up, but we left him in that state, for him to explain it to Old Bill. Then we got to work on three big upright safes. As usual, I'd sent Ronnie to a waste dump to get a couple of old flock mattresses, which were always damp and ideal for muffling the noise of safes being blown. I had safe-blowing down to a fine art. If I had to blow big padlocks (which I found quicker than struggling to snap them with crowbars) I would use a couple of cushions. I would use just enough gelignite to blow the padlock and the cushions would deaden the sound.

Ronnie Clare trusted me. He knew that I knew what I was doing, but he had given me the hump. He must have been on 'smoke' because after trussing up this big night watchman like a chicken we needed to get on with the job, but Ronnie was strutting like a zombie in slow-motion. The whacky baccy was giving him false courage. He was walking around like he was on a film-set, and he's gently going, 'Uumm . . . the doors to the safes are over there.' And I've said, 'Come on! Hurry up!', because when I was on a job I was hyperactive, I had to get it all done quickly. In – Bang! – And out.

I always felt it was like when you're driving slowly, you're thinking slowly, but when you're driving fast, you're thinking fast. For me everything had to work with the precision of a Swiss watch. But here was Ronnie, ambling around, taking his time and undoing the wiring for me right slowly. 'Come on, for fuck's sake,' I said, but as I knew by now that he was under the influence of this crap, I deliberately put in three times the amount of gelignite that I would normally put in. Then I said, 'Right, Ron, hold the mattress up now!' And bosh! The fucking door came right off and Ronnie flew across the room. He ended up almost on top of our transvestite night watchman who was tied up on a chair only 20 feet away from where I was popping the boxes, so I could keep my eye on him too while I was working. So now Ronnie's arm swelled up like a barrage balloon but, although I thought I'd taught him lesson, mugs like him never learn.

Despite Ronnie being so spaced out, I agreed to go to Bournemouth with him to have a look at a bit of work. My two close pals, Tony Samms and Davey Norman, were also in on the scheme and they showed me the place they fancied. I said, 'No, I don't fancy that, I fancy this place', and it was the Bournemouth branch of Harvey Nichols which was the biggest store in town. It was a weekend and I figured there was plenty of money in Bournemouth so there would be plenty of takings. That night we waited for all the lights to go out and stayed watching the premises for hours for signs of patrolling security staff. Davey climbed up and looked through the windows into the main store but he couldn't see any activity, so we assumed there was no resident night watchman. This seemed odd to me. I would far rather know there was a watchman on duty, so we could grab him and wrap him up, than worry if one was still on the prowl when I should be concentrating on the explosives.

We were in Bournemouth only that evening but, while we were waiting, we had time for a drink and I found this lovely little bird. I was always finding birds, I couldn't help it. We got on well and I took one of the cars and shot off with her while the others had a couple more drinks. I told her I'd come down and meet her another time and then we said goodbye.

Now it was time to oblige Harvey Nichols. Ronnie and Tony drove ahead in the van, and Dave and I followed in a big Yankee car with a bag full of tools. When I felt ready and the coast was clear, I said to Dave, 'Right, it's time to go in.' We took out the gear, in we went and quickly found all the safes.

While I was inside working on the safes, Dave was using a new walkie-talkie system and communicating with Tony Samms, who was up on the roof and meant to be keeping a look-out. What we did not know was that Tony was making use of some scaffolding that happened to be there to carry off some bits and pieces that had caught his eye from the retail part of the store.

We had no idea that several times that night he went up and down the scaffolding, transporting all sorts of gear that he'd nicked for himself and putting it all in his van. We were going to get plenty of money out of the safes – that was the whole point of the job – but unfortunately some people's minds work this way.

All this time down in the vault we were working away on the safes, happily thinking Tony was on watch on the roof and blissfully unaware that he was preoccupied with his own side venture. It all seemed to be going well, especially as such a big store had all these lovely carpets and soft furnishings on hand for me to wrap around the safe doors to deaden the sound each time I blew one.

Bang! I blew the first box and got a bag of money out. Then I did the next door: more money. Then the next one: bang! And they were all going open: all good old boxes, all the same age. So once I'd done the one, they were all going to flop. Sweet as a nut! I'd done the lot and there was plenty of readies and it was all going fine. The vault looked like a train carriage alongside a station platform, with all its doors open. Lovely jubbly.

All of a sudden, all fucking hell broke loose! All the lights came on in one hit. The whole place was floodlit. So the other two dropped the bags of money they were holding and everyone dived for the exit.

And the reason? As I found out later, it was all down to Tony's noise as he went up and down that scaffolding . Every five minutes he was going up and down and he had woken up the night watchman, who'd fallen asleep that night. Yes, there was meant to be a watchman on site all the time but we had not seen him on patrol when we were recceing the store because he had sneaked off next door to get a kip. It was our misfortune that his place happened to be right next to this scaffolding that Tony was clanking up and down, so he had heard Tony, he'd got straight on the phone and now the entire Bournemouth police force had turned up to greet us.

I managed to get into the alleyway when three Old Bill have jumped me. Then I heard, 'Help!' and it's Ronnie Clare who's jumped off a wall, hit a clothes line and landed on some bread that a woman had thrown out for the birds. It had got wet, he'd slipped on it and broken his hip. So he's lying there and they've let the dogs in, and they are ripping away at him and he's shouting out, 'Help me!'

And you know how your mind works? I'm thinking: I've got three Old Bills hanging round my neck and he's telling me he needs fucking help! What about me? You're not on your fucking own! Pal!

So I've taken the truncheon off one of these coppers and bosh! bosh! and I'm away. And as I've managed to pull myself free I've gone diving through this hedge and picked up this great big lump of cement, waiting for one of the coppers to put his head through, but he didn't. Then I took my shoes off and, because there were dogs everywhere, I've gone straight into that park in Bournemouth that has a stream running right through the length of it. So I've run all the way along this stream and thrown the dogs off my scent. In the background I could hear the police yelling and whistles blowing but I've run a bit and, towards the outskirts of the town, I've come up near a front garden where I saw a kid's bike. Fuck it, I thought, and I grabbed the bike and I'm peddling and my knees keep hitting the handle bars. I could have been a kid doing his early morning paper round.

I peddled right out of Bournemouth but up ahead I could see a road-block, so I did a right and somehow I've ended up in the New Forest. It was freezing cold, my eyes were running and my nose was running, but my biggest worry was what had happened to my pals Dave and Tony, especially as I had a poxy feeling that Tony would get nicked again. I kept peddling along and I got all the way to Ringwood, where I dumped the bike in the River Avon so the police couldn't get hold of it and use it as evidence.

In Ringwood I found a phone box. I rang my wife and I said, 'Get hold of Billy Cotterell. Get him to pick me up' and I said where I'd be. A few hours later, they turned up and took me home. I'd never been so glad to see anyone before in my whole life.

The following morning I'm in bed with my wife and all of a sudden the front door of our old prefab gets kicked down and in comes Inspector George Groombridge and his little mob from the Flying Squad. They dragged me out of bed and they dragged her out of bed too. And he says, 'I'm nicking you for the thing in Bournemouth.' Then Groombridge spotted this photo of Ronnie Clare sitting next to me in the prefab. This just tied us in even closer because of course they'd captured Ronnie on the spot in Bournemouth with his broken hip. So they dragged me back down there and they said, 'We're charging you for the Harvey Nichols job. You were the jelly man. You did all the safe-blowing.'

So they've got Ronnie Clare and they've got me. Davy Norman got away by climbing up a big advertising hoarding and hanging up there all night long until the police moved off. Then he slipped down, walked away to his Yankee car and drove home. He was never picked up. As for Tony Samms, he had got away too but, typical of Tony, he went back the next morning to get his old van with all the crap in it that he'd thieved from Harvey Nichols. So he unlocks the van, gets in and just sits there for a while – I don't know why – until all of sudden, bomp! It's on top. The police have been sitting watching the van for hours and now he's nicked again. With all that Harvey Nichols gear, he had to be nicked. So once more he's got himself towed off.

Now I was remanded in custody in Dorchester jail alongside Tony Samms and Ronnie Clare. They were pleading guilty and just waiting to come up for sentencing. They weren't even going to argue. How could they? They were caught bang to rights. But I'm going to fight it. I've told the local police and Groombridge's Flying Squad mob in London that I wasn't there and it was nothing to do with me. In my entire criminal career I've never, ever held my hands up. If my old woman had caught me in my own bed with four birds, I would have claimed mistaken identity. If I'd been caught in a vault with jelly in my hands, I'd have said, 'Sorry, I thought I was in Bethnal Green underground.' I could be walking down Mile End Road with a safe on my back and I'd say, 'What safe, officer? I thought it was an old oven!' I would never hold my hands up. It's a matter of principle. You've got to put up a struggle.

When I was being questioned, the Bournemouth police said, 'We've got a witness.' It turned out to be this little bird I had met down there the evening we did Harvey Nichols. Somehow – and this could only have come from Clare who'd obviously done a trade – the police had heard that I had been seen with this girl, who again could only have been identified by him. So they paid her a visit and one clever copper turned the story on its head. She said they told her that I had been accused of a crime in London but I was claiming that on the night in question I was in Bournemouth with her, so I needed her as a witness. She said, they said if she would swear that she saw me in Bournemouth that evening, it would get me out of the charge I faced in London. Of course she didn't realise what was going on. They conned her. She was green and did not realise how odd it was that the police, rather than a solicitor, were helping to prop up my alibi. So she says, 'Yes, he was here. I was with him', and she described me to a tee.

So now I'm in stook, dead trouble. Or was I? Maybe not, because she was the only witness and I thought this could be turned to my favour. As usual, my brief, Jimmy Fellowes, was in my corner and had got me bail, so I was free to approach the bird myself. I told her she could have a grand and go on a holiday. So she took the grand and changed her story. At the trial she would now say words to the effect that, 'No, I didn't say it *was* him, it just looked like him. He looks like the fellow but I can't be sure.'

At the same time my then business partner Joe Wilkins got hold of a local councillor from Stepney whom we used to do a bit of business with. Joe also had a pal who was the chairman of the dockers' distress fund, known as 'Admirable Harry'. They were both persuaded to testify that I was with them in London on the night of the raid.

Now, with the bird saying she wasn't sure and these two pillars of society saying I was definitely in London with them, my prospects are looking rosy. When the trial starts, my pal Joe takes these blokes down to Bournemouth and they book into a hotel. And where does Joe go to buy some clothing and other bits and pieces? Harvey Nichols! While he's in there he also buys a suitcase, but throughout this expedition he's keeping these two witnesses with him. Of course he's paying for everything he takes, but what he doesn't know is that these two fucking nutcases were kleptomaniacs. None of us knew. So while he's in some other department of the store, they get hold of the suitcase and they're filling it with shirts, pants, socks, everything. Fucking unbelievable. How I ever had these men as my witnesses I do not know. Then Joe goes to the paypoint, the shop assistant takes the price tag and rings it up on the till, Joe pays up and off he goes.

When he gets back to the hotel, he opens up the suitcase and he sees that it's loaded up with gear. Straightaway he realises what these two soppy bastards have done. What idiots! They were worse than criminals, they were compulsive thieves. They could have got my pal Joe nicked, themselves nicked and me totally fucked. By the skin of our teeth none of this happened, so with their evidence I still had a hope of coming out of that trial a free man. Sure enough, the jury believed me – or at least they had reasonable doubt that I was there. They found me not guilty and I walked free. So I had to forgive the councillor from Stepney and the Admirable Harry for all their fucking stupidity. I'll always be thankful to them and to Joe for that help they all gave me. Without them I would probably have been starting ten years in jail instead of driving back home for a celebration.

And ten years was certainly on the cards because I was being portrayed in deepest Dorset as Mr Big from London. When I'd been led into the dock, I could hear some spectators in the crowded public gallery shouting, 'Here he is. Here's the ringleader.' I was the one they had come to see. Two hundred years earlier I would have been hanged in public for this kind of crime (not that there was any jelly about in those days) and I had the feeling that some of these people would have liked to see me hang there and then.

As for Ronnie Clare and Tony Samms, I suppose they had the hump over my acquittal. Why should I walk free when they're doing time? But it was their own fault. I am the survivor.

When I got home, I returned to my three great passions in life – apart from safes. They were guns, of course, fast convertibles and . . . you know what the third one was, but I'll get back to that later.

As you can tell by now, I was making a lot of money from crime but there were always additional expenditures. The downside of this business is that you tend to get fitted up. And every single time I got fitted up, it cost me a lot of money. But I still had no idea how bad a real fit-up can be, when villains and cops jointly conspire to put you out of business forever. Yes, I'm a self-confessed criminal, but I have always stolen my own money – if you get my meaning. I've never leeched off other villains. For instance, I've never had any of the Great Train Robbers' money – unlike some other people in this story.

Except for my time on the boats, I've never done a day's conventional work. On his deathbed I clearly remember my stepfather saying, 'Learn a lesson from me. I've worked like a cart-horse all my life and I haven't got a penny to show for it.' By then I had already retired – I'd retired when I was 14 – but I took his advice anyway and blew my way to a nice few quid many times over. But you know, I would have done most of those jobs for nothing. I got to the stage that I loved the work so much, it became my vocation and most of the time it was a pleasure. I didn't care if there was no money in the box, I just wanted to blow the bastard.

To show what I mean, I recall one job I did very early on in my love affair with safes. At the start we weren't blowing safes, we were nicking them out of walls and ripping the square-backed ones open with chisels, crowbars and sledgehammers. One day a job like this was put my way by Davey Norman. He said, 'I know where there's a lovely little box in a big builders' yard in New Cross.' Dave would have known about this because he lived close to New Cross, in Ossory Road, not far from the Thomas à Becket pub in the Old Kent Road. At the time this was Charlie Richardson territory but, as it happened, it was Charlie Richardson who had introduced me to Davey. I've always thanked Charlie for that because Dave turned out to be one of the best pals I ever had.

So on this particular weekend we decided to hammer and chisel this old safe out of the wall. We didn't take any tools because we knew we would find everything we needed in the builders' yard. So we drove over, parked the car round the corner, got in there and started work. We thought we'd prize it out in a few minutes but we had to work on it for ages, sweating bullets, right through until the early hours. And when we finally get it out of the wall, we find that it's stuck to a bloody long scaffold pipe. Can you imagine?

So we drag it away from the wall into the yard, but we can't break off this pipe because it's welded on, so we can't get the safe in the boot of the car. We can't even chisel the back off and do the job on site because it's not a square-backed safe but a round-shouldered one. So now we've only one option: we've got to lug it all the way back to Dave's home. It would have been quite a long bike ride, let alone foot-slogging it with a big safe.

It was the middle of winter so at least we still had the cover of darkness, and we were dragging it, carrying it, we even got it on our shoulders. Then we got it round one turning and waited, listening for anyone else on foot or any approaching cars, until we felt it was safe to nip across the road. Then a bit further a car did come by so we ducked in a doorway, then a gateway and all the way down this street till we got to the Old Kent Road. Then we dragged it all the way along there, dodging car headlights every now and then until eventually, around four in the morning, we'd just got it to his turning and we heard bells ringing. Fuck me, it's a police car coming down the Old Kent Road! So we've run to his doorway – luckily, his was the first house on the left as you turn in – and we slung the safe into the 'area': the basement well. Clunk, clunk, clunk, down the cement steps it went, while Dave and I stood dead still. But the police car went straight past. It didn't turn into Ossory Road, it just kept going. The siren was nothing to do with us. Were we relieved! The sweat was pouring off us but at least we made it home to Dave's.

So we ran down the area, to tuck the safe out of sight, intending to chisel it or drill it open later that day. But when we got down there, we saw that the fucking door's open. It had come open when we slung it down. We looked inside and there was nothing in it, not even stamps. It was absolutely empty. All that work, all that smashing and chiselling, all that dragging and carrying, all that heart-stopping panic over police cars. And it's come to this!

Then we looked at each other. We'd only just begun working together and now we've had this fucking fiasco. Then we looked at the damned safe and we knew it wasn't over, because we couldn't leave it there. We've still got to get rid of it! So we looked at each other once again and then . . . we burst out laughing.

It was this, really, I suppose, that made me like old Dave right from the start. We were bruised and aching all over, only to find out that the poxy door would come open on a jolt, which we could have given it back in the builders' yard. And all for nothing.

But you know, we didn't care. In a sense, we weren't even at it for the money, not all the time. We were at it because we were criminals and we *had* to be at it . . . in those good old days, or should I say, nights?

SEVEN

Gun-Crazy with the Krays

IF the good old nights were for safe-blowing, the good old days were when I put my other criminal passion to work. My love of guns wasn't just a hobby. It was a tool of the trade. And just as I enjoyed applying the explosive skills, timing and concentration demanded of a safe-blower, I loved the buzz of daylight robbery. The safe-blower works under cover of darkness, like a mole. The bank robber performs out in the open, in the public gaze. It's show business.

As a safe-blower I never took a gun with me. As a robber I had to have one. At first I worked with people who thought they could fake it. I remember us getting chased away on one job by some mug in his private car. He even had his little son with him. He was trying to be a hero and we couldn't easily shake him off because the little mob I was with were only waving an engine crank or some other bent bit of metal about, making out it was a gun. If they could have fired one shot, even in the air, there wouldn't have been a chase. So I said, 'Don't make out you've got guns. Bring guns!'

From that point on we did bring guns. I'd jump up on the bank counter, fire a shotgun into the ceiling and blow a lump of it away, taking out the lights. Then everyone – all the staff and any customers – would go down on the floor. Sometimes we'd steam over the counter and empty the tills out, or if the vault was open we'd dive in there. When you show you mean business, anyone with brains doesn't want to get involved. They'll wipe their mouths and look the other way. Unfortunately, there's always that one bloke who will try to be a hero, but you just have to get him off your tail without turning him into a martyr. Sometimes we had close ones because we didn't stop 'have a go' vehicles behind us, so I reckoned that it was always best to have two motors: one in front with the readies in it and one behind to block anyone trying to get his picture in tomorrow's newspapers.

Still, we never got caught and we never shot anybody. We just waved the guns round to cover our getaway. But the getaway isn't the end of it. In the days after a bank raid I always expected a visit from the police, looking for both the cash and the weapons. They often came and searched the prefab but always left empty-handed, which made them a bit sore. I have always taken a pride in my appearance. Just as I used to have top-of-the-range cars, I used to have plenty of smart clothes. This probably got up the local Old Bill's nose, as I found out when a pal of mine from Homerton, Siddy Hogg, ran into a copper from Hackney nick.

'How's The Duke?' asked the copper.

'Who's The Duke?' said Siddy.

'Jimmy Evans,' said the detective.

'Why do you call him The Duke?'

'Because every time we go to his home to give him a spin, loads of clothes come tumbling out the wardrobes.'

What the CID never found was any guns, even though I always kept at least three guns in the prefab, plus loads of ammunition. One was a beautiful Colt .45 with white bone handles. I also kept a revolver, a little Colt Cobra, and a high-powered Browning. The .45 gave me a hard-on just looking at it. I hid them all in the door of the refrigerator. I'd wrap them in grease-proof paper, applying a bit of Vaseline, then I'd take the packing off the inside of the door, stick the guns inside and put the packing back. This made the door a bit heavy but all fridge doors were heavy in those days and no copper ever sussed it.

One day old Jimmy Grainey from Hackney nick spun me with his sidekick, Len Hopkins, over a job that had just been done on the Barclays Bank on the corner of my street. Someone had obliged but these detectives couldn't work out how anyone had got in. Their suspicions fell wrongly on a bloke who lived above the bank so they spun his apartment. I was friendly with the wife who looked a ringer for Anita Ekberg: long, blonde hair, a Dolly Parton size bra – all round a very good-looking woman. And what did they find? A photograph of me! I did not even remember giving her one – a photo, I mean – so straightaway I'm the number one suspect.

Now, along with the three shooters tucked inside the fridge door, I had put ten grand in banknotes, fresh out of a safe that I'd obliged a few days earlier. They were all new and most had consecutive numbers so they were ready for changing up, but in those days I used to have another little hiding place for, say, a pair of expensive watches, a camera, cufflinks and two diamond rings. These were hidden under the sink units only a couple of feet from the fridge, so any coppers would find them very soon, as they were meant to. I'd be standing there watching and, as Jimmy Grainey dragged this stuff out, I'd put a look on my face like I'd just crapped myself. 'Hello, hello! What have we got here, then?' Grainey would say, just like an old-time copper. He'd have a big beam on his face, and he'd think he'd got a result.

But no. These were all straight gear. What's more, I had a receipt tucked away for each item. I never had anything crooked. I would go, 'Oh . . . er . . . umm . . .' And he'd say, 'Right, we're taking this lot away. And you'd better come up with a bit more than oh-er-umm or you're nicked.' And off Grainey and Hopkins would go with their little bit of stuff. The next day I'd take the receipts round to the local nick and get it all back. They'd be mad but they'd have been a lot madder if they knew they'd missed the ten hot grand, especially as it wouldn't have taken them two minutes to find out where it had come from. Not from that branch of Barclays but just as bad. Then it wouldn't have been ten grand for me but ten years. Maybe more, with those guns in the fridge door too. And they were just for starters. I used to keep other guns in big tool-boxes in different lock-up garages, and every now and then I would bring some home to test-fire: Lugers, Polish Radams, Berettas, Smith & Wessons, Storm Rugers, .357 Magnums and the occasional .22 micro-grooved barrel lever-action Marlin. At the time we had a wrap-around 'Miami' suite so whenever I got a new gun home, I would lay along the sofa and fire it through the kitchen into a target that I'd stuck on the back door. Some people might stick a dartboard on a door (dangerous enough) but I used to shoot right through it, knowing that a few yards beyond was a brick wall which would stop most bullets.

One day my wife said, 'My mother comes round the back door sometimes. You might shoot her.' So I said, 'Tell her to use the front door then.'

Another day I came home and she was doing some washing-up in the kitchen She said, 'I've never felt so embarrassed in my whole life. The painters came round from the council today and when they reached the back door they said, "Looks like a bad case of woodworm you've got there, lady."'

Every now and then I would take those three guns out of the fridge door, to make sure they were working, then I'd clean and polish them. I used to sit on the Miami sofa, facing the fireplace, while my wife would lie in front of the fireplace on her stomach with her feet up behind her, reading. One day she was lying there, as usual, when I had the guns out. I had placed them on a pouffé next to me and I was cleaning away when she said, 'I'm going to put the kettle on', and got up. One second later I pulled back the slide on the .45 and let the hammer go back, but I had no idea that there was still one .45 bullet in it so, without realising, I had jacked it up. Then I squeezed the trigger. I slammed it back and crash! The bullet went right into the woodwork flooring, eight inches away from the side of the hearth. If she had still been lying there, the .45 would have hit her spine. She was a slightly built woman and this would have cut her in half. However, by now she was safe at the sink in the kitchen. When she heard the bang she thought it was just another gun going off, which was an everyday happening in our house. She was wholly unaware how close she had been to another world. It's only now I look back and realise that at this time not only did I lead a charmed life; it must have rubbed off on the people around me.

I was surprised that the CID never did a really thorough search because the uniformed police knew as far back as 1957 that I had at least one firearm in the prefab. There were lots of little shops and factories round our way and whenever it was windy some of the alarms used to go off, including one in particular on the wall of a clothing factory in Belsham Street, 100 yards away from our bedroom. One very windy night this alarm started ringing. It went on and on until it got so bad, I couldn't put up with it any more. So at four in the morning I got up, pulled out my Bernardelli shotgun and put in a clip with five Brenneke slugs – the kind they use to kill lions. It was freezing cold but wearing just my Y-fronts and slippers – nothing else – I walked out on to the pavement across the road up to the factory and shot this alarm three times. The second shot reduced the sound to a chicken's squawk, the third smashed the alarm right off the wall and left it dangling on a piece of wire. It stopped ringing. Peace at last.

Great, I thought, but as I turned round to go back inside I saw a copper sitting behind me on one of those silent motorbikes they used in those days. He was just looking at me. So I said, 'Bollocks' and walked straight past him back into the prefab. He never said a word. He just shook his head from one side to the other, throwing his eyes upwards as if to say, 'Bloody vandal.' Then he just rode off. I never suffered any repercussions, even though he must have told his pals back at the nick. When I walked back into the bedroom I found my wife rolled up on the floor, holding her stomach in hysterics, laughing uncontrollably with tears in her eyes. She thought it was funny. I thought it was a liberty that I had to leave my bed to silence that firm's poxy alarm in the middle of the night.

My wife laughed then but she herself had several more narrow escapes. I bought her a ladies' shotgun, a Holland and Holland .410, and one evening I had left it lying around when a pal called Kenny Neill – 'Posh Ken' – happened to turn up. I had just slipped into the bathroom when he casually picked up this .410 and accidentally fired a cartridge. Now while I liked living in the prefab, the internal walls were only made of plywood and this cartridge had gone through one wall into our bedroom where my wife was already in bed. We rushed straight in and we saw all these pellets stuck in the headboard – and her sitting bolt upright and motionless. 'I've killed her! I've killed her!' screamed Kenny, but he hadn't noticed that she was holding up a cup of tea. Close examination proved that not a single pellet had hit her. The headboard looked as if someone had created a dot-to-dot puzzle, with her head in the only space with no dots. But she had barely blinked. Just mad Jimmy up to his usual pranks.

At least that was an accident. Sometimes it got deliberate. When I went out in the evening – not on a safe-blowing job but, say, for a night out in clubland – I used to carry a .22 Derringer in my front hip pocket. One night I came home in the early hours to be greeted by my wife moaning and groaning because she thought I'd been playing around with another woman or something. There she was, standing in the passage, screaming and yelling. 'Do you know what time it is? Where have you been?'

I got a bit annoyed and I said, 'Fuck's sake! I can't stand it!' And, as I had this little Derringer .22 on me, I pulled it out and fired. I made sure I wasn't going to hit her but I wanted the bullet to go near enough to bring her to her senses. And it did. It passed her about two inches from her face and it went through the wall. I must say, this did shut her up.

The following morning Stan the bookmaker, who lived in the next prefab, knocked on my door and said, 'Do me a favour, Jimmy. Next time you want to take a shot at your old woman, point the gun in the other direction.' He must have heard her yelling and raving too. Then he took me in his place and, stuck in the wardrobe door, was this bullet. 'It went right across my old woman's head while she was in bed.' Imagine. It had gone right through two prefabs. Luckily my neighbour had a sense of humour.

At some time I picked up two dozen .25 Baby Brownings. This little automatic is so small – only three inches long and light as a feather – that you can put it in an empty cigarette packet, but it can shoot five shots. I kept one of these little fellows at home and I used to leave it in a gap between the seats of that Miami settee, where it curved. One day Tony Samms (who was nicked on the Harvey Nichols disaster) and my old pal Dodger Seabrook (the target on the job that landed me in borstal) were there with half a dozen other pals. Dodger's standing in front of the mirror, doing something with his hair, when Tony happened to find the Baby Browning under where he was sitting so, as a joke, he got up and put the gun to the back of Dodger's head. He was about to squeeze the trigger when I said, 'Stop, for fuck's sake. There's one in it!' Tony was just playing around but still he could have killed Dodger.

Looking back, I can see it was careless of me to leave these things lying about. I should have had more respect for them, especially as my little daughter used to run around on top of that settee. Any day she might have picked up the Baby Browning and started playing with it, but luckily that didn't happen. Mind you, kitchen knives and caustic soda can do terrible damage too – and think how many people get killed by Old Bill roaring their way recklessly to an incident or in hot pursuit of car thieves.

Through my obsession with firearms both my wife and Dodger Seabrook only narrowly escaped accidental death, but someone else wasn't so lucky. I've already mentioned a man from Clapton called Tony Mella, who had established himself as a substantial figure in the Soho underworld, and his pal, Big Alf Malvin, who lost out in that plate-smashing game with Tommy Smithson. Alf Malvin thought the world of Tony Mella but Mella often treated Malvin with contempt. In front of other people he would tell Malvin, 'Wash your fucking hands and make me a sandwich, Alf.'

One day I bumped into Tony Mella in the Regency Club – not the Barrys' place in Stoke Newington but the one in Leicester Square. I gave him one of these little Baby Brownings because I knew he liked guns too. He said, 'Is this my little present?' and I said, 'Yes, Tony, it's yours, and I've got half a dozen more if you know anyone who wants to buy one.' He really appreciated it.

Two days later Tony was upstairs in his Soho office, above the Bus Stop club in Wardour Street, humiliating Big Alf as usual. This time it was over £380 that Tony owed Alf, when suddenly Alf snapped. He seized the Baby Browning that he had found earlier that evening in Tony's desk and he shot him. Instantly realising what he had done (though we all assumed he'd never intended to do), Alf put the gun in his mouth, squeezed the trigger and bang! He shot himself dead. Meanwhile, Tony had struggled to his feet and staggered down the stairs saying, 'I've been shot.' The receptionist thought he was joking, as he had performed this routine dozens of times before as a lark, only this time it was for real. And Tony died, just like his old pal upstairs. This tiny little .25 had killed two really big hard men – over nothing more than a dispute about Big Tony's attitude and petty debt – so what would it have done to the back of old Dodger's nut?

I bought many of my shotguns over the counter, legitimately, so I was a very welcome customer at the biggest gun store in Europe: Cogswell and Harrison in Piccadilly. Actors like John Wayne and Robert Montgomery and loads of other American stars would also buy their guns there. I knew the manager who would let my buy anything legal. I had no licence to keep handguns but I did have a shotgun licence and I often used to take pals out shooting in the country. We would set off at five in the morning and head down to the New Forest where we'd shoot pheasants. Thinking back, I don't know how I did that because I don't like hurting animals. On the other hand, I did get pinched for inflicting grievous body harm on a game warden who caught us at it.

But some people were even nuttier with guns than I was, and I mean Ronnie and Reggie Kray. I'd first met them in the 1950s through my close pal, Tommy 'Ginger' Marks, who was also a pal of theirs. I was one year younger than Charlie Kray and two years older than the Twins and, as I lived in Hackney, only a mile and a half from their home in Vallance Road, we would often bump into each other. During these years Smuggler Bill and I were friendly with a farmer who let us shoot on his 500 acres at Nazeing in Essex. On Saturday mornings I'd go to Cogswell and Harrison and buy boxes of 1,000 rounds of different ammunition, and very early on Sundays I'd lead them into the van and drive to the farm with Posh Ken, Smuggler Bill and Davey Norman, who hated guns but used to come for a day out with the rest of us. Then from half-five until just after midday, we'd have a roam around and a shoot-up.

One day I was with Charlie Kray in the Grave Maurice pub in Mile End Road (a few yards from the Blind Beggar) and in passing I told him about these days out. This proved to be a mistake because a few days later Ronnie and Reggie said, 'We'd like to come up to that farm with you one morning.' 'Yeah, OK,' I said, 'but I'll have to pick you up right early.' So one day we all met down the East End and off we went to the farm. I took the Twins and their cronies there twice, I lent them my guns and gave them plenty of ammo but they had no idea how to perform and they went crazy. At the end of their second trip the farmer took me aside and said, 'Look, Jimmy, I don't mind you and your other pals but, please, don't bring these people up here any more. They shoot my pigs and anything else that moves.' And it was true. I was there when Ronnie spotted a pig lying on the ground a few yards away, half asleep, and he just took a pot shot at him. Then there was the time Ronnie had just emptied his gun in the direction of anything that moved when he turned and saw Reggie 40 yards off, sitting on a stile taking a break, his gun in one hand and a cigarette in the other. All of a sudden we heard Ron shouting: 'Reggie, don't just sit there. Get up and kill something!'

I tried to tell the Twins this wasn't the way to behave. I'd even gone to the trouble of providing them with something else to aim at. As we were driving through Stratford on our way to the farm, I'd seen a milk delivery bloke disappear down an alleyway, leaving his float unattended, so I said to Dave Norman, 'Pull up, Dave', and the Krays and their little mob pulled up behind us.

Then I got out and lifted a crate of milk off the float and stuck it in Dave's boot. And as we drove off, I could hear Ronnie telling Reggie, 'Oh, nice bloke, Jimmy. He's bought us all some milk.'

But the milk wasn't for drinking. When we got to the farm, I made Posh Ken carry the crate over to some land where I could stick these bottles on some posts. Then we used them for target practice because, when a bullet smashes into a bottle full of milk, the effect is spectacular. Now he realised that was why I'd nicked a crate-full, Ronnie liked me even more.

If the Krays were like ducks out of water in the country, they were totally at home in the city, especially London's West End in the early 1960s when it was throbbing with gangsters. In this underworld – so blatant it had become part of the overworld – I was now known as a capable thief, a skilled safe-blower and an expert with guns. This reputation helped put me on good terms with the dominant gangsters of the day, even though I was not a gangster myself. I had no one on my payroll. I was a sole trader operating outside the gang structure. I was an independent but if I was 'with' anybody, it was Albert Dimes. In 1955 'Italian Albert' had got the upper hand over Jack Spot, the boss of a previous generation of London thugs, in a celebrated knife fight in Frith Street. By the time I knew him he had established himself in the new world of legalised gambling. I got involved in a small way with him and a few other pals in the fruit machine business. We had some interest in a little spieler called the West End Sporting Club opposite Ronnie Scott's jazz club (which was then in Frith Street) and Ronnie himself sometimes dropped in to play poker at one of the tables. I was also on the firm in case anything naughty needed to be done, then me and my little team would fix it. My understanding of explosives sometimes came in handy but maybe those stories are for another book.

I also knew Billy Hill, another legendary gangster and club-owner. I had first come across him in the early 1950s when I'd just come out of Portland Borstal and I needed somewhere to stay with my wife and kid. We moved into the house of a bloke called Billy Smith. 'What are all these suitcases doing here?' I asked Smith. 'Oh,' he said. 'They're from the Eastcastle Street mailbag robbery. They hid the notes in them.' He said it so matter-of-fact but I was impressed At £287,000 in used notes, the 1952 Eastcastle Street job was Britain's biggest ever cash robbery at that time and it was put together by Billy Hill. Later I got to know Hilly himself through his Soho clubs. He had a long-time mistress, Gypsy, and I was a bit pally with her brother Michael.

Hilly retired in the mid-1950s, just when a lot more dodgy clubs were springing up all over the place. And where there are clubs there are protection rackets. The Krays protected some places but we were involved in many more. When I say 'we', I mean myself and Joe Wilkins, whom I'd met through the rag trade when I bought a clothing factory. Later Joe became the king of the clubs. He owned the 400 Club and his uncle Bert Wilkins had the Nightingale Club in Berkeley Square. Bert was also partners in Wembley Stadium with the old boxing promoter, Harry Levene.

Joe Wilkins, with my back-up, took over Winston's which, from our point of view, was the finest club in the whole West End. At that time Winston's was owned by Bruce Brace but to move in on the place we had to get a man called Billy Howard off Bruce's back. Billy owned a club himself, the Beehive in Brixton, but up West he was 'protecting' Bruce. So I had a scheme to goad Billy into a confrontation. I was taking a risk because, make no mistake, Billy could have a fight. This particular night he came into Winston's with a young girl, no more than 18. When he went down to the toilet, I followed and as we stood a few yards apart over the washbasins, I pulled out my comb and made as if to smarten myself up in the mirror, but at the same time I was concealing my little Derringer in the palm of my right hand, alongside the comb.

I said, 'Lovely young woman you've got there. Bit young for you, eh, Billy? Why don't you step aside for someone a bit younger?' I thought he would come at me but he let it go. In my arrogant way I guessed this was because I was 30 and he was maybe 15 years older.

'Yeah, I suppose you're right,' he said, but at the same time he did some dazzling nifty footwork, like a boxer sparring, and he smashed one fist into his other open palm as if to show how fast he could move. And he was fast. In a fair fight, even with my age advantage, he would probably have done the business on me. But it would never have come to that because I had to cheat, like when I was a little kid and I always had to win at brag otherwise I'd kick the wheelchair with that old man in it Well, my little Derringer had twin barrels, so there would have been one for each of Billy Howard's knees. My best friends have usually been dogs but that Derringer was my friend to. It couldn't wag its tail but it had a right bite on it.

Later on I got to know Billy well and we became good pals. It turned out that he had married that young woman and so eventually I apologised for trying to wind him up over her all those years before in Winston's. Somehow the conversation turned to guns and he let drop a remark like, 'Don't worry, I know all about you and guns.' The way he said it made me think that the reason he didn't have a fight with me that night was because he knew I'd be tooled up.

I told him, 'You're right, Bill. I ain't got the patience for all that fighting bollocks. I like something that barks here and bites over there.'

Through the clubs and the crime I had a few dealings with the Kray brothers. Today Ronnie, Reggie and even Charlie Kray are cult figures, icons, but to me they were just three blokes. Yes, they had a gang but, as I say, I prided myself on being independent. And when they tried to consolidate everything in their hands, eliminating the competition, I felt like the last of the independents. I lived on the fringes of 'Krayland'. I knew what they were up to, but they never muscled in on my activities and there was never any gangster trouble between us.

On the contrary, sometimes they wanted me to help them when they had troubles. They used to drop into a clothing shop I had in Islington, in Essex Road opposite Cross Street. It was a front, a place where we would plan things. They'd ask me for ammunition or they'd want to buy a few guns. Sometimes they might want a ringer – a car with false plates – and I would oblige them, because at any one time I'd have several cars laid up in various garages for use on my own jobs at a moment's notice. I'd do this as a favour to the Krays – no charge – because they were so pally with my pal, Tommy 'Ginger' Marks, and Dukey Osbourne, who worked with me and Tommy. We had other pals in common, like big Ronnie Knight from Canning Town (not Barbara Windsor's ex-husband), and if you're friendly with someone, their friends are your friends, sort of. But although I was of some value to the Twins they were of no value to me. They would have been no use on a bank job because they weren't robbers. I could do whatever they did but they couldn't do what I could do. I could be one of them but they couldn't be one of my people. I didn't compete with them in their game and they could not compete with me. I was a thief. They were leeches.

Ronnie Kray, in particular, knew of my passion for guns. He had seen me in action on the farm with all sorts of weapons and he knew I had access to many more. He was quite good at shooting low-level thugs and members of his own firm, but he never pulled a gun on me. He also knew that what had happened to a bloke called Norman Hall was supposed to be down to me, and whoever did that didn't even use a gun.

I had first met Norman Hall in Portland and by the late 1950s I was doing a lot of work with him. That was until he suggested we rob two safes in an office block in Chiswick. Curly King, Charlie Reader and I took up the idea and on the night we turned up in our usual nondescript old clothes, only to find Norman decked out in a red tie, white shirt and blue jacket. We looked at him as if to say, 'What the fuck are you dressed like that for?', so he volunteered, 'Oh, I've got a bird to meet afterwards.' This didn't ring true. His ridiculous gear reminded me of the startling red dress worn by the girl who set up John Dillinger in that Chicago cinema, so the FBI were sure to spot the couple coming out. As soon as they saw that red dress, Dillinger was done for and shot dead.

Straightaway I suspected this was another 'ready-eye', another ambush, like that Loughton job back in 1948 when 'Frogs Eyes' Fox set us up and I got three years in Portland. I had never forgotten that lesson but this was far worse because I could get eight years just for having a small residue of jelly on my clothes. That's why we used to get rid of all our clothing after every job – and also why we'd never wear expensive gear like Norman's that night. So I crossed the road and I looked up at this office block and I saw a quick glimmer of light. It was someone drawing on a cigarette. I said, They're in there,' meaning Old Bill. Now I was sure we were being set up. And when I'm out of earshot, Norman said to Charlie, 'That fucking Jimmy. He doesn't miss a thing.' So Charlie, Curley and I all quit, leaving Norman to answer to his bent coppers.

A survivor yet again, I drove home to the prefab and talked the whole business through with Charlie. I said, 'That was a ready-eye', and I recalled the time when Norman Hall had asked me to screw his own cousin Freddie Want's house, also in Morning Lane. Then I told Charlie, 'You know what we've got to do. We can never trust him.'

I won't go into all the details of how we dealt with this matter, but it involved a visit to Norman's home in Hoxton, a Korean army knife with a huge blade, a swipe down the chops, his thumb getting sliced off and him leaking blood all over the council block.

The following morning who should turn up at my house but Bob Whitfield – Dodgy Bob – the crazy thief that I'd met on the *Samaria*! He came round to collect a set of skeleton keys that a key-maker I knew had made for him, but I wanted to know what state Norman Hall was in, so I told Dodgy Bob that Norman had the keys and he should get them off him. Two hours later back he came saying, 'Wha . . . wha . . why did you send me up there? There's cops everywhere, there's sawdust all over the landing, and they say Norman was crawling all over the floor looking for his thumb. What's happened?'

'Don't worry about that, Bob,' I said. 'Did he have your keys?'

Norman Hall had to stay in hospital for five months while the wounds healed. In the meantime his father went to Ronnie and Reggie Kray to ask them to take retribution on Norman's attackers. But when they heard what had happened, they told old man Hall, 'Well, he must have done something bad to have that done to him. Whoever did that did it for a fucking good reason. He must have asked for it, so we don't want to know.'

Of course, the Twins already knew who had done all this to Norman, and why. They would have done the same themselves. Besides, this wasn't their problem and old man Hall was never going to get any joy from them. So the Krays and I understood each other. But as the 1960s went on I became suspicious that they might be tied in with senior police officers. In 1968 these suspicions were confirmed.

I was in Winston's one midnight when in came Reggie Kray with his shadow-cum-driver, little Tommy Cowley, and another fellow. As soon as Reggie saw me he called 'Jim! Jim! Over here a minute! I want you to meet someone.' So I went and shook hands with this someone who straightaway beckoned the barman, Ray 'the Yank', and asked, 'What's Jimmy drinking?' 'Jimmy only drinks Coca-Colas,' said Ray and poured one out. As this stranger turned to pass me the drink, Reg said, 'He's very high up at West

End Central.' So I looked at the bloke and said, 'I don't drink with fucking coppers,' and I've turned and walked away. I wouldn't have drunk with any copper at the best of times but at this particular moment I had only recently came out of jail for a crime I had not committed, so I was even angrier with the police than usual.

Now Reggie came over to my side to smooth things down, but I walked away in disgust. I heard the copper say, 'It's all right, Reg, I've got a car waiting for me outside anyway,' and out he went. By this time I was back at my table in the corner so Reggie walked over, with dopey little Tommy Cowley, and he's sitting astride a chair that he's just turned round so he's leaning over the back and he's glaring at me. 'You've just took a right fucking liberty with me,' he growled, so I said, '*I* took a liberty with *you*, you cunt! *You* took the fucking liberty: introducing me to Old Bill when I'm sitting here in the shadows minding my own business. I really need you to fucking point me out to these bent scumbags! I'm on bail now for something I ain't done. I'm lucky to be sitting here at all. As far as I'm concerned all coppers are crooked. If I saw a horse kicking a copper to death, I'd give the horse a lump of sugar.'

Then little Tommy Cowley said, 'You've got a chip on your shoulder.' I said, 'Go on, fuck off. You're only a driver. Go away. I want to talk to *him*,' and I pointed at Reggie.

Now it was open – if Reggie wants a row, he's got one – because I was annoyed. But instead he mumbled, 'Well . . . Look . . . We . . .' He just couldn't get anything out, except a look of apology. He's gone the other way: one moment he's full of fury and temper, the next he has realised he was out of order. Within seconds he'd realised he wasn't going to win any medals here. Typical Reggie. If it had been Ronnie, depending on his mood, it might have been a different thing. But all the Krays knew that I would not stop to argue. I would just pull out a shooter and, most likely, use it. Reggie must also have guessed I had something in my pocket and I think that's why he wisely let it go. Instead he blurted out, 'We need all the help we can get.' And I said, 'I know, Reg, but I don't think even the Commissioner of the Metropolitan Police can help you and your brothers now.'

Two days later the entire Kray gang was nicked over three murders and the Twins got 30 years each. Reggie served even longer than that and was only allowed out to die. Ronnie never got out at all and died in Broadmoor.

But I'm getting ahead of myself. Back in the early 1960s I was on good terms with not just the Krays in the East End but also the Richardsons in

South London. There was supposed to be a war going on between these two mobs, glaring at each other from opposite sides of the river, but I took no side. As it happened, I liked Charlie Richardson. He was a capable villain. He had more brains than all the Krays put together, and he had far more money because he was a good businessman. Everyone talks about the Krays' 'empire' but that was all bollocks. The nearest the Krays ever got to any empire was the Hackney Empire, my local music hall in Mare Street. But Charlie Richardson? That's a different story. He really did have an empire, in terms of the size and spread of his business interests. What's more, he had the bottle to do a bit of the other kind of business, like a blower or something. He came with me, old Dave and Tony Samms on a couple of jobs. That's more than the Twins had the bottle to do.

It was Tony Samms, my pal from Portland, who introduced me to Charlie. It turned out that my old lady knew his old man and, within ten minutes of meeting, we were talking guns. I must have impressed him because straightaway he called out to his mother, who was in the office at the time, 'Mum, go home and get my gun for me. I want to show it to Jim.' And she did. This made me like Charlie straight off.

Charlie was always on the look-out for new businesses. He even bought himself a chemist's shop, off Camberwell High Road. The bloke who ran it for him was a lovely old fellow called Tommy Knight. When Charlie introduced us he told Tommy, 'If Jim ever wants anything, give it to him.' I found Charlie to be generous that way, if he liked you. I certainly liked him.

But drugs was never my game. I have never taken drugs, just as I've never smoked cigarettes and never been drunk in my life This is why I'm still fit, even though I'm over 70. No strokes or triple by-pass operations for me.

I've never even trafficked in drugs. In the early 1960s only a few London villains knew anything about them, and they only bought stuff for their personal consumption. These were still the days when the biggest moneymakers in crime were robbers – if they didn't have their profits nicked off them by other villains. And that's were the Great Train Robbery comes in.

THE SURVIVOR

EIGHT

The House of Peacocks

WHEN we first moved into the prefab in Morning Lane in 1945 it was brand new, with all the 'mod cons' of the day, but prefabs were only meant to last ten years so by 1962 it was showing its age. Not that the council had any immediate plans to demolish it and I had no wish to move. I liked living in the prefab. I loved its memories. It only had two bedrooms but we didn't need any more. It cost almost nothing to live in, we paid a small rent and I had no responsibilities. And it was handy. I'd lived in the neighbourhood nearly all my life and I knew every inch. You might think that my flash Yankee cars -- Chevrolet Convertibles, Ford Thunderbirds and the like -- would arouse jealousy if you parked them on the street in a poor place like Hackney but the only car of mine that was ever vandalised was my first, a white Ford Consul convertible. One night I parked it round the corner. When I came back in the morning someone had nicked the wheel trims. So I went and bought a tarpaulin-style car cover, I put on new trims and in the evening I took a chopper and got in the car. My wife pulled the cover over me and went home. I sat under there for three nights in a row, hoping the petty bastard would come back, but nothing happened. Lucky for him because my first little car was my baby and this fellow would have got a right going-over.

I never had any other trouble. Anyhow, I could always park in one of the lock-up garages I had all over the Hackney area. So, overall, it made sense to stay put in Morning Lane.

On the other hand I was getting plenty of money – enough to buy ten houses – and I was looking around for somewhere new. A year or two earlier I was on the point of buying a home with a swimming pool in Golders Green. In those days it would have cost me just £8,000 – less than a night's work sometimes – but I changed my mind. Still, I kept looking, and when I finally did buy a place, I found I liked it so much that I wondered why I hadn't done this years ago.

One day Dave Norman, Posh Ken and I were driving round Norwood in deepest South London, along a road called Beulah Hill, when we went round a bend and I saw this house with a fine stone chimney and a speedboat and an American car parked in the drive. It looked just right for me. It sort of put a finger out and beckoned me over saying, 'Buy me!' So I said to Posh Ken, 'If ever that house comes on the market, I'll buy it.' A year or so later Ken called me to say, 'You know that house in Beulah Hill? It's for sale.' So I phoned up the agents and I went straight over to view it. It was beautiful inside. It had a very large reception room, two bedrooms (which was all we needed), a beautiful staircase and even a minstrel gallery. It also had a nice garden. It was a long way from Hackney but I had some good pals in the area so I did the deal right away and bought it.

The very first day we moved in, my little girl was so happy, playing in the garden with her little corgi dog. Then she came in crying. I said, 'What's wrong, Denise?', and she said that the neighbour in the bungalow at the end of our garden had told her, 'Shut up!'

I was upset. I had just spent a lot of money on this house for my wife and kid and there's this mug spoiling the day for them, putting the dampers on it. In those days I wasn't famous for my patience. I walked straight across the garden, dived over the fence and bashed on this bloke's door. The moment he opened it, I grabbed hold of him and nutted him. Just as I've dragged him out of his house, to oblige him with a real beating, his old woman's come to the door and starts yelling, 'Don't hurt him any more. He's a cripple.' Then I looked down and saw that this bloke's wearing a big club boot – for a club foot – so I had to let him go. But I said to him, 'Don't ever upset my kid again!'

Then I went back and sat down to take stock of the situation. Straightaway it hit me. At the bottom of this garden there were two apple trees, right next to this raspberry's bedroom. I'd once heard something about peacocks making a big noise early every morning so I made a phone call to my favourite petshop, the one where I had bought a chimpanzee and a little monkey while we were still living in the prefab. I knew this bloke would find me some really good specimens. Sure enough, two days later a pair of lovely peacocks arrived. They were magnificent, especially when I put a long pole between those apple trees for them to roost on. From that day on, every morning about five, they would scream their throats off and wake this miserable bastard up. A few months later he moved.

But I kept the peacocks. That's why our surviving neighbours started calling my home 'The House of Peacocks', and somehow it stuck.

The place not only had a fine stone chimney outside, it had a large fireplace inside, built out of 150 rocks. It was so big that I constructed a secret armoury within it, large enough to store 12 guns and thousands of rounds of ammunition. The only way to release the door panel was to activate a gate spring by pressing a button which I concealed under one of the rocks. When people looked at the fireplace all they would see was an electric fire with fake coals, a teak mantelshelf and, above it on the wall, a painting of an angel-fish, which had a small safe behind. I convinced myself that the concealment was so skilful no one would ever crack it. I was wrong. The first day Joe Wilkins came to visit, he was casually fiddling around when he found the one rock that had the button underneath. I hadn't even told him the armoury was there so I said, 'You bastard, you've been looking through my window!' I wasn't really upset but I thought that if Joe could find the button that easily, so could Old Bill. That drove me to find another hiding place for the guns, which later turned out to be another good decision.

Not that I had moved house under the delusion that I could escape the attentions of the Metropolitan Police. I knew they'd have their eye on me wherever I lived. My reputation had spread far beyond Hackney, as I found out one night when I was in the Thomas à Becket pub in the Old Kent Road with the landlord Tommy Gibbons. Tommy was a good pal of mine and when I got back home he called me on the phone to say that, as I walked out of his pub, a local detective had walked in. Tommy said that this copper had come straight up to him and said, 'Do you know who that was who's just left? It's one of Britain's top safe-blowers!'

So why the armoury in the House of Peacocks? Was I hiding all those guns so I could shoot cops? No. I had the guns partly because they were my hobby but mainly because a violent protection war was going on at the time. It was all tied in with the newly legalised business of slot machines which was bringing in plenty of money. I was in the game with Albert Dimes and Joe

Wilkins in the East and West Ends, but in South London another outfit was muscling in. This was led by Eddie Richardson (Charlie Richardson's brother) and Frankie Fraser (during the short periods when he wasn't in jail). But they weren't having it all their own way.

One day I had a phone call from Eddie and Frankie and they asked if they could come to my home to see me. I sent my wife out, then I decided that I would lead them up the stairs into this open-plan minstrel gallery where I had a pony-skin-covered bar and ocelot-covered seats. It looked great but I put a Colt .45 under a tea cloth on the bar and I wedged a Baby Browning in my back. I'd also hidden other guns behind every drape all the way up the stairs.

Just as I'd expected, when Eddie and Frankie turned up they didn't come alone. They had five other men with them. I was on my own. They knocked. I let them all in and led them upstairs as I'd planned. Then they said they had come to see me about a man called Moishe Cohen who was a bookmaker in Soho and they wanted to do business with him. Moishe had had a bomb put in one of his shops and they thought that maybe I had put it there for Italian Albert Dimes. They didn't raise any other topic, they made no threats and they made no moves, so I have a feeling that Eddie and Frankie sensed I was well tooled up and it wouldn't be wise to take any silly chances.

All this may sound melodramatic but these were times of high tension throughout the London 'underworld'. There were several wars going on, not just over slot machines but also over who controlled the West End clubs, and there was the rumbling dispute between the Krays and the Richardsons which might break into open warfare at any time. Of course, I was friendly with both the Krays and the Richardsons but there was always a chance that I might have to get off the fence and choose one side or the other. Tricky, especially as I was an East Ender now living in South London, so maybe neither side would think they could trust me. But gang warfare just wasn't my game. I wasn't a gangster. As I've said before, I was the last of the independents. Even the slots and the clubs were just sidelines to me. I was still, first and foremost, a safe-blower.

But on 8 August 1963 a new war of sorts broke out. That was the day of the Great Train Robbery when a gang of more than 20 men stole £2,500,000 in cash from a Glasgow-to-London Royal Mail night train. It seemed so simple. Near Cheddington in rural Buckinghamshire, under cover of darkness, they climbed up the embankment from a road passing underneath and placed a false signal alongside the track. At 3.03 in the morning they turned it red just as the train was approaching. When it halted the fireman was grabbed, the driver was coshed and all the mail-workers were frightened into co-operating. The gang then unloaded 120 mailbags containing the money and passed them down the embankment and into a lorry on the road beneath. Then everyone drove in convoy to their hideout a couple of miles away, Leatherslade Farm, where they counted out the money and split it into shares of around £90,000 each after 'expenses'. Then all the robbers went their various ways, fully expecting that any traces of their presence at the farm would be removed.

That was their first mistake, because the man who was paid £35,000 to do this – to wipe any fingerprints, get rid of the mailbags, dump the vehicles and, if necessary, burn the whole place down – never did anything of the sort. As I've said earlier, the culprit was a bloke who was with me in Portland. We called him 'the Tortoise' because he had a strange, tortoise-like way of moving his head, but the Great Train Robbers should have called him the Tortoise because he was so bloody slow he never turned up. Anyhow he pocketed the money and ended up a country squire, so I was told.

I only found out about his role years later. I had nothing to do with the Great Train Robbery. The nearest I've ever got to trains was lying under them as they rumbled over me when I was a kid. I'd never even worked with anybody who's ever admitted being on the robbery. Just like any non-criminal member of the public, I only heard about it after it had taken place.

It took all of five days for the police to find Leatherslade Farm but everything was still there, including the mailbags and the vehicles. Worse still, according to what the newspapers and the courts were told, many of the gang's fingerprints were found at the farm and that's supposed to be what led to their rapid arrest. Four months later 13 men went on trial for the crime. One was acquitted. The other 12 all got heavy sentences. Some got 30 years.

The police operation was hailed as a great success but right from the start I had my doubts. For instance, even if so many robbers really did leave their prints all over Leatherslade Farm, was that really what led to their arrest? And consider how neatly most of the others were picked up in the next five years. Was that really due to the brilliance of the leading detectives on the case, Chief Superintendent Tommy Butler and Inspector Frank Williams, as newspapers said at the time? They hailed Butler as a genius and he rode on the robbers' backs to become Head of Scotland Yard's Flying Squad, but did he make all those headline-grabbing arrests as a result of pure Sherlock

Holmesian powers of deduction? Not according to my East End villain's powers of deduction. To me, the whole thing stank of underworld treachery from the moment I heard that the police had found the farm. Many other villains came to the same view: the entire robbery had to be a ready-eye, a set-up, so the robbers were really nicked before they ever went on it. Like I was nicked at Loughton at 17 but on a far bigger scale. That was how Scotland Yard worked in those days: it created many of the crimes that it solved because it was a far easier way to catch villains than by solving genuine crimes. And my guess is that it works that way to this day.

It's been said since, by people who say they were involved in the robbery from the start, that it took 'only' nine months to set up. But where was it set up? In whose premises? Who knew about it in advance, other than the blokes who were nicked? If it took as much – not as little – as nine months to set up, you can be sure lots of other people knew about it. It's been rumoured for years that both the scheme and the team were put together in a couple of South London clubs, so who owned and controlled those places? They must have been in the 'know' in advance but did they go on the robbery itself? If not, why not? Who else were they working with?

Did they have friends in the police? Did they have partners in Scotland Yard? I'm sure the self-styled leading players really did do a lot of careful planning, and they may have come up with the original idea, but who fed them the specific information? Who told them that so much money would be on board that train on that particular night?

Consider this. Who knows anything about movements of really big money, other than key security people in the companies doing the moving? Probably only top coppers and the villains they tip off. In the days before credit cards, only they knew exactly where and when all large amounts of cash were being shipped. They had to be told 'for security reasons' – and because big outfits like banks and the Royal Mail trusted them. So no one was better placed than high-ranking police officers to feed such information into this motley crew and then pounce on them as soon as the job was done, grabbing the glory and a good deal of the cash for themselves while they're at it.

So did senior detectives have someone close to the heart of the gang who was feeding controlled information in and feeding hot intelligence back out? Not anyone who later got jailed, of course, but maybe someone who ducked out of going on the robbery, preferring to act first as counsellor and later as intermediary for those robbers who dodged the first round-up and then went on the run. Someone who brokered deals with the Yard when these men were finally driven to surrender their money, themselves or both. Someone who could find out where the final few were hiding and then pop them straight into the clutches of Tom Butler – in front of a posse of photographers and in time for the next day's front pages. Some Siamese Viper: a two-headed Judas snake with a smile on one face for the 'chaps' and a copper's helmet on top of the other one.

Some of these thoughts first struck me at the time of the robbery. The others matured over several years as I gradually realised exactly which underworld figures were associating with Butler and Williams. For a long time I scarcely thought about the robbery. I couldn't help reading about all the arrests, trials and escapes – the newspapers were full of this stuff, day after day – but I didn't know any of the robbers and, from what I read, I couldn't admire them. Apart from Bruce Reynolds there didn't seem to be an ounce of brains among the fucking lot of them. You'd never catch me going on any job that involved so many people – too great a risk of betrayal. And it was such an outrageous crime, the state couldn't allow the named suspects to get away with it. The state wanted 'bodies', show trials and banner headlines saying, 'Thirty Years'. It didn't care much about getting the money back. And that was a perfect recipe for kick-backs, pay-offs and downright theft by certain senior detectives and their buddies in the underworld.

Anyhow, in 1963 I just carried on with my own activities: decorating the House of Peacocks, riding around in my Yankee cars and safe-blowing. It wasn't until late in 1964 that someone made me an offer which had everything to do with the Great Train Robbery. Through Joe Wilkins' uncle, Bert Wilkins, I met a man called Johnny Tilley. Sad to say, John's dead now but in those days he used to have a big car business down towards Shepherd's Bush along Holland Park Road. John knew a high-ranking detective called Bob Anderson. They were very close friends. According to John they did plenty of things together, even though he had a serious criminal background and Bob Anderson was a top cop. Indeed by now he was Tommy Butler's deputy at the Flying Squad.

One day in early December 1964 Johnny Tilley handed me a little stainless steel key. It wasn't a locker key, it was a key to a safe. Nothing out of the ordinary there, I thought, until Johnny told me, 'That's the key to Tommy Butler's own personal safe at Scotland Yard.'

'Tommy Butler's safe?' I said, 'How did you get hold of that?' John told me that his pal Anderson had given it to him with these words: 'Get hold of someone game, John. Slip him in there, open up Butler's safe and you'll find 36 grand in there.'

In those days there was no such thing as security cameras, not even at London's police headquarters. As John said, 'Anyone can walk in there. It's a doddle', so I said, 'But won't there be murders if someone steals all that?'

'No, there won't,' he said. 'Bob's told me there won't be any scream because it's train money. It's come from the Great Train Robbery.' And as Anderson had told John, if Butler had come by this money legitimately, it shouldn't still be in his safe. The robbery had happened 16 months previously and he should have stuck any such money straight in a high-security vault, to be kept until either it was produced in evidence in any trial or it could be handed to its rightful owners (probably the Royal Mint).

Naturally, as soon as Johnny Tilley had this key, he had come to me as the man most likely to be game for it, but he also told me, 'Get it done quickly.'

Now I don't like any of that 'hurry up' business. It puts me on edge. So I said, 'Why? What's the rush? If Butler doesn't know that someone's planning to nick it off him, he'll just keep the 36 grand there. Besides, if we leave it a bit longer, he might put even more in there.'

'No,' said Johnny. 'There's something going on. They're keeping an eye on Butler.' He indicated that, according to Anderson's information, Butler was under some sort of observation, not over his handling of the Great Train Robbery round-up but over some other aspect of his behaviour, maybe something in his private life. Anderson may have seen some papers he shouldn't have seen and that's how he knew Butler was in some sort of trouble. Clearly he didn't like Butler, otherwise he wouldn't have given Johnny the key. Few of Butler's colleagues did like him, it seems.

So this is the proposition: Butler might get lifted any time, so the money had to be nicked 'quickly' or not at all. Straightaway I got flashing lights. As much as I liked Johnny Tilley – and I had taken part in a few things he'd stuck up before – I wasn't going to be rushed into anything. I had to think this out. Getting into Scotland Yard wouldn't have been a problem. After all, we're not talking about New Scotland Yard today, that fortress off Victoria Street. We're talking about the previous Scotland Yard: down Cannon Row, opposite Big Ben by Westminster Bridge. It was wide-open at all hours, like churches used to be. In theory I could just stride in and go straight to Butler's private office. It sounds ridiculous but in those days it really would have been that simple, especially as I would have had help. As

Johnny said, 'We'll let you know when he's not there, out of town on some distant inquiry, then you just walk in.'

I was torn. On the one hand, Johnny was reliable. He was very close to some very good pals of mine and they had a bit of respect for me because I did things for them that other people wouldn't do. So I was sure this wasn't a ready-eye. On the other hand, it was all a bit too rushed. It appealed to my sense of bravado – walking right into the lions' den and walking out ten minutes later with 36 grand – but I had things on my mind. Not just other jobs but domestic problems. I was having trouble concentrating. I was distracted. I wasn't able to put a hundred per cent effort into this bit of business, like I normally would. So I had to let it ride for a while.

One week later all my domestic problems would come to a head. All my suspicions would climax at the same time. Everything would fall into place, fall apart and explode.

THE SURVIVOR

NINE

Inspector Evans Calls

WHEN I was 14 my old stepdad said to me, 'Now you've left school, what do you want to do with yourself?'

I said, 'I want to put my prick out the window and fuck the world.'

He laughed and said, 'Oh well, there's nothing I can do for you. You'd better get on with it.'

So I did. I couldn't help myself. I had too much energy. I had a huge sex drive but I was also in a line of work which meant I never knew when my liberty or my life might suddenly end, so I packed every minute with intense, pleasurable experiences, usually involving women.

I'll explain it another way. You know when you watch a boxing match – especially on old newsreels – you only see the boxers themselves. All the onlookers are blurs, their faces little smudges. Everyone in the audience is faceless. Only the principals are identifiable. That's how it was in my world of crime. Blurs, blurs, blurs. Everything out of focus except for stark clear close-ups of individuals fighting to the death, or so it seemed. Straight people can't understand that being a practising villain is like living in a war zone.

Just think what World War II did to the morals of straight women of all classes – decent, respectable women who would have been shocked at the mere idea that they would ever have strayed from the path of virtue. Then the war came along and they began working in ammunitions factories, driving ambulances, working on the land, and they went the other way.

They started smoking, drinking and getting fucked by Tom, Dick and Harry because they never knew if there'd be a tomorrow. They never knew if, the very next moment, another siren would go, another bomb would drop and they'd be killed. So fuck it, they fucked!

It's just like that when you're a criminal. You never know if, the very next day or night, you're going to get shot by Old Bill, blow yourself up or get nicked and go to jail for the next ten years. So you make the most of it, especially when it comes to women. I've only ever known one villain who stuck with just one woman throughout his life. As for me, even if I'd been married to Marilyn Monroe I would still have been looking around. I can't help it. It's the way I'm made. I could be married to the most beautiful woman in the world but it wouldn't be enough for me. I would still be nutting around. I still couldn't help looking if I saw a pair of lovely legs walk by.

So there was me and my old woman. She had all the attention in the world. There was never a day when I didn't make love to her. Every day of my life. I'd take a bird home from a club, pump her, come home, wake up the missus and pump her. I couldn't get enough. I was a fuck machine. I loved women. And strangely enough, women liked me.

One day I drove Dodgy Bob down to Redhill where he had some business. He was just about to break into this place when a bird came along on a bike and she started talking to me. I tried to shake her off but she kept following me even when we were climbing up and over walls. So I had to take her on a long walk to get her away from what Bob was doing. Then I realised there was only one thing for it. After that, we came back to find that Dodgy Bob had finished, so I just said goodbye. I think she guessed we were villains but that only turned her on. Later Dodgy Bob did me no favours by telling my wife, 'Birds follow him around.'

Then there was the lovely summer day when I was driving through Shoreditch in my Thunderbird with the hood down, and little Curly King next to me, when a bird pulls up behind us in a little car. She followed us right up to Oxford Street, through three or four miles of quite heavy traffic, and then I ran out of petrol. In those days you could stop anywhere, so I parked right opposite Selfridges in the middle of Oxford Street. Then she pulled up behind us and said, 'Anything I can do?'

'Yeah,' I said, 'I've run out of petrol.'

'I'll take you to the petrol station.' So I told Curly to stay with the car and I left him sitting there in the sunshine with the hood down.

When I got in her car she said, 'I've been following you.'

I said, 'I know, I saw you in the mirror. So what are you following me for?'

She said, 'I like the way your hair curls at the back of your neck.'

So now I figured, the petrol can wait, Curly can wait and she can drive me straight to the White House Hotel by Regent's Park, where I kept a permanent suite. By the time we had finished and got back to the Thunderbird, Curly was so tanned he looked like Louis Armstrong.

Can you understand women's logic? Just the curl of your hair can turn a woman on to the point where she'll do anything. I'll never understand it. It was so easy. I couldn't help myself. I was weak. I wasn't addicted to cigarettes or drugs or gambling – gambling gives a lot of villains a rush. I was addicted to sex.

Throughout this time I was married. Don't forget, when I first met my future wife, she was 15 and I was 17. At our wedding she was just 17 – and eight months pregnant – and I was still only 19 – and in borstal. So by the time we moved to Beulah Hill we were still barely in our thirties but we'd been together for 15 years. When we were younger, she naturally assumed that I was never going to have other women, but as the years went by she wised up. She was no genius but she couldn't help noticing things and when she thought she'd found evidence that I had been playing around, she went potty.

It got to the stage that she surrounded herself with so many alarm clocks that, if I came home in the early hours of the morning, she'd moan and groan and say, 'Look at that clock! What time do you call this?' Whether we were in the prefab or in Beulah Hill, I'd come in and she'd be sitting at the other side of the room and I'd see her face moving and little nerves twitching. 'You've just been with a bird,' she'd snap. And she'd smell it, she'd smell another woman on me, from right across the room. She had an acute sense of smell.

Then she'd get the keys to my car, she'd open it up and she'd look for clues, armed with a pair of tweezers and an envelope to stick the evidence in. This would happen time and time again, till it got so bad that when I came home I would leave the car somewhere else, streets away, anywhere she couldn't find it. And of course I always drove convertibles, which were sure to attract admiring looks from women, so when we were driving along together, if my head went this way or that way, her head would go the same way too, just to see if I was ogling someone. She was obsessed.

I couldn't take all this. It was too much. With all her clock-watching, my old woman was driving me mad. I had to have my freedom. I was like an albatross, flying all over London, fucking everything. It was a lovely life, I had plenty of money and in those days I could pull.

There was another angle to all this. Women can get a little bit jealous of their husbands and in a way, I think, she was jealous of me. Yes, on a lot of those late nights I was hard at work, blowing safes, while on a lot of others I was hard at play. When I wasn't blowing, I was being blown. It got to the stage that I was out every night but by then the blowing was taking precedence. There was so much villainy, I had to be out all the time. But I don't remember her ever complaining about living off the proceeds of crime: the clothes, the house, the cars. On the contrary, one day she said, 'How come you've got a Thunderbird? Why haven't I got a Thunderbird?'

So I said, 'Well, you can have a Thunderbird, if you want to go out and rob banks and blow safes. No one's stopping you. If you do what I do, you can have cars like that.'

See, it's easy to sit back and have cars bought for you, to have a lovely home bought for you. It's nice to have all these things done for you, if you ain't got to do it yourself. She didn't have to go steaming into banks and on ram-ups and blowing safes. And she wasn't going to end up going to jail. She was going to be there tomorrow, whatever happened, whereas I could have been locked up for the next 20 years. That's if I wasn't shot by Old Bill.

You might think that when I bought the House of Peacocks in Beulah Hill, I would have eased up on my criminal activities, become a kind of suburban country squire, sat back, relaxed and rested on my laurels. But no. I was more active than ever. In the course of 1964 I was so busy on work that I even gave up women. I wasn't larking about with any girls. Until the move it had been out every night for me – clubbing it and taking birds on my arm – but now I was in the House of Peacocks I had more important things on my mind: my wife and my kid, my home. And, despite all her clock-watching, I had a better-looking wife, a better home life and a better way of life than almost any other villain I knew.

So now I was splashing out on all sorts of fancy domestic goods that I'd never bought before. I bought the first Blaupunkt radiogram that entered the country. I had a carpet specially made for that minstrel gallery and then had it flown down from Scotland by helicopter. And I bought even more expensive cars. At a time when there were only seven Thunderbirds in Europe, I had three of them. And, being a criminal who had dodged all those burglar-detection systems, I bought the first internal sensor alarm ever to be installed in a private house in Britain. I knew what was best for my home and I liked living the way I lived. But to live that way, you need the money, which was one reason why I was blowing more safes than ever.

So now she was living a good life too. I didn't give her a Thunderbird but she had plenty of other cars. When we lived in Hackney, her red Ford convertible was stolen. The insurance money took some time to come through so, in the meantime, I went out and bought a grey convertible. All of a sudden the police found the red one. It had been used on a caper, a robbery – bloody criminals, you can't trust 'em – so now she's got two convertibles. A few days later we were driving down Seven Sisters Road and we stopped at a car showroom and saw a turntable with a brand spanking new convertible MG Midget going round. So she climbed in it and, sitting there with her blonde hair in this little car, she looked right. So I said, 'Do you want it?' 'Yes,' she said, and I said to the salesman, 'I'll have that! Wrap it up.' Brand new. This is the sort of thing that I would do. Yes, we had a lot of arguments and I had a terrible, violent temper then, but she didn't have it so bad. Life was good for the pair of us and for our kid Denise.

At the same time, and in return, I expected my wife to keep a low profile. I felt that if she had the know-how and the expertise to keep me in a life of luxury, then she could lead the life of Riley and I would be keeping a low profile at home. But that wasn't how it was. I was well pissed off when I went into Billy O'Dare's club one night – the Speakeasy in Margaret Street – and I saw her in there with Smuggler Bill's wife, Peggy. So I went down and grabbed her by the hair, dragged her upstairs and slung her out of the club. Billy O'Dare and his father, who was a professional wrestler, came running up the stairs behind me and I've pulled out a truncheon. I said, 'If you don't mind your own business I'll cave your fucking skulls in, the pair of you.'

I didn't want her in there because I didn't want anything to happen to us. I knew that if she went out clubbing it on her own – or with a girlfriend – she was going to breathe trouble. Now you might say that, when I dragged her out by the hair, I was exhibiting a caveman attitude, but I don't think so. How else are you going to get the little bastards out? With the life I was leading, I didn't need this kind of complication. She was living quite a good lifestyle on my efforts and she should have been satisfied with that.

But she was changing. In 1962 when we first moved into Beulah Hill, I was still fucking about with different women. Then there came a period when I'd get up the morning and have my breakfast and she'd be crying her eyes out. 'What's the matter with you?' I'd ask, and she'd say things like,

'You were at Charlie Richardson's party last night with two black girls!', which was totally untrue.

So I thought to myself, 'Who's she getting this crap from?' Someone was filling her head with a pack of lies. She's got women friends – other villains' wives like Dave Norman's wife Ann – but this kind of thing must have come from someone else, someone who's trying to poison her against me for their own sake. Must be a bloke, I thought, must be some geezer trying to get in her knickers.

Yes, I had been at Charlie Richardson's party but not with two black birds. I might have been there with three white birds, but someone was deliberately twisting the truth because they thought that this would cause me an even bigger problem with her. That's only one example. She was getting this crap put in her mind all the time. Someone was continually pummelling away at her mind – 'Your Jimmy's been with this bird last night . . . that bird last night . . .' – keeping on and on until it made her ill.

It was towards the end of 1964 – at the very time when Johnny Tilley handed me the key to Tommy Butler's safe in Scotland Yard for me to go and empty it – when I found that, all of a sudden, I had a problem with my pissing. I went to my doctor and he told me that I had urethritis. He said it was nothing too serious – 'It may never bother you again, or if it comes back, you just take a few pills and it goes' – but he said it can be picked up from sex.

I had been on the ships for ten years and I thought I knew the signs of every venereal disease – gonorrhoea, syphilis and the rest – because we'd had it all explained to us. Not that I'd ever had anything like that in my life, but I knew other blokes who had. To sailors they are occupational hazards. I also knew the gestation periods. So I asked my doctor, 'How long after you have sex does this urethritis take to show itself?' He said, 'Only four or five weeks.' So I thought back and I realised that I hadn't had sex with anyone but my wife for the previous four or five weeks or, indeed, for quite a few weeks before that, because I'd been so preoccupied with crime and with refurbishing the House of Peacocks that I hadn't had girls or sex on my mind.

This realisation now dawned on me. I'd always assumed that, whatever I'd been doing with other women – and however crazily I'd been acting, like taking a pot shot at her in the prefab – my wife would always be faithful to me. I had always made a fuss of her so, to my mind, whatever I was doing on the side shouldn't have had the slightest impact on our relationship. That was separate, that was special. Whereas she only had to do one thing and the relationship would be finished. One fling and our marriage would be over.

Not that I was leaping to any conclusions. Yes, I had caught a dose of urethritis but I had no proof that it was down to her. After all, doctors can be wrong. But, as I couldn't come up with any other explanation, this thing kept gnawing away at me to the point that it was affecting me professionally.

I wasn't into bricklaying. I wasn't a gardener. I was a safe-blower and I could not afford to make mistakes. I had to concentrate one hundred per cent on what I was doing. At this time I was using all sorts of volatile explosives. Bellex or Polo-aman or Belamex, for example, are several different types of gelignite. They are made up of differing combinations of gun cotton and nitro-glycerine, and there comes a time when the nitro-glycerine can start oozing out. This makes it a very dangerous substance so I had to watch out for any such deterioration, just like a munitions officer in the heat of battle. And it wasn't only my life at stake. I had other people relying on me, especially as now, no matter who was with me on a job, I always had to blow that safe. Even when I went out with other experts at the blowing game, like Wally the Goat or Meggsy, I would blow. Just like if I went anywhere in a car I couldn't let anyone else drive me. I always had to be in the driving seat. I couldn't let anyone else blow safes.

All this meant that I had to have a clear head, but now that was impossible because I couldn't get a long string of questions out of my mind. Has she really given me this condition? If the answer's no, then by now she must have it too, so how come she's never come to me and said, 'I've caught something from you' – especially as she's always going on about me playing around with other women? But she hasn't, so does this mean she knows she's caught it from someone else? If so, who the fuck is he?

I had to get all these questions answered soon or I'd have to stop work. One mistake by me when I'm safe-blowing and I could lose a limb or two. At worst, I could get killed. During these years I had a one-track mind. Whichever obsession I was pursuing at any one time – guns, gelignite, cars, women – that was all I could think about. I had tunnel vision. So now I was obsessed with finding out if my old woman was seeing someone else, I couldn't be in a fit mental state to blow a safe. I'm going to make a mistake and either blow myself up or get nicked.

To make things worse, I found I had a sixth sense about her activities. Nobody had told me anything. I just sensed something wasn't right. Still, I wasn't going to accuse her outright because I knew that, whenever she did that to me, I denied everything. So I carried on as normal but watched out for anything she might say or do that could give me a clue.

For instance, a couple of times I told her I was going out of London overnight, indicating that I had a professional assignment in some other town, but instead I deliberately came back home to find she wasn't there. She stayed out all night on both occasions. Again, I comforted myself by thinking she might have been staying with Dave Norman's wife or with another girlfriend, after parking our daughter with my mother-in-law. So that still wasn't evidence that she was seeing another man, but things were beginning to pile up.

I was at an age when I was very fit and my mind worked overtime. I could put two and two together very quickly. My mind was at its sharpest, like never before in my whole life. My senses were spot-on. I would file things away in that little mental filing cabinet without even realising I was doing it. My brain was in turbo.

Then one Sunday morning in the House of Peacocks I was sitting up at the big breakfast bar reading the newspapers while she was lounging on the settee reading something else. I was leafing through the *News of the World* when I came across a story which for some reason I read it out to her. It was about a surgeon who suspected his wife of having an affair, so he followed her to a secret rendezvous in his car and caught her with her lover in the act – 'bang to rights', as we criminals would say.

'It says here,' I continued, 'that he followed her in his car.'

Quick as a flash, she said, 'Nobody could ever follow me.'

'How come?' I said.

She said, 'I'm always looking in my mirror.'

That's how it came out. Bomp. Straight away I'm analysing what she's said. Why would she be looking in the mirror? What the fucking hell is she worried about being followed for? She ain't doing anything wrong. I'm doing it all. I'm the one who's very, very active. I'm the professional and I've got good reasons to look in my mirror: flashing lights, police cars and unmarked cars. I'm the one who has to be aware. You may think that I was paranoid, but paranoia is just over-awareness really, and I'm over-aware to an extreme degree. When I was on a job, I would check and double-check everything – and everybody.

But my old woman? Does she have Scotland Yard following her? Not on your life. Even in our own little family, she's the hunter, not the hunted. She's always checking on me, so what's new? What's with this, 'Nobody could ever follow me!'? What does that mean?

Right. That remark goes into the little filing cabinet up here in my head. That's a challenge. When the right time comes, I shall follow her. And she'll be the last person to know it when I do.

But there was more. Around the middle of November 1964 I was in Bermondsey, South East London, with my old pal, Davey Norman. We were standing talking to a bloke called Roy who owned a car front in Jamaica Road. Roy had sold me the Galaxy Convertible and I often dropped by there. It also happened to be on the route between my home in Beulah Hill and my old home in Hackney, because Jamaica Road leads to the Rotherhithe Tunnel, which goes under the Thames and straight into the East End.

So I was talking to Roy and Dave with my back to Jamaica Road when, on an impulse, I turned round just in time to see a blue Vauxhall, driven by a woman in a headscarf. I don't know what made me turn just then, in mid-conversation, but it was a kind of intuition, as if someone had tapped me on the shoulder. And now, on another impulse, I started running after the car. I caught it as it stopped at some traffic lights that led into the tunnel, and I've run to the door. I've looked in and the driver looks at me and it's her! It's my old woman!

So what's made me chase that blue Vauxhall when she had a red Ford Classic? Was it another flash of intuition that's propelled me? Anyhow, now I said, 'Pull over, where are you off to?'

'I'm going to see my mother,' she replied, as she might well have been, because her mother lived in Chingford across the river. But I could see that her knee was trembling violently.

So I whistled to Dave Norman and I told him to get in my car and follow me while I'm in this blue Vauxhall. And as we're going through the Rotherhithe Tunnel I said to her, 'Whose is this car?'

'It's been leant to me.'

'Where's your own car?'

She said, 'It's got back axle trouble.'

Oh yeah. This won't do at all. If her red Ford really did have back axle trouble, or any other trouble, she would have told me immediately. That's the way she was over the slightest mechanical hitch, let alone something as serious as a back axle. She never even cleaned one of her cars, let alone put one in for repair.

So I didn't believe this for one moment. I knew straight away that someone dodgy had given her it to prevent me from spotting her driving along. Just like she was wearing that headscarf. Till now she'd never worn headscarfs. She must have been wearing this one so she couldn't be recognised. Being clever again. Another fact sheet for my old mental filing cabinet.

So while she was still driving, I started searching around and – intuition again – I said, 'What's in here, in the glovebox?'

She said, 'I don't know.'

I opened it and there was one solitary piece of paper inside. It was a summons for a motoring offence and so it gave the name and address of the car's owner. I turned it over and on the back, written in eyebrow pencil, were four digits. Part of a phone number, I guessed, because in those days London numbers consisted of seven characters: three letters followed by four digits. Then it hit me that these four digits were the same as Dave Norman's Bermondsey number: BER 6985, let's say, but without the BER for Bermondsey.

I did not think for one moment that Dave was playing games in my wife's life, but I knew that she was friendly with Dave's wife Ann. In fact she was so friendly with Ann that she knew their number off by heart, so why had she written down Dave and Ann's number on the back of this person's driving summons? There could only be one explanation: she had given it to him, so he could ring there and leave messages for her. Obviously she had told him not to ring her at our house in case I picked up the phone. So Ann Norman must have been in on this arrangement. The name on the summons was George Foreman.

George Foreman? Means nothing to me, I thought. I hadn't heard of a George Foreman since the one I knew at school, the kid who helped me thieve all the carpentry tools. Then I remembered. A few months previously my wife – not being very canny – had asked me, 'Do you know a Georgie Foreman?'

I said, 'Yeah, he's the one who robbed the tools from school with me that night. His name was Georgie Foreman.'

I described him and she said, 'No, that's not him. Never mind. I just wondered.'

Strange how this conversation was stockpiled in my memory, so I could pull it out of that filing cabinet the instant I saw the name on that document.

So I said to my old woman, 'What's this fucking number then?'

'I don't know,' she mumbled, which obviously was bollocks because it was done in eyebrow pencil, like women do.

So I made her pull round and I told her, 'Get in Dave's car.' In we climbed and Dave drove us to the address on the summons: Bland House, Lambeth Walk. It turned out to be in a grubby block of council flats in Vauxhall. When we got there, I looked at the summons again and this time I really focused on the surname: Foreman.

What the hell. Time for some guerrilla tactics. Time to open up a can of worms.

I left her with Dave Norman while I went up to the first floor landing, where this Foreman had his flat. I was quite formally dressed, with a grey suit, shirt and tie, and I was holding the summons in my hand. There was a group of women on the landing and one said, 'Can I help you?' I said, 'Mrs Foreman?' She said, 'Yeah' – she had curlers in her hair, a fag in her mouth and slippers on – so I said, 'I'm a police officer, Inspector Evans. I was in a squad car and we had to stop a blue Vauxhall on suspicion and we've apprehended the female driver, a young, attractive blonde.' I thought this will start the tempers flying, so I continued, 'She wouldn't tell us whose car it is, but when we searched it at the station we found this summons, with your husband's name and address. Can I have a word with him?'

See, I went up there to do the bastard there and then. I wanted to get hold of him and say, 'Right, you've been fucking around and now let's put this thing right.' But she said, 'No, he's not in.'

OK, then, I figured, I can do him another sort of damage, so I said. 'Well, when will he be in?'

'I don't know, he goes away for days at a time.'

So that was the sort of relationship they had: away for days at a time. So I said, 'Well, tell him I'll be back. Thank you very much, Mrs Foreman. Just be sure to tell him Inspector Evans called. Goodbye.'

That should have started the ball rolling. Now I was sure the next time he came home she would give him an earful about this Inspector Evans and the blue Vauxhall and the little blonde bird. It would have gone something like: I've had the cops up here, so who's this young, attractive blonde you've been lending your car to? Christ knows how he would have dealt with that, but if he lied to his old woman like he used to lie to mine, he may have got away with it. Anyhow, I knew I'd done enough to let George Foreman know I was on his case.

So now I went back down to this car and I asked my old woman who'd lent it to her, and she said, 'I borrowed this off of Pat Riley.'

Pat Riley, eh? This set my mind off on an another track, because Pat Riley was married to Freddie Riley. I had first met Freddie in Portland – where else? – and now he was a well-established thief. He was also a detonator and jelly man. Usually if my little pals and I wanted detonators we would go down to the Kent quarries and steal them ourselves, but sometimes I would call on Freddie Riley who always had a stock put away. He lived in Wandsworth, not far from Vauxhall, which was a lot easier for us than going all the way down to Kent. And Fred was OK, reliable, to the point that I introduced my wife to his wife, Pat, then I would send her along to pick up the gear whenever I needed it. Freddie would drop detonators and jelly off at their flat, then my wife would go and collect them.

That must be how it started. All the local villains used to congregate round at Riley's and George Foreman lived close by. My wife must have been down there to collect detonators or some gear one day, he must have been hanging around and Pat Riley probably introduced them.

So when my old woman told me that Pat had lent her this blue Vauxhall I said, 'Right, let's go to Pat's home', which was only a few minutes away. So as I'm walking along the landing towards the Rileys' place, I let my wife walk behind me, and as soon as Pat opened the door I looked around and saw her signalling to Pat to back up her story. So Pat asked, 'What's the matter, Mary?' and she leapt in, 'Pat, you know that car you lent me?' But Pat said, 'What car?' So I said, 'Pat, I know you never lent her the fucking car, so don't say you did.'

Then I said to my old woman, 'Right, come on', and I drove her home with me to Beulah Hill. As soon as I got there, I've slung all her clothes out of the wardrobe, put the whole fucking lot in a pile on the bed, picked the bedspread up, carried the bundle out in the garden, thrown half a gallon of petrol at it and set the whole thing alight.

But even in tragedy, you get some comedy, because when I'd dumped all her clothes on the bed, I'd forgotten that I'd just thrown my jacket down on it too. So when I'd gathered up the bedspread and set everything alight, my jacket had also gone up in flames, along with a few hundred quid in the pockets. All that money – worth maybe £10,000 today – and my jacket.

Over the next few few days I made a lot of inquiries about the name on the summons. I had got bad reports. Even so, I had to be sure, so for the time being I hadn't taken any action. A week or so later I was back in Jamaica Road, driving along the one-way system towards the bend where Roy had his car front. This time I was with Tony Samms, my close pal from Portland, in his Hillman Husky kind of a hatchback, and in the boot we had a double-barrelled shotgun. As we turned the bend I could see three men 80 or 90 yards away, outside the car front. One of them was the manager. The other two I had never seen before: both tallish, one with dark hair, the other fair. As we approached I looked at the back of the one with fair hair and something told me this was George Foreman. All that previous week I had been asking about him and maybe someone had said he had fair hair. And maybe now he was there enquiring about me, asking how I'd identified his blue Vauxhall, perhaps. Anyhow, as we drove by, I looked up at them and those three looked down at us.

Tony was doing the driving but he'd looked at them too, and when we'd got 50 yards further on, he said, 'Do you know who that was?'

I said, 'Which one?'

'The geezer with the fair hair.'

I said, 'Yes, Georgie Foreman.'

He said, 'Yes, but how do you know? You say you've never seen this fucking geezer before.'

I said, 'Aah, I just know.'

Then he said, 'Yeah, but be careful. You're not going to have a row with him, are you? They're really fucking serious, these people. They call them the Underworld Undertakers.' He went on to tell me what a fearsome mob they were.

So I said to him, 'I don't care about reputations, so turn the car round, stop there and I'll go straight in the office. You know him well enough to talk to, so I want you to pull him over and take him to the back of your car, open the boot up, show him what's in it and tell him my pal Jimmy says, "Do you want to buy a shotgun?"'

This was my sort of logic of letting Foreman know that I'm on his fucking heels, because I want him to know. Don't forget, I'd already been round to his house, deliberately disclosing my real name and telling his wife about the blonde bird. Now this is the second incident, at the same spot as I saw her go by in that car. It was as if it was all ordained, like a pattern, or a game put together by my own personal demon.

So Tony turned round and drove up to the car front. I got out but by now the three men were disappearing into the office, which was in the middle of all the cars. So I've followed them in and I see this Foreman scratching his arse and looking up at the ceiling. He knew who I was straight away. That's why he was trying to edge past the door and get out, but when he'd got out, I heard Tony say, 'Here, George.' Then I could see that Tony's got him at the back of the car with him and they're talking. Half a minute later I heard the boot go down.

Then suddenly I heard car wheels spinning and it was Foreman driving off like a maniac in his own car. A few minutes later there were brakes screeching and it's Foreman back again with Stevie Murphy, who just stood at the wall. Now Stevie Murphy was a big lump, about six-foot-odd, chewing gum and giving us all that menacing bollocks look. So I said to myself, 'You're just about the right size. I'll do both you and Foreman right now and get it over with.' After all, it was a double-barrel.

But before I can do anything off they both go, which didn't surprise me because at no point did Foreman have the guts to look me in the eye. He couldn't face me and he was looking double-guilty. I had never seen him before but now I felt I had some real proof that he was the one. I was on to him. Things would move a bit quickly from now on. But I still had to be 100 per cent sure for me to do what I had in store for him.

So I got in the car and Sammsy told me that, while they were sitting together, he'd asked Foreman, 'Do you know Pat Riley?', and Foreman said, 'Who's he?' See, he was trying to be clever because, of course, Pat Riley was a woman. Sammsy's gone on to ask him about this blue Vauxhall and Foreman said, definitely no, he didn't know anything about it. So I asked Sammsy, 'What else have you said to him?'

So Sammsy said, 'I told him that his name's come up and you suspect him, and then he said, "Well, what will happen if it was me?" So I told him there and then, "He will shoot you." He said, "Oh, he'll shoot me!" "Yes." So Foreman said, "Well, anybody can do that." Then I showed him the shotgun and said what you told me to say, and that's when he screeched off and came back with his pal.'

So, you see, Foreman was told. We had marked his card. But if, as he said, 'anybody' can shoot anyone, how come he didn't shoot me right there? What about that big, dark-headed guy he had with him? If he's got help why didn't Foreman and his pal do something straight away, instead of diving off and fetching Murphy back? See, I think they were all Mickey fucking Mouse gangsters.

So now it was all fitting in, like pieces in a jigsaw. The blue Vauxhall. Ann Norman's number written in eyeliner on the summons with Foreman's name and address. My old woman's feeble denial. Her failed attempt to get Pat Riley to lie for her. His clever-stupid denial that he knew Pat Riley. His furtive shifty manner, scratching his arse and looking up at that office ceiling. His flight at the sight of the shotgun. Then there

THE SURVIVOR

were her unexplained nights away from home. That odd question a year ago about whether I knew a George Foreman. The unexplained dose of urethritis. And, of course, that provocative boast of hers: 'No one could ever follow me. I always look in the mirror.' Uh huh. That's what she thinks.

Time to put that to the test, but how? I can't follow her myself – she's bound to spot me – and I can't ask anyone else to do it. No one's ever told me my wife's fucking around so if I tell any other bloke of my suspicions now, it'll be as if I'm making a public declaration. No one likes admitting this kind of thing to his pals and I don't want to embarrass myself.

But I'm still torn. One side of me doesn't want to know if she really is playing around because, if it's true, there will be no marriage. It will be over. But the other side of me has to know because I can't keep on blowing safes with this thing clouding my brain. I have to sort this out. Whether she's going with this creep Foreman or with anyone else, I've got to put a stop to it, get it over and done with, get back to work and get on with my life.

So I gave her one last chance. I said, 'If you're screwing around, stop it. Hit it on the head. Otherwise something terrible will happen.'

But she said, 'You're imagining things.'

And that's when I decided to hide in the boot of her car when she went on one of her secret drives. Then she could look in her mirror all she liked but she wouldn't see me. I'd be so close behind her, she couldn't know I was there. But I wasn't just going to climb in the boot. I had to make sure I could climb out again, she couldn't open it up and I could hear everything that might be said up front, especially if someone climbed in beside her when she was on her meet.

So I came up with a scheme. First I bought an intercom from an electronic store in Tottenham Court Road. Then on the morning of 17 December 1964 I told her, 'I'm off to Manchester today, so I'm going to clean my car. Shall I clean yours too?' She said, 'Yeah', like I knew she would because she never cleaned cars. So while she had a shower and tarted herself up, I cleaned her red Ford Classic in my own way. First I rigged up the intercom between the boot and the dashboard, then I broke off the car aerial so her radio wouldn't interfere with my hearing any conversations.

I attached a belt to the underside of the boot lid and stuck a metal strap through it so that when I climbed in I could pull the lid down. I could use a spanner to unlock it from inside and I could also stop anyone opening it from outside. Then I spread out my sheepskin coat to lie on. I stuck in a few tools

– a truncheon, a cobbler's knife, a meat cleaver, a double-barrelled shotgun and some ammunition – and shut it.

I went back in the house. I got myself smartened up to look business-like and, as I was at the door on my way out, I called up and I said, 'Mary! You'll never believe it. Some vandal's snapped off your aerial. Anyhow, I'm off now. I'll be away for a few days. And don't forget: don't go seeing any boyfriends while I'm away.' She said, 'Oh, you're imagining things again!' And that was that.

Then I got in my big Galaxy convertible and drove off, but I left it just two blocks away and came back. I could hear the shower still running, so I got in the boot. I lay down on my sheepskin coat and clamped the lid shut. Then – trot, trot, trot – out she came and off she drove at speed. By now I've got the boot slightly open, to get some idea what's going on. She stopped to make a telephone call – she was calling Foreman at the betting shop where he worked – then she drove on through the Rotherhithe Tunnel so fast that I was worried she'd have a crash, smash me against the tunnel wall and cause the shotgun to go off while I was still in the boot.

I survived the tunnel and, now she was on the north side of the river, I could tell that she had turned left and was driving east towards the City of London, along Cable Street. Then she slowed, made a couple of turns and finally manoeuvred into a parking place. By now I knew she intended to be here – wherever that was – for some time because of the time she took to park – the usual 15-point turn. I waited for her to get out and then I peered through the gap of the boot until I saw her walk to a nearby corner. Then I climbed out, gathered up the bits and pieces that I thought I might need – including the doubled-barrelled shotgun – and I sped to the corner. When I got there she had disappeared, so I walked quickly in that direction along the side of a block of flats. And there up the first flight of stairs, I saw her about to put a key in the door of one of these dirty little Cable Street hovels, the kind of place which for a hundred years the poorest immigrants have moved into, before moving out again as soon as they can afford it.

I walked quickly up the stairs and, as I always did in a moment of crisis, I pulled out my comb and ran it through my hair (like Cookie in *77 Sunset Strip*) just as I came up behind her. When she saw it was me, she had a look of terror on her face. She couldn't work out how I had managed to follow her and now she feared the worst.

So I grabbed all her keys, I unlocked the door, opened it up and pushed her in front of me, only to discover a terrible little dump, a pigsty. What a khazi!

I've seen better accommodation in Cardboard City on the Embankment underneath Charing Cross station. I looked around and I could see a set of double sleeping bags on the floor, and a few bits and pieces which I recognised as my things from my home: some pots, some pans and a couple of vases.

The only things that came from Foreman, apart from a blue camp bed on the floor with a kind of yellow slimey stain in the middle (now I knew why I had to go to my doctor), were a load of Christmas cards addressed to the Great Train Robbers – Charlie Wilson, Tommy Wisbey, Ronnie Biggs – all then in jail. What the cards were doing there, rather than in the postbox, or whether he had addressed them to these sorry but celebrated villains just to impress her, I had no time to check because by now she had screamed and run to the door of another flat opposite, belonging to someone else. She slammed the door in fear, I kicked it in and I dragged her out.

When we stepped back onto Cable Street, I saw Georgie Foreman and six or seven of his pals waiting there, alongside a big old Humber Super Snipe. I was in a state of controlled fury and I walked her right past them. Foreman and his half-hearted mob didn't intervene or come to her rescue, perhaps because they could see the shotgun I was carrying. But now they had all seen me tumble his secret little love nest they knew that it was all 'on top'. I didn't care if they also guessed that I'd soon be returning to his home over in Vauxhall, though not this time as Inspector Evans. I didn't care if he summoned an entire army to defend him, I was going to do what had to be done just as soon as I could stick the fool that I once regarded as my wife in a place where she couldn't get in my way.

In the world of crime you've two types of people. On the one hand you've got your contenders and on the other hand you've got your pretenders. George Foreman and his brother Freddie were pretenders. Those Christmas cards to the Great Train Robbers, for instance. The fact that he'd written them goes a long way to explain what the Foremans were really up to at the time – but how pathetic of him to try to impress her by displaying them in that stinking hole. Why didn't he leave them lying around his own family home for his own dear wife to savour?

Real people don't do these things. Real people don't meet their women in Jack the Ripper-style hovels. If they've got the money, they take them to a hotel with a poolside bar and a bit of style. That's why I used to take my birds to the White House in Albany Street, while Cheapskate George would take his to a shite-house in Cable Street. And real people don't live in hovels either. Real people try and give their wives and kids a nice home to live in, even if most of them do without peacocks.

But I wasn't dealing with real people. I was dealing with the 'Underworld Undertakers'.

TEN

Necessary Surgery

SHE wasn't a bad-looking woman but nowhere worth losing your bollocks over.

I was the last person he ever saw when he was a happy man.

It wasn't as if he hadn't been warned. Remember how he'd reacted when Tony Samms gave him the clearest possible warning only a week earlier, at Roy's car front on Jamaica Road. 'Well, what will happen if it was me?'

'He will shoot you.'

'Oh, he'll shoot me!'

'Yes.'

'Well, anybody can do that.'

She even warned him just before it happened, because I had made a miscalculation which could have cost me my life. When Davey Norman and I set off for George Foreman's flat that evening – Thursday, 17 December 1964 – we thought we had left my wife in a place where she couldn't get hurt and where she couldn't interfere. Don't forget, it was that same afternoon that I'd hidden myself in her boot and trapped her going to that cesspit in Cable Street – and when I'd yanked her out along with me as I strode back to her car past that do-nothing creep and his cronies. She knew war would break out any minute and, left to her own devices, she might have got caught in the crossfire, literally. She might have been foolish enough to come between me and the shotgun I was going to fire at lover boy.

So when I went to pick Dave up from his home in Ossory Road, off the

Old Kent Road, I took her along with me and I left her there with his wife Ann. Then Dave and I went off to do what I had to do. As we were leaving his house I told Ann, 'You keep her here. I've got a visit to make.' Later I realised my wife may have phoned Foreman straightaway from Dave's and told him I was on my way round, so he would have known that Dave was on his way round too, because Dave had been with me a week earlier when I caught her in the blue Vauxhall with the summons and I went to his flat as Inspector Evans. Dave was also with me when I dragged her up to Pat Riley's to prove she'd been lying over the car. So in the ten or 15 minutes it took for us to get from Dave's place to his place, my old woman might just have told him Dave was with me. It's the first question he'd have asked: who's he got with him? Make no mistake, when Dave Norman knocked on his door that night, claiming he was 'Mary's brother', Foreman knew damned well who he was, even with the hat and glasses. Dave's skinny Don Quixote face – with his long nose – was unmistakeable.

That night, after I had shot Foreman, I went back to Dave's house to take her home. She said, 'What happened?'

I said, 'Well, he's fucking shot and you can join him in the next ward, if you like, in the next bed.'

Then she broke down and said, 'I told him what would happen if ever you found out. It's not like he hasn't been told.'

See, George Foreman thought he could just get away with what he had done. Although I only found out later, he and his brother Freddie thought they had an overall licence to do whatever they liked, because of the help Freddie had from very senior detectives. So, of all the people that my wife could have got involved with, no one else in this world could have given me more headache and hassle in the future than these people. It's not just so-called gangsters, it's corrupt Scotland Yard.

I remember Ann Norman saying to me years later, 'You know, Mary came over and she'd sit down and have a drink with me and say, "Oh they're bastards, these people. They're all running round with guns and they've got all the police with them."' So Ann said to her, 'Well, you know what Jim's like. You don't think he's just going to walk away like that. It doesn't matter who they are.' And she said 'I know.'

So my old woman knew what she was doing to me and she knew what she was doing to him. She knew she was endangering everybody. She wasn't like the Brain of Britain but she was not that stupid. She knew that, sooner or later, somebody was going to either die or wish they were dead, because I had warned her only a month or so beforehand, 'Mary, whatever you're up to, drop it out. Otherwise something terrible will happen.'

In France they might call what I did to Foreman a crime of passion. In Sicily they might call it a crime of honour. To me it wasn't a matter of passion or honour. I never shot the mug out of jealousy. I wasn't crumpled up at discovering someone was 'digging my potatoes, trampling on my vine', as that old song puts it. I hadn't gone nutty because I had lost my one true love. I shotgunned Foreman for three reasons. First, as I've already explained, this matter was distracting me when I needed all my powers of concentration for the dangerous science of safe-blowing. Second, I did it for my own personal pleasure. This man thought he could take liberties with anyone he liked and get away with it. He was insulting my intelligence. So he had to be taught a lesson. Third, I had to get in first. Once George Foreman knew I knew all about him, I had to strike. If I hadn't done what I did when I did it, I would have gone on the missing list within days because even then I knew that his brother Freddie was running the English version of Murder Incorporated. Or, at the least (as I later realised), Fred's police friends would have fitted me up and I'd have got plenty of bird for something I had not done. I wouldn't even have known where the fix had come in from. But my main concern was that I could have gone for a walk and never come back. Oh, and the little question of that urethritis. Whoever gave that to me was going to have his donor card destroyed.

But though I didn't give a damn about the odds that night – I knew that a dozen of George Foreman's cronies would be waiting to try and kill me – I took a far bigger chance with my own weapon. I figured I might need to fire more than one cartridge so I had to have a double-barrelled shotgun, but I had no time to get hold of the ideal weapon. That's why I slipped into Tony Samms' house and took what was really a museum piece off the wall where he had it on display. I was very lucky it didn't blow up in my hands. It had Damascus barrels – made with a bit of iron, a big metal rod and metal wire stripped round – perfectly adequate for the kind of cartridges Arabs used to fire in desert warfare, but a modern-day cartridge could 'blow'. It could unleash the whole mechanism. That wire could whip round and whip out. And that night I used a long-reach Eli cartridge – nearly four inches long. Probably the only thing that saved the gun – and me – was that when I chopped it down (turning it into a 'sawn-off'), all that was left of the barrel was very thick. Otherwise, the shot would still have hit him but the gun could have blown up and done a lot more damage, especially to me. I took a chance but then I used to take chances. Lucky? Maybe, but I was the survivor.

Meantime, so I was later told by Hungarian George, who had casually walked into Foreman's flat a few minutes earlier to the sound of that old shotgun going off like a Howitzer, all his supporters panicked 'jumping out of windows and running for their lives'. I didn't see any of that. As I walked down the stairwell and out into the forecourt there was just a deafening silence, then screams from other flats and lights coming on all over the block. I expected to see a load of faces with guns peering out from his place, on the balcony above me, but they were all lying flat out, fearing there was more to come. And there could have been because I'd used only the one cartridge and I still had another in the Damascus barrels, plus six bullets in my little back-up Colt .38 Cobra that was down my belt. But the cowards never showed their faces, let alone fire their guns.

When I walked out Davey Norman was still there, sitting in his car with the engine running. He opened the door and said, 'Get in! Get in!' He was a good old mate. He not only looked like Don Quixote, with his long face and hooter, he acted like him too. Imagine hanging around there that night, when I had told him to go on home and he knew what was going to happen. He was brave to the point of being foolhardy. He was well aware that I wasn't shooting to kill Foreman. But he also knew that anyone could bleed to death from having a shotgun fired at him point-blank. Then the stakes would have been raised for both of us. In spite of this penalty clause, Dave had stayed on to take me back to his place where I collected my wife before we returned to Beulah Hill.

So as George was being carted off to hospital with almost nothing left downstairs, you might think that she'd be rushing to his bedside. That would have been a bit difficult because he'd got a wife and family of his own to do all that stuff – unless his wife stayed away because she believed he'd got what he deserved. But I didn't give my old woman the chance to visit him. The very next morning I moved her and our daughter straight out of the House of Peacocks. We drove right across town and went to stay with my mother-in-law, Wag, and her other half, Harry. Wag was a very nice little woman and I always got on well with her. She had a good-sized house in Chingford on the outskirts of North London, near Epping Forest. We went there to get our heads down. I felt sure that Freddie Foreman would attack the House of Peacocks without warning, with guns or firebombs or whatever – in a few weeks I would be proved right – but at this particular moment I

THE SURVIVOR

wasn't concerned about those creeps. My main concern was to stay out of sight of Old Bill who, at this time, were far more likely to send me to an early grave than anyone else.

I didn't want George Foreman dead. I wanted to give him a life sentence. I had aimed deliberately at his bollocks so that each day he would suffer the consequences of his actions. But I didn't want him dead for another reason. Remember, in 1964 you could still be executed for murder. In August, only four months before this shooting, two blokes from Cumberland had been hanged for killing a man while burgling his home. They had used a cosh and a knife on him and he died. I doubt if they intended to kill him but they still swung. So, if George Foreman croaked, how much worse would my crime be judged? As premeditated murder with a firearm at point-blank range. No way out of that one. String him up!

So, if he dies, I'm in for a topping (I didn't know this at the time but I might even have been the last person to hang in Britain – capital punishment would be abolished a year later). That's another good reason for me to staying at Wag's. At least, if he bleeds to death, I have a chance of bolting abroad. In the meantime I want him to live.

That's why, a few days later, I rang Charlie Kray from a call-box. He was very cheery and he said, 'Jim, I've seen his brother. He says Georgie's had two operations and he's got a few more to come. I'm surprised he survived. It went through his groin like a tennis ball. Blew away his prostrate, half his arse and half his cock. He'll never fuck again.'

That's good news, I thought, he's not dying, so they won't need a rope for me. But Charlie seemed to be egging me on to finish the job. Why else did he tell me that George was in St Thomas's Hospital – not once but several times? As if he didn't realise that I'd already done all I'd wanted to. If I'd meant to kill George I would have killed him but what I wanted was for him to wish he was dead. That's why I shot him in the balls, not in the bonce.

Charlie thought I'd still want to murder George in his hospital bed. He even started sympathising with me: 'It was only a matter of time. If you hadn't done it someone else would have done. That's the type of person he was. People couldn't leave him in their wives' company for two minutes.' And he gave me some advice: 'Jim, keep a low profile, they're looking for you. Four of them, driving around in a motor.'

I said, 'Don't just say four people are looking for me. Tell me who these four are, Charlie, and I'll look for them. I'll save them the trouble.'

So he said, 'Well, you know I can't do that, Jim, because one of them is my partner.'

Word for word, that's what he said. So no Kray–Foreman loyalty there. Charlie Kray was happy to tell me that his business partner – Fred Foreman as he well knew I knew – was looking for me. If those two had been real pals, Charlie might have tried to set me up. It would have been so easy for him or Reggie Kray to say they must see me about something right away. They could have fixed to meet me some place and then told Foreman, 'He'll be there tonight', but they didn't because they never liked this self-styled 'managing director of British crime'. To them he was just there to be used.

If anything, the Krays were on my side. Ronnie was, for sure. Like Charlie said during the same conversation, 'Ronnie sends you a message. He says: tell Jimmy Evans he did well. That will show those South London mugs what the East End is all about.' A couple of years on they pretended to help Fred Foreman but it was all fake, as I'll explain later.

For a few days the shooting got a lot of publicity. This is how one local newspaper, the *South London Press*, wrote up its front-page story:

BET SHOP CLERK IS SHOT BY GANG

George Foreman, the bets shop clerk who was shot when he opened the door to five men at his Bland House, Vauxhall St, Lambeth, home on Thursday is still in hospital, although his condition is not so serious as when he was rushed there for an operation.

Police are still searching for the men who shot 44-year-old Mr Foreman in the groin with a shotgun, and investigations into a 'protection racket' have proved negative. Someone might have shot Mr Foreman to settle a personal grudge, it is thought.

Both Mrs Foreman and Mr Foreman's employer know of no reason for the attack. Mrs Foreman was not at home when the shooting took place.

Mr Foreman is well known in Vauxhall and New Cross betting circles. There have been a number of 'fire bombs' thrown through bets shop windows, but it is unlikely that such an attack would be made on an employee.

See, a myth in the making. The press are already being force-fed the fib that five men attacked brave lone George, not just little old me. There was even a TV reconstruction, showing two pairs of feet going up the steps, not one pair. And there was never a mention of the mob of eight or so that Hungarian George found there, all ready and waiting to blow me away.

Not that the Foremans wanted publicity, because such stories showed them up in a bad light. If, like Fred, you're the boss of the 'Underworld Undertakers' – contract killers by appointment to gangland – it doesn't look good if you can't defend your own brother. You call yourself an enforcer when you can't even deal with a lone gunman whose wife your brother's been messing with! So while local detectives made their inquiries, the Foremans put it around that they weren't going to name the gunman because they would never 'squeal'. Instead they would deal with it in their own way, pretending to abide by the underworld code of silence. But no such code exists. How could it, with people like Fred Foreman around?

Of course, Fred had to make a show of coming after me. But I wasn't going to wait for him. I was thinking, 'If you've got one lot of retaliation in first, get another lot in before they have a go.' As America's Teamsters Union boss Jimmy Hoffa said a few years later, 'Do unto others what they would do unto you – but do it first and do it harder.' The trouble is, Hoffa didn't practise what he preached. He didn't do what I'd already done. Instead he was 'disappeared', plucked off the street and never seen again, like several people in this story.

Now something else was eating me up. I wanted to know who else my old woman had been keeping company with during her time with George Foreman. On Christmas Eve 1964 – a week after I'd shot him – I was driving through Camberwell with her, when she used the phrase, 'Oh, you're lovely, ain't'cha?', which means the very reverse: you aren't lovely at all.

At that time the only person I'd ever heard using that phrase was Charlie Richardson. It was an expression that had gained currency only in that little area of South London. Different parts of London had different expressions so I leapt to the conclusion that she must have picked this one up in the Charlie Richardson circle. I didn't dislike Charlie. I didn't distrust him either. As I've said before, he was a bit of a pal. He'd introduced me to Dave Norman, for which I was forever grateful, and he was a game fellow. He had been on a couple of things with me and Dave. But when I heard her using this phrase, 'Oh, you're lovely, ain't'cha?', I suddenly felt that old temper rising up in me and I've gone bosh! and hit her on the chin.

And it happened that at that very moment we were driving by one of Charlie Richardson's premises, the Pickfords metal yard in Camberwell, so with my Colt .45 down my belt, I stopped the van, got out and whacked the door to the yard. That's how Charlie did it – he was always in a hurry in life – he never used a key, he whacked the door and the Yale lock would spring open. I've gone bursting into his office, where I saw four or five people with their feet up on the desk, all drinking. Well, it was Christmas Eve. So I said, 'Hey, Charlie, come here a minute', and we went into another office, down a couple of steps, where he kept his big safe. He's looking a bit concerned, especially when I pulled out the Colt .45 and said, 'Where does your fucking pal Freddie Foreman live?'

So Charlie said, 'You must be fucking mad! That's Old Bill in there! I'm having a Christmas drink with them.'

I said, 'Well, you shouldn't be drinking with fucking coppers. Where does he live?'

He said, 'I'll take you there. I'll show you where it is. I've got the needle with him myself. He owes me 14 grand.'

I said, 'I don't want you to take me anywhere. Just tell me.'

He said, 'It's the Prince of Wales in Lant Street.' It was a pub and he told me how to get there.

I went to the Prince of Wales but not that night, in case Charlie had made a warning call. I left it for two or three nights, then I went there with a short micro-groove lever-action Marlin .22 rifle, a carbine, with a silencer and a scope. It was about ten-forty as I walked up the stairs of a block of flats from which I could overlook a window of what seemed to be the kitchen of the living accommodation on the pub's first floor. It was so close that I didn't need the scope.

There I stood with my gun, wearing the same coat that I'd worn when I shot his brother. I saw him come into that room. He turned to go towards a fridge or a cupboard. I was just going to have a crack at him, when 'Clink! Clink!' A woman had opened the door of a flat beside me to my left, and was putting out milk bottles. As I looked round, she looked up at me and the light from the passage lit up my face. So I said, 'I'm sorry, lady, I've had a few drinks and I was taken a bit short', and pretended I was about to have a piss. What other excuse could I have for standing there? Then, using my coat to conceal the Marlin at my side, I made out I was doing up my flies and I walked away. But if this old girl hadn't opened that door, I would have hit Fred Foreman in the back of the head. Later on – when I realised what an evil scumbag he was and the damage he was doing to lots of families by murdering fathers and husbands and 'disappearing' their bodies – I wish I had killed him, even at the risk of her picking me out on an identification parade. Mind you, if she had known what he was really like, she might have been only too pleased to pull the trigger herself.

So where did my wife and I stand after I'd shot her friend George? She would still have stayed with me if I'd been prepared to put up with her. She told me so during a trip we took to Spain a few months later with Tony Samms and his wife and our kids. We were waiting in a pharmacy when she sat on my knee, put her arms round my neck and said, 'Can't we just stay down here forever and never go back to England again?' She really didn't want to go back, she wanted to pretend it had never happened.

Later she told me what they had got her to do for them. She said, 'The only reason I got involved was because he was giving me suitcases of ten-bob notes to change up. I did it because I wanted to make my own bit of money.' Whether she knew it or not, these were ten-bob notes from the Great Train Robbery. She'd fallen for this business because I'd told her that, if she wanted a Thunderbird like mine, she'd have to pay for it like I did, by taking risks.

Remember, at that time George's brother Freddie Foreman was running with the hares and hunting with the hounds. He was kidding the Great Train Robbers he was one of their chums while being even chummier with the top Flying Squad detectives who were busy nicking the robbers on 'information received'. Back in 1963 when the robbery occurred almost nobody in the underworld knew Fred was a double-dealer. At that time the robbers were grateful to anybody who could change ten-bob notes because they must have had a million of them among their total haul of £2.5 million in cash. In those days we were still using the old 'lsd' or pound, shilling and pence currency, and ten-bob or ten shillings was equivalent to 50 pence, but today its real value would be around £15.

So when my old woman was shown suitcases full of money to go out and change, that was one way George Foreman hoped to win her round. This wasn't a case of picking up some tart in a club, taking her in the back of a car and humping her. This thing would have taken a lot of time. That was probably why he was displaying all those Christmas cards from Ronnie Biggs, Charlie Wilson and Tommy Wisbey in that dingy dump in Cable Street. Suitcases full of notes and gangster Christmas cards: all part of the same bizarre 'charm offensive' to beguile both my wife and the Great Train Robbers. Not that they saw much of that money. By December 1964 they were locked up or on the run, so Freddie Foreman would have been creaming off most of the profit from any changing my old woman and other mugs were doing on his mob's behalf.

And at the same time, of course, brother George was continually pummelling away at her, feeding her with lies about what woman I'd been seen with last night, at Charlie Richardson's parties and the like. Dead easy, really. You can see how it happened. But, like they say, it takes two to tango.

So when my wife said, 'Can't we stay here in stay in Spain and never go back to England?', I didn't give in to that idea. If she did not wish to share Foreman's impotent future that was up to her, but I wasn't interested. I don't ever try to glue something together. When something of mine gets broken, it gets thrown straight in the bin. Finished. If anything's smashed, dump it. That was how it now stood with our marriage. And that's why, even though the idiot was no good to her that way any more, she was no good to me either. But our marriage still had stormy months to go.

THE SURVIVOR

ELEVEN

The Shooting of Ginger Marks

WE had spent Christmas 1964 at Wag's place. I'm not religious but we performed the usual festivities for the sake of our kid. Now it had to be business as usual. My pals and I had a meet. Davey Norman, Ginger Marks and a couple of others were there and they drove me mad to oblige a jeweller's in Bethnal Green Road, called Attenborough's. I didn't need to do the job. I didn't want to go to work but they said, 'We're all skint. We've blown all our money over Christmas.' I wasn't skint. I had plenty of money, but no one except for me could have blown those safes and they wanted me there. We were going to work together that night as a firm.

So on Saturday, 2 January 1965 – two weeks and two days after I'd shot George Foreman – I set off for Tommy Marks' home in Redman's Road in Stepney, about a mile from our target. Tommy was a close pal, quite tall, heavy-set but not fat. His nickname to those who didn't know him so well was 'Ginger', but I always called him Tommy. So first I went over to his place and, while we got ready, I had a chat with his wife Annie, whom I also knew well. We loaded detonators and jelly from his stockpile into the car. Then I took a crucial decision: I decided to leave my little Colt Cobra .38 at his home, above his drinks bar. I was carrying that gun for personal protection – vital at this time, I'm sure you'll agree – but if we were nicked on this job and they found a gun on me, we would all have been charged with armed robbery. That could bring 20 years in jail rather than, say, just five for burglary, and I couldn't get these blokes into that kind of trouble. A few hours later I'd be wishing I'd kept the gun on me, but at least I was wearing a bullet-proof vest under my sheepskin jacket.

We set off for Attenborough's thinking this was going to be a quick in-and-out. I would just put the jelly in the hole and bosh! I would blow three safes, I'd say goodnight and I'd collect my whack later. At the start Tommy and I had nothing to do. First the rest of the team had to break in through the roof and by-pass the alarms, but it was such a cold night that Tommy and I and another bloke went to a pub close by to have a drink. We let the others know where we were, and whenever they had any progress to report they would send us a message.

So we were sitting in the pub, chatting about my confrontation with the Foremans, when Tommy raised the name of an old pal of ours, Dukey Osbourne, a colourful, flamboyant fellow who, like Tommy, was quite pally with the Kray Twins. Tommy started laughing and said, 'Oh by the way, Dukey Osbourne sends you a message. He came over the other day and he said, "Tell Jimmy not to pay too much attention to the Foremans. It's only a matter of time before the little mob who were on the train job put two and two together about what's been going on between Freddie Foreman and his pal, Tommy Butler."'

We knew who Tommy Butler was. At the time he was Britain's most famous policeman. He was in the newspapers day after day because he was the head of the Flying Squad and for the last 18 months he'd been targeting any Great Train Robbers who weren't nicked in the original round-up. At least that's what Scotland Yard was telling the press. As I've said before, I had always thought the train job was a ready-eye, a sting so cunningly constructed that any conspiring detectives deluded the robbers into thinking it wasn't a ready-eye, even after they'd been captured. That's because it may have been a ready-eye with a difference: the bent boys in blue never intended to catch the robbers in the act; they wanted them to get away with the money so they could steal it back later, publicly declare they'd seized a small part of the £2.5 million haul, but share a far bigger chunk with their co-conspirators in the underworld. Just think: only a measly £500,000 or so was ever recovered, officially. The other £2 million stayed missing. I wonder how.

All the other detectives on the train robbery investigation were honest and hardworking, but this theory would explain how Butler had all that train money in his Yard safe, which I was asked to empty with the key that his deputy Bob Anderson had given to Johnny Tilley. Johnny had stuck that key in my hand only a few weeks before Tommy was giving me Dukey's message about Butler and Foreman. When he told me that, I told him about all the Christmas cards to and from the Great Train Robbers that I'd discovered at George's filthy little hole in Cable Street. Then Tommy took the thought on and he said, 'If Fred Foreman is such a good pal of the mob who were on the train – and at the same time he's Tommy Butler's pal – how come they've got 30 fucking years? Do they want them to die in prison?'

Exactly. Even with our limited knowledge at the time – and a lot more has come out since – we could tell that, if there was this Foreman-Butler connection, it would be like a disease for the underworld, infecting everyone, although very healthy for the pair of them.

But we still had a job to do. I had to focus my mind on the safes that I'd soon be blowing so I didn't pay Dukey's message the attention it deserved. We left the pub and went back to the geezer who was keeping watch for us opposite Attenborough's. He told us they needed more tools, maybe a wood bit and brace, so Tommy and I went back to his place to get them. I stayed in the car while he went up to his flat, then he came back, got in the driving seat and started up. I looked in the side mirror, as I had throughout this evening already, and I saw lights come on from a car about 100 yards behind us. When we began to move off, that car came out too and followed us. I was watching it as we crossed Jubilee Street and did a right into Sidney Street where I said, 'Tommy, I think we're being bottled off.' And as we drove on, so did this car. It was a red Austin 1100. I said, 'Tom, they're on us.' They were still following us half a mile later as we came up Bethnal Green Road.

Now Tommy parked his car, we got out and we turned into Saint Matthew's Row where he glanced at the car himself and he said, 'It's Old Bill. That's a Q car number on that 1100. There's Old Bill in there. Plainclothes.' 'Q cars' was what the police called their unmarked undercover surveillance vehicles but Tommy could outwit them with his extraordinary memory for car numbers. These cars used to follow us all the time and he would remember all their numbers, whether they were moving or just parked. Once we were walking in the East End and being tailed by a car when he said, 'Have you looked in the back of that?' And there, laid out on the rear seat, were photographs of all of us: Tommy, me and the rest of our little team. Then he revealed that as we'd been driving around he had logged this car's numbers, suspecting the occupants were Old Bill. And he was right.

Not this night, though. Because I had got a good look at these characters and I knew they weren't police, so when Tommy said, 'There's Old Bill in there', I said, 'No, it's not. That ain't Old Bill. It's the other firm. It's the scumbags.' And what Charlie Kray had told me a few days earlier flashed through my mind: 'Jim, keep a low profile, they're looking for you. Four of them, driving around in a motor . . . one of them is my partner.' That's who it is, I thought, that's Fred Foreman and Co.

We turned into Cheshire Street when suddenly they came round again. They slowed to within six feet of where we were standing. I heard someone shout, 'Ginger! Come here a minute!' And Ginger stopped.

I stood to one side. I knew what these people were capable of. I recognised their white faces but I had no gun. I had left my Colt Cobra .38 at Tommy's home. What a mistake. I'd been carrying guns on me every day for years, but at this moment in my life when I really needed a weapon, I was defenceless. I'd always said, it's better to have a gun and not need it than to need one and not have it. But now I couldn't defend myself, let alone Tommy.

There were three or four flashes from .22 automatics. They hit Tommy more or less together. This made no sense to me. I was standing right beside him. Why didn't some of these blokes shoot him and some shoot me? But instead they all went for one target – Tommy – and when everything hit him he went, "Ooouff", as if all the air had been knocked out of him, like he'd been hit hard with a big baseball bat. He was a big bloke, he weighed around fourteen and a half stone, but he went straight down. Boomph! He just dropped. When he was hit in the chest – probably the heart – he couldn't stay standing.

At that moment I'm gone. No time for me to drag Tommy to safety, I had to run for my life, literally. I ran along Cheshire Street, keeping my head low to make a smaller target of myself. I heard another shot, then bomp! They've hit the wall in front of me. If I had moved the other way they would have found it easier to take a clear shot. As it was, the little .22s were flying all around my head. One went so close to the front of my nose that I got a load of brick dust in my eye from the crater it made in the wall beside me, but every bullet missed me.

I kept going until I reached the corner of Cheshire Street and Wood Close when what seemed like a sledgehammer whacked me in the back, just above the belt-line on my right. I'd been hit. I was wearing that bullet-proof vest and my sheepskin but my ribs were hurting and I couldn't run any further. I went up to the pub, then changed my mind – it was too obvious, they would follow me in – so I slipped left into Wood Close and rolled underneath a small van. They came tearing after me in their car but they did not realise I was under the van. They drove right past it to the end of the close where there's the wall and railings of Saint Matthew's churchyard. They must have figured that I'd gone over the railings into the churchyard where they'd never find me. You can be sure that if they had had any idea I was under that van, they would have bent down and gone bosh! bosh! bosh!, emptying their .22s into me. They would have done the business. I would have been dead. But no, the car did a turn round the close. As it came round, I looked up and saw the driver's white face and the offside rear door swinging open.

The car passed within feet of where I was lying. It almost ran over me as it turned back up Saint Matthew's Row and back again into Cheshire Street. It stopped right where Tommy had been dropped. I heard one more single shot, bosh! I peered out and saw them drive away fast, with that offside rear door still open and Tommy's legs being dragged in. They were still dragging him in as they drove off. When they were well away, I rolled out from under the van. I got to the corner in time to see the car going east towards the T-junction with Vallance Road where took did a right.

I had survived once again, but what about Tommy? I thought he might still be alive. I reasoned that, if they had taken the trouble to cart him off, they might dump him at a hospital. If not, and if they had killed him, what were they going to do with his body?

I went over to the spot where he had first been shot. I looked around for anything that might confirm what I had just seen. I spotted his hat and his glasses and some of his shirt buttons. I scooped them all up. Then I thought, what do I do now? I can't go back to Attenborough's and blow the safes as if nothing's happened. What if these bastards come back? I've got to fucking move. The Krays only live a couple of hundred yards from here. I've got to go and talk to Reggie.

And that's what I did. As I looked up towards Vallance Road, I could even see their little two up, two down house to the left. I went straight there. I could see their father, little old Charlie, looking through the upstairs window. He was easy to spot because he always wore a white scarf round his neck, like a gypsy. By now it was after midnight, the place was dark and gloomy and old Charlie was just standing there, his face like a little moon in the shadows. I was surprised that he wasn't in bed by now; it was as though even he sensed something was up. After all, as Fred Foreman and Charlie Kray junior were business partners, even the old man might have known something like this was going to happen.

I shouted up to old Charlie, 'I know you can see me. Tell Reggie to open the door.' Within seconds Reggie's opened up. I used to get on pretty well with him – he was half-sensible, not like Ronnie – and he said, 'Come in.'

I walked down the short hallway into the little scullery out the back. I told him what this Foreman mob had done. Then I said, 'Reg, what have they done with Tommy? Where have they taken him?'.

Reggie said, 'Jim, take my advice. Forget it and go home.'

And I walked out.

As I'd been talking to Reggie I'd been thinking, why is he so negative, what does he know? Then I realised that the last single shot – the one I'd heard while I was still under the van – must have been a headshot. I had only heard it, I hadn't seen it, but it had to be a headshot. To make sure he was dead. Tommy was always telling everyone we had plenty of guns and ammunition, so that mob in the 1100 must have been thinking, 'We can't take any chance, we've got to kill him now or he might try something, he might even have a gun.' Yet even while I was thinking all this, I was clinging to the hope that by now he was getting intensive treatment in some casualty ward.

Whatever these bastards had done, right now I had to go and tell Annie Marks everything. I was the last person she'd seen him with and I owed it to her. I walked straight back to Dave Norman who was still working his way into the jeweller's, I told him we'd been hit by the other mob and I got him to drive me to Tommy's flat in Redman's Road. When Annie opened up I told her, 'Tommy's been shot. They've taken him away. He must be in one of the hospitals.' Then I gave her what I'd found – his hat, his glasses and those shirt buttons – and I said, 'You'd better phone Terry.' He was Tommy's brother and he came straight over. I took him to Cheshire Street and I showed him where it had happened. That's when we came across an empty .22 cartridge case. That proved they were using automatics, because a .22 revolver – or any revolver – wouldn't have ejected one. After all the shots they had fired from within their Austin 1100, it must have been full of empty cases. The one left on the street meant that someone had got out to fire that final shot before they heaved him into the back.

Terry Marks and I drove straight to Mile End Hospital because the car had driven off in that general direction, but Tommy wasn't there. I was so worried about him I'd almost forgotten that I'd been hit too. My back was giving me hell. Terry could see I needed treatment. He said, ' I'll carry on without you.' Then he or Annie called the police and I went back to my

THE SURVIVOR

mother-in-law's. I went straight upstairs to our bedroom. I stripped off the top half of my clothing – jacket, shirt and bullet-proof vest – and I asked my wife to take a good look at my body, to check if there were any bullet entries. When those little .22s fly into your body, your skin can almost close up over the point of entry, so no blood can flow out. One of them could have passed through the vest, bounced inside me and penetrated a vital organ. I could be bleeding to death with no outward signs. It wasn't until 36 hours later, on the Monday, that I had an x-ray which showed that the bullet had snapped a rib off my spine. The loose rib had somehow jarred against the top of my right lung and stopped me from running, which was why I had to roll under that van. I still have the x-rays. I couldn't believe my luck. It was just a broken rib. By the thickness of a bullet-proof vest – and my sheepskin – I had survived yet again.

Now I knew I was OK, it was time for cool thinking. What was that all about? This bunch of mugs – Freddie Foreman and his three death squad mercenaries: I recognised them all – were hareing around in a car with a Q number, so they probably had corrupt cop connections. And they were using automatics, so they really meant to kill someone. But who was that? Sure, this foursome had me on their death-list because I'd shot the bollocks off Freddie's brother, yet they hadn't taken any interest in me. Remember, when I first saw those flashes from their car, point-blank, all the guns were shooting at Tommy. None at me. They didn't know or care who I was. It was only after they had dropped Tommy that they drove after me. Maybe by then they had realised who I was but, more likely, they just didn't want to leave a witness behind. Either way, it was another of their Mickey Mouse fuck-ups.

I don't think they had the slightest idea I was going to be there that night. Everyone on that job was staunch and stumm – absolutely leakproof. Not even Tommy would have shot his mouth off. He was a great talker, but he'd never tell anybody what job he was going on in advance. They didn't know where he'd be that Saturday evening. That's why they had to stake him out at home. Remember, they weren't pratted up there when I first turned up. They only showed up when we came back a little before midnight: the sort of time Tommy would usually get home after a night out with Annie.

I didn't even get out of the car that time, so they didn't know I was in it. What's certain is that someone in that car knew what Tommy looked like and where he lived. I knew who that someone was. He knew Tommy well and he was also a close pal of Foreman's, but none of them knew what I looked like. So it had to be Ginger Tommy they were after that night, not me. After all, they didn't shout, 'Jimmy! Come here a minute!' They shouted, 'Ginger! Come here a minute!'

But why kill Tommy? I was still feeling my way on this mystery when I realised that Freddie Foreman must have conned the others by telling them that Tommy had been with me when I'd shot George. That was rubbish but it was the only 'legitimate' reason he could come up with for wanting him silenced. He couldn't tell them the real reason, which was that Tommy was telling everyone what he'd heard from Dukey: 'It's only a matter of time before the little mob who were on the train job put two and two together about what's been going on between Freddie Foreman and his pal, Tommy Butler.'

If Foreman had revealed that to his gunmen, he would have been admitting that Tommy's tale was true. Why would you shoot the man if it wasn't true? You would just ignore him or give him a slap. Of course, if any Great Train Robbers did have the sense to put 'two and two together', they would have paid someone to shoot Freddie himself.

But how would Tommy's tale have reached Fred's ears? Tommy was a freelance villain, like me. He had worked with almost every team in London and he knew everybody. But as I say, he was also a great talker, he would talk to anybody, and in the days between him talking to Dukey and his disappearance, he would have told a lot of blokes about Foreman and Butler. One could have been Stevie Murphy, who was close to George Foreman at the time. Remember: who did George get to protect him when Tony Samms showed him my shotgun at the Jamaica Road car front ? Stevie Murphy from the East End. And Tommy knew him very well.

I know that Tommy had spoken to Stevie recently because, when we were sitting in the pub waiting to do Attenborough's, he mentioned that he'd gone to see Stevie a few days earlier, so I said, 'I want to see him as well!' Tommy replied, 'Stevie's a nice fellow. I see him regularly.' Then he's laughing and he went on, 'When I saw him, I told him you've got the fucking hump with him too, not just with George Foreman. You ought to have seen his face. He said, "Tell your pal Jimmy it was nothing to do with me. I was walking along the Commercial Road and all of a sudden this car screeches to a halt and it's Georgie Foreman shouting, 'Get in! Get in!' He was panicking so I just got in, he dashed through the tunnel, and we ended up at that car front. I didn't even know what I was going there for." '

Until Tommy told me this I'd been thinking, I'll go and see Stevie because he shouldn't have made himself busy in a personal thing which had nothing to do with him. Now I didn't blame him. And Stevie hadn't finished. According to Tommy, he went on, 'Tell your pal Jimmy he did the right thing. But tell him to keep a low profile.' There was Stevie Murphy telling me exactly what Charlie Kray had told me a few days earlier: 'Jim, keep a low profile. They're looking for you.'

See, during that kind of conversation there's a free flow of underworld gossip. Often things are said that would be better left unsaid, and Tommy could easily have told Stevie what he'd been told by Dukey. I'm not saying Stevie would have repeated it to Fred Foreman – he probably said nothing – but you can be sure Fred heard it from someone pretty damned quick. And as soon as he realised his entire applecart of police connections was going to be exposed, he would have coldly resolved that Tommy had to go. We know what he did later to two other 'gangsters': Frank 'the Mad Axeman' Mitchell, murdered on the Krays' orders on 23 December 1966 by Fred Foreman and 'disappeared' by him; and Jack 'the Hat' McVitie, murdered by the Kray twins on 28 October 1967 and 'disappeared' by Fred Foreman.

So if he was killing mugs for wages on the Krays' behalf, how much more effort would he have applied to someone who posed a real threat to himself? He killed Tommy not because I'd shot the bollocks off his brother. Tommy had nothing to do with that, and the Foremans knew it. No, Tommy was killed to shut him up.

Looking back through stories written at the time, I see a remarkably accurate comment in the *Sunday Times* a week later. The reporter Cal McCrystal wrote, 'Marks had a habit which some people found irritating. He was apt to shoot a line about people he knew and of things they had done. Much of what he talked about was taken with a pinch of salt. Lately, however, several of his friends believe the salt may have given somebody severe heartburn.'

But if he killed Tommy for telling the truth about him and Butler, why didn't he kill Dukey Osbourne at the same time? That's simple: I was the only one – bar Tommy – who knew Dukey was the source, because he had asked Tommy to tell me. In Tommy's words, 'Dukey Osbourne sent a message: "Tell Jimmy not to pay too much attention to the Foremans."' Dukey understood that I had a special need to know because Fred and his mob were out to kill me. Only I needed to know the source, but every villain needed to know that Foreman was in bed with the copper who was nicking the train robbers. In the legitimate world that's called a conflict of interests.

I've often wondered whether, years later, Foreman finally found out about Dukey's role. In 1979 a lorry full of 'Paki black' cannabis was parked up on the Commercial Road in Stepney when the driver shot and killed a customs officer called Peter Bennett. The driver was later jailed for 25 years but, just six weeks after the shooting, on 1 December, Dukey's body was found on Hackney Marshes. It seemed he'd had a heart attack elsewhere and had just been dumped there. Customs believed Dukey had been running the cannabis racket. So did people in the underworld but with this extra spice: they believed Dukey was only halfway up the chain of command and the real boss was Freddie Foreman. They also claimed Foreman had held a gun to Dukey's head while he wrote a suicide note and then forced him to swallow enough pills to cause the heart attack. He was then stuck in a deep-freeze until Fred or his pals dumped the body on the Marshes. That was the rumour.

A year or two later, a senior detective from Dorset Police came to see me. He explained that he was working on Operation Countryman, a wide-ranging inquiry into corruption among London detectives. This had started out with high hopes but would end with low returns – only two coppers were ever convicted as a result of Countryman. He explained that he had heard about my complaints over the years regarding bent Scotland Yard cops and me being constantly framed. Then he produced a photograph of two people. I could see that they were Freddie Foreman and Dukey Osbourne.

He went on to explain that the photo had been taken during the drugs operation that ended with the customs man's murder. So, both customs and Countryman had proof that Fred was working closely with Dukey on his last job. 'All very interesting,' I said, 'but I can't help you.'

Fred must have got very angry over this murder because it brought a lot more 'heat' on Fred himself. Angry enough to kill Dukey? On past form, yes, but maybe Fred had finally found out it was Dukey who, 15 years earlier, had betrayed his bonds with Tommy Butler. I've been told, indirectly, that at Scotland Yard there are informant dockets – taken from sources close to Foreman and written up soon after Dukey's death – that state exactly what he did to Dukey, but he was never arrested for it. As always, he's had police protection.

I keep thinking back to the night he and his mob killed Tommy. Even then they had the protection of driving round in a car with Q number plates. Some influential copper must have cleared them to use that number, not just

138

to deceive us but also to make sure they would have safe passage right across London. If you've got a dead body in the back of the car with you – and those Austin 1100s didn't have a self-contained boot – you want to make sure you won't be stopped and searched. But with the right number, no copper would have stopped them. For absolute safety's sake, Fred's police pals may have given him a warrant card too.

Then when they picked the body up, stuck it in that car and took it away, they acted like they had a licence. They might just as well have had Butler in the car with them. They went on to kill time and again but were never convicted. The only time Fred Foreman was convicted of anything like it was when Nipper Read did him for disposing of Jack 'the Hat' McVitie for the Krays. But Chief Superintendent Read was a fine example: a top copper who refused to compromise with his bent colleagues at Scotland Yard. Foreman got ten years in jail for that but he was out much sooner. In 1983 the police believed he was involved in the robbery of £6 million in cash from Security Express in London but it wasn't until 1989 that he was whisked out of Spain to face trial back home. He was convicted of receiving £363,280 and jailed for nine years, but he got out in six. That was in 1995. By then his pal Butler had been dead for 25 years but even if he'd been living he couldn't have saved Foreman this time. The fool had put the money in bank accounts in his own and his wife's names. How Mickey Mouse can you get?

TWELVE

The Gospel According to Freddie the Fib

IN 1996 Freddie Foreman came out with an autobiography, *Respect*, which contains long overdue admissions about a few of his murders. When he mentions the deaths of Ginger Tommy Marks and Dukey Osbourne, in typical Freddie the Fib fashion he takes a few morsels of truth and wraps them in lies. As for what he says about Tommy Butler of Scotland Yard, he must think his readers are as naïve as the Great Train Robbers when they were on the run, desperate, and turned to him for help.

In one chapter he finally owns up to killing my pal. It starts with brother George in Saint Thomas's Hospital, after four operations, and Freddie whispering into his ear, 'Give me a name', to which George replies, 'Ginger Marks.'

Here beginneth the big lie, for Ginger had nothing to do with the shooting. On my daughter's death-bed, he was not there. He was at home in Redman's Road. Only Dave Norman was with me and there was no confusing the two. Tommy was big and well-built, fourteen and a half stone, Dave was tall and thin, like Don Quixote. He was skinny. Tommy was just as distinctive. See him once and you'd recognise him again straight away. He was unmistakeable.

Besides, George Foreman would have known who Dave was. It was Dave's wife Ann who (unknown to him) was taking his messages to pass to my wife – remember that phone number she wrote in eyebrow pencil for him? And it was Dave who had been with me all that day when first I'd caught her in the blue Vauxhall, then I'd gone to Foreman's home as Inspector Evans and finally I'd dragged her over to Pat Riley's. It was all Dave, and my wife would have told George that. And that very evening when I went to shoot him, after we had left Dave's, she would probably have phoned George again, to say I'd be at his door in minutes with Dave.

Fred Foreman goes on with this lie, saying that while Dave acted as the getaway driver, 'Evans and Marks went to do the business'. Nonsense. And it wasn't Marks who, 'wearing his usual hat and glasses', knocked at the door and 'gave a moody name, pretending he was looking for someone else'. It was Dave who knocked and he stuck to my script (he said he was her brother to draw him out so I didn't accidentally shoot the kid). Sure, Dave was wearing a cap and glasses – like Tommy – but the sole point of this feeble disguise was to prevent nosey neighbours from seeing Dave's face. It wouldn't have fooled George, because he must have known I was on my way over with Dave before we arrived.

Lie two starts a few lines later: 'My brother George, who is one of the chaps, stuck to the time-honoured code of the underworld: he told the police nothing. The comeback was our business.' That is rich: a few months later George would give evidence that left it open for the jury to believe that I'd shot him. And see how Freddie uses the phrase, 'one of the chaps', to describe him and his brother. On the cover of his book 'chaps' is defined as 'an almost mythical grouping of criminals' with an 'ethos' which includes 'professionalism in the pursuit of crime; loyalty to others of their kind; hatred of and non-co-operation with authority; and courage'. The definition comes from the ex-lifer turned writer, Norman Parker.

'Hatred of and non-co-operation with authority'? What a nerve. For years Foreman revelled in co-operating with authority. He's even been on TV saying he had a 'working relationship' with policemen. I was the one who hated authority and didn't co-operate, when all the while he was in bed with Butler and other coppers. As for 'loyalty to others of their kind', remember what Dukey said about how Foreman was betraying the Great Train Robbers.

I'll come back to Dukey later but first here are more lies: 'Evans had a monkey, which he dressed as a policeman and, to the amusement of his friends, he'd whack this poor animal with a rubber truncheon. "Hit the copper. Hit the copper."' Rubbish. I love animals. Yes, I did have a stump-tailed monkey, which I sold to Charlie Richardson, and I did have a chimpanzee. I never hit either of them. Let Foreman produce one witness to say I did. Yes, I did dress the chimp up as a copper, with a helmet and truncheon, but that was just for laughs – like they used to dress those chimps up in the PG Tips adverts on TV. Maybe Fred's upset that I didn't name the chimp after him, but Sally was female.

He then says that when I jumped out of the boot of my wife's car outside George's dirty little hole in Cable Street, I 'pulled a knife on her and demanded to know whose flat it was'. Wrong again. I already knew whose flat it was and I didn't pull a knife on her. I did produce a single-barrelled shotgun but that was to shoot anyone who stood in my way when I got in that khazi. As for the origins of that shotgun, he says I got it from Dave Norman, but old Dave hated guns and he never lent me any shotgun. A small point, perhaps, except that Fred Foreman's already giving Dave a far bigger role than Tommy Marks ever played, so why didn't he shoot Dave as well?

He also says that before I shot George I removed the bulb from the landing outside his door. Rubbish. Would I do that when, as soon as I get up those stairs, I can see his door is already open? No, his mob must have done that. They had prepared it all.

Then Foreman writes, 'Evans returned to his home and told Pat [the name he uses for my old woman] he'd killed George.' I never said I'd killed George. It was Dave who broke the news and he just said, 'He has shot him.' I did say that George was in hospital and she could join him in the next bed if she wanted to. Then Fred writes, 'She was kept a virtual prisoner for the next ten months.' I didn't keep her prisoner. She could go anywhere she wanted. She still had her own car. We even took that break in Spain when I needed a bit of space. That was when she sat on my lap and put her arms around me, in a pharmacy, and said, 'Can't we just stay down here forever and never go back to England again?' And how could I imprison her for ten months, when – as you will see – I was in a real jail myself for two of those months?

Foreman also writes that after I'd shot George, Tommy Marks was seen sitting with a shotgun across his lap, saying, 'Send the fucking Foremans across here, I'll deal with them.' Well, there's no chance he would have said that because he wasn't on the shooting and, as far as he knew, the Foremans had no reason to take it out on him.

Foreman claims he was 'tipped off that Evans's firm were going to rob Attenborough's', but he had no such information. If he had, why didn't he take his crew straight to Attenborough's and wait for Tommy there, instead of loitering outside his home? No, the truth is they had no idea what he was going to do that night, nor did they care. Fred's sole mission that night was to kill Tommy and he would have shot him there and then, outside his home, if his Mickey Mouse mob could have got their act together.

Fred even scores an 'own goal' by admitting that, as he heard later, Tommy told the others on the burglary they were being followed by a police car, because Tommy 'had the registration number at home'. Foreman doesn't deny they had a Q car number. He just says it was 'nicked and rung specially for the job'. 'Rung' means it had false number plates, but how did Foreman choose a number secretly allocated to a local unmarked police car when none of his team lived on that patch? Did a friendly detective give him the number so we would be 'disarmed', mentally as well as physically? We would be annoyed by the sight of a car-load of cops but we wouldn't expect them to shoot us.

Foreman then goes on about he and Gerard stalking me and Tommy:

> My right-hand closed on the .38 revolver . . . Alf [Gerard] gently eased the car forward and drew alongside the pair . . . I leaned out, my gun at the ready: "Ginger!" Marks stopped in his tracks. Unsure of who we were . . . and startled by the recognition, he stepped towards us. I let fly a hail of bullets.

But it wasn't just 'Ginger!' that they called. It was, 'Ginger! Come here a minute!' And as for a .38, I never heard a .38 that night. It was all .22s. A .38 shell would have made a terrible racket and woken the entire neighbourhood. He never had a .38 that night but I know why he can't remember: he was so stoned, he wouldn't have known the difference between a .38 bullet and a 38 bus.

> There was no sound from Marks but Evans reacted instantly. He crouched behind Ginger and gripped his shoulders using him as a shield. The pair of them performed a macabre dance of death in the street trying to avoid the volley of bullets.

I don't even dance with my wife, let alone dead men.

> Ginger took most of the bullets although one entered Evans's coat missing him by a hair's-breadth. Evans could no longer support his shield. He let go of Mark's shoulders. The man dropped to the pavement as Evans ran away. I dived out of the car

and stood over Marks with my gun pointing to his head. He didn't move.

Foreman expects people to believe that, despite shooting his first 'hail of bullets' point-blank, he fails to hit Tommy. Miraculously Tommy is still standing so I grip his shoulders and use him as a shield. We perform a dance of death to avoid Foreman's second volley, only this time Tommy gets most of the bullets and I can no longer support him. So now, when I have no shield, what are Fearless Fred and friends doing? I am a sitting, or rather, crouching duck, less than six feet away, so how come they didn't shoot me dead, there and then?

In some other place he has written that while we were doing this so-called dance of death, a bullet went right through Ginger into the brick wall. But if I'm right behind him, how come the bullet didn't go through me as well?

How could Foreman and his pals – whom he airbrushes out of the shooting so he looks like the lone avenger – miss the first time, when Tommy was less than six feet away? The truth is, they didn't miss. He was hit straightaway and he just dropped. That's what .22 bullets do to you. A .38 would have knocked him right back against the brick wall and that didn't happen. A .22 will do the job well enough. No way could I prop Tommy up as a shield after one bullet, let alone a volley. I was around ten stone at that time. Ginger was fourteen and a half. That's a difference of over 60 pounds. I couldn't hold him up alive, let alone dead. I would have been flat on my back underneath him, where Saint Fred the Avenger could have shot me like a dog.

Next, so he says, I ran and hid under a lorry, not a small van. Well, if he knew I was under a lorry, why didn't he get down and fire a few of his .38s under there to keep me company?

Marks was still lying on the ground. We picked him up and slung him in the back of the car and tore off in the direction of Vallance Road.

Strange. Tommy 'was still lying on the ground'. Where did Foreman expect him to go with at least a dozen bullets in him? But if he was still alive, this would account for that last shot, the head shot to finish him off. Foreman doesn't mention this, but it definitely came from a .22. I heard it and that was the size of the only cartridge we found at the scene. He says he had a .38 revolver which, like all revolvers, doesn't eject cases. Fine, but no .38 went off that night. All I heard was .22s and, believe me, I do know the sound. So if, as he says, he was the only one who shot Marks, he must have had a .22 but was too doped up to know. The difference between a .38 going off and a .22 is like a Great Dane's bark and a Jack Russell's yap.

> Evans . . . drove round the corner to Vallance Road and knocked up the Kray Twins telling them what had happened. Reg and Ronnie told him: "If you've any trouble with the Foremans, you get on with it yourself, don't come to us for help" . . . They knew the sort of person I was and no one could have stopped me from making a comeback to avenge my brother.

But Ronnie wasn't there. As I've already explained, I was talking to Reggie alone. I said, 'Reg, what have they done with Tommy? Where have they taken him?' And he said, 'Jim, take my advice. Forget it and go home.' By the way, I'm still waiting for this 'comeback'. It's been almost 40 years. I wish he'd hurry up before he has another heart attack.

So does Foreman have any regrets about Ginger and me? 'Yes. I regret that I did not shoot the two of them.' That is true but think about it again. His target that night wasn't me, it was Marks. Otherwise, why did he shout 'Ginger! Come here a minute!', not 'Jimmy!'? Why shoot the monkey when I'm the organ grinder? I blew the bollocks off his brother, not Ginger. No, this shooting had nothing to do with the 'War of George's Balls'. It had everything to do with Ginger's loose talk about Foreman being in bed with Butler.

He says, I seemed 'to live a charmed life'. Two of my accomplices on the Attenborough's job got six months for breaking and entering, but 'strangely the case against Evans only got as far as magistrates' court and he was acquitted'.

Nothing strange about that. I was never inside Attenborough's. He fucked that up and got us all nicked. Thanks to him I never crossed the threshold, I neither broke nor entered and no safes were blown And there he goes again, breaking the so-called 'code' by saying we were on a bit of work that night.

He dares to say *I* had a charmed life! When he boasts of doing at least two murders for which he was never convicted! Thirty years later, he comes clean and the police still don't nick him – not even for perjury. So who had the charmed life, him or me? Yes, I've been lucky and I have survived, but I've never had any help from Old Bill like he has over far worse crimes than I've ever done.

He can't even tell the truth about what he did with Ginger's body. When he writes about how he got rid of Jack McVitie, he says, 'as with Ginger Marks and Frank 'the Mad Axeman' Mitchell, McVitie was buried far out at sea', thanks to a 'friend on the coast who wrapped him up in chicken wire attached to weights . . . Many people prefer burial at sea.'

But not even people close to Foreman at the time believed this was true. In December 1966 when he shot Mitchell for the Krays, and their lieutenant Albert Donoghue came to pay him off with £1,000 of Charlie Kray's money, he told Albert of his surprise at seeing the size of Mitchell's brain. According to Albert, 'he said that when they took Frank to pieces, they were surprised that, for such a big man, he had such a small brain, and he cupped his hands to show me. And he described how his heart was all ripped and torn from the three bullets that went through it.' But in his book Foreman claims he was dumping whole bodies trussed in chicken wire, not headless corpses. And even if he cut off Mitchell's head to make identification more difficult (which he never says he did), did he also break his skull and take out his brain? If so, why? Some kind of ritual, perhaps? How many brains had he handled before to know the difference?

Albert Donoghue said all that when he testified against Foreman and the Krays at their 1969 trial for murdering Mitchell. He repeated it in his own book, *The Krays' Lieutenant*. But back in 1966 Foreman had said the same thing to Mickey Inglefield, who had been in borstal with me. Mickey came from Clapham and he knew both Foremans very well. He was always in Georgie Foreman's Red Sail Club but he was a very good pal of mine and a dangerous little bastard. A year or so after Mitchell disappeared, we both found ourselves in Wandsworth prison. One day he came up to me, laughing, and started talking about how he and his pals used to pull Georgie Foreman's leg. He said, 'We'd all be sitting round a table and we'd nudge each other and say, "I had a terrific bird last night, I tell you what I done to her", and we'd go into the details. Then we'd turn to George and say, "Ain't that right, George?", because of course he was incapable. We used to call him "Spanish George". And if anyone asked why, we'd say, "Los Coblos!" – meaning, "Lost Cobblers" [cobblers being Cockney rhyming slang for 'balls' – cobblers' awls]. So George would say, "I don't know about those things any more", and he would slink away.'

Then Mickey Inglefield said, 'You know, back around that Christmas time, George's fucking nutcase of a brother came over to me and he coughed that he'd killed Frank Mitchell. Then he said, "Funny thing about Mitchell, as big as he was, when we took his brain out of his head, it was only that size [cupping his hands very close]: a tiny little brain in a fucking big bloke like him."'

Now Mickey Inglefield did not know Albert Donoghue – they lived on opposite sides of London and moved in different circles – yet they both said Foreman had told them the same thing about Mitchell's brain, and at around the same time: Christmas 1966. Mickey was a very serious little fellow, he was not the sort to make this up. So how could both he and Donoghue come up with this same line from Foreman – ' As big as he was, he only had a little brain' – unless he really did say it?

What's more, at that Mitchell murder trial another Kray henchman, Harry Hopwood, testified that in the afternoon before he shot Mitchell, Foreman had come to Hopwood's flat to meet Charlie Kray. Hopwood then overheard Foreman talking about an incinerator. Nothing about dumping Mitchell at sea, it seems Foreman was simply going to burn him.

Then there was what Reggie Kray told me in August 1968, just after our set-to over him introducing that copper to me at Winston's. When we'd both calmed down we sat together and I said to him, 'You know, old Ginger thought the world of you and your two brothers. What did those scumbags do with him after they shot him? His old woman and the family are entitled to know.'

Reg said, 'I don't really know, Jim, but one day after it had happened, Charlie was talking to me and Ron, and we said the same thing. And Charlie said, "No one will ever see anything of Tommy, no trace of him, because they [Foreman's mob] have access to a crematorium in South London. They've got the old janitor straight."'

At that moment I felt that Reggie, knowing my temperament, would rather please me than offend me. It seemed to me that, although he was telling me something that didn't help, he was marking my card.

There it is. I'm sure Foreman had Tommy burned or cremated close to home in South London, not taken 60 miles to the coast, in convoy 'with a back-up vehicle minding me off', loaded on a trawler, wrapped in chicken-wire, attached to weights, then given a naval send-off far out in the English Channel (all of which crap he later unloaded on a television show). Who would risk car breakdowns, or getting stopped by the police, spotted by other seafarers, fingered by members of the public, or intercepted by customs and coastguard officers as you're humping big men like Ginger Marks and huge Frank Mitchell aboard? Far safer, surer, quicker and easier to slip him into a crematorium furnace in your own backyard. And you would involve far fewer people. No need for a whole trawler crew singing,

'Fifteen men on a dead man's chest, Yo-ho-ho and a bottle of rum'.

So if Foreman's told a pack of lies about Ginger, what does he say about Dukey Osbourne? He claims that in the late 1970s Colin 'the Duke' Osbourne, 'an old friend from the East End and a good pal of the Twins', was losing vast sums in an illegal gambling house or spieler in the old Kent Road – more than £50,000 on some days 'so he had to be into something big to have that kind of money'. Out of the blue in October 1979 the Duke called him at brother George's minicab office in Peckham. He said he was in 'a bit of trouble and needed a flop to put his lorry down'. Fred Foreman denies knowing that the lorry had £2.5 million worth of cannabis aboard or that customs were bugging and following the vehicle, but he admits knowing the driver, Eddy Watkins: 'Apparently he'd been doing a profitable cannabis run for some years.'

Foreman says he met Dukey and Eddy on Blackheath where Eddy revealed they were surrounded by surveillance teams. 'I was angry,' says Fred, 'because it meant we were probably being photographed and I had no wish to be deeply involved in their enterprise.' But instead of leaving the others to stew in their own juice, he told Eddy to use the lorry to block the end of the northward Blackwall Tunnel where they would pluck him from the customs' clutches. But Eddy didn't show up there – he'd gone through Rotherhithe Tunnel instead – so Freddie dropped Dukey off, drove home, switched on the television to hear, 'Scatty Eddy had shot a customs officer dead. We never even knew he had a gun. It was completely out of order . . . They would now be turning London upside down like lunatics . . . All the people closely involved with Duke and Eddy were arrested but as I had played virtually no part in this enterprise, no one mentioned my name at that stage.' And I'm supposed to be the one with the charmed life!

Foreman says that now he and Dukey went into hiding miles apart, but 'he was dead before I could help him. To my dismay, I was telephoned and told to buy a newspaper. Duke had been found lying on a football pitch on Hackney Marshes . . . all suited and booted and laid out on the ground. He had committed suicide and left a note taking full responsibility for any evidence that was found . . . After he had killed himself, friends took his body to the Marshes and laid him out, rather than face police questioning about the safe house where he had stowed. But the Duke need never have died. His [false] passport came through a couple of days later and he could have been away with me.'

Foreman says he fled to Tenerife, then on to America. He returned to England in 1981 when he was grassed and arrested over that container-load of cannabis. After six months on remand he was given a suspended sentence of two years but immediately released. 'I was highly delighted,' he tells us, especially as the prosecution had produced a photograph of him talking to the driver Eddy Watkins, just before he killed the customs man, and Dukey Osbourne, not long before his death. And wasn't that suicide note convenient?

Dukey's death had served Foreman's interests. Without him around, there was little chance of anyone proving Foreman's true role in this murderous racket. That's why he only got a suspended sentence. And Foreman had reason to fear Dukey would have grassed him: it was Dukey who had grassed him to Ginger over Butler and the train robbers 15 years before.

Which brings me to what Freddie the Fib says about Butler. Again, it's a mixture of truth and lies but it helps reveal Foreman's contorted behaviour towards the robbers. First he reveals that around May 1963 he was drinking in a South London pub 'when in walked Buster Edwards, Gordon Goody, Bruce Reynolds and Tommy Wisbey . . . I was asked if I would like to go on some work. I thanked them for the invitation but said the firm was having a little rest for a few months. Once I had refused their offer they didn't elaborate on what they had in mind. It was none of my business but I wished them luck in their enterprise. Three months later, on 8 August, 1963, they had pulled off the Great Train Robbery.'

So Foreman says he knew this team were working together on something, though he didn't know what. And when Wisbey and Goody were sentenced in March 1964, 'I felt outraged that they had been given 30 years for the robbery. That was a fucking liberty. Nothing short of barbaric. I still believe to this day that someone probably sweet-grassed them.'

Someone grassed them, eh, Fred? That's just what I'd been saying when they were first nicked. But Fred had a front-row seat because he'd had that earlier meet with the prime movers. Even though 'Buster Edwards, Tommy Wisbey, Gordon Goody, Johnny Daly, Jimmy Hussey and Bruce Reynolds were all good pals of mine', says Foreman, 'I had knocked back the chance of becoming one of the Great Train Robbers and the likelihood of a 30-year prison sentence'. Lucky man. So again, who had the charmed life?

He then outlines how he helped hide the most famous Great Train Robber of all, Ronnie Biggs after his escape from Wandsworth jail in July 1965 with a man called Eric Flower. Originally they had been hidden in Dulwich by a man called Paul Seabourn but Flower was worried about security and called Foreman to come and move him. When Foreman turned up with Alf Gerard, Paul Seabourn 'was not too happy. He recognised Alf Gerard immediately and took Biggs into another room and told him [as Biggs confirmed in his book, *Odd Man Out*], "I know Alfie and he's bad news. They're not here to do you any favours and they know you've got lots of dough tucked away."'

So Seabourn recognised that this mob were treacherous parasites, just like Dukey did and like I do today. Unperturbed, Foreman goes on, 'we had no designs on Biggs's money. We were only doing this as a favour to a friend. We didn't need the money and all "fees" for services went directly to the parties involved and not us.' His mob then shipped both men to Amsterdam and supplied them with passports. 'We did not profit from the transactions and that was the end of the firm's involvement with Biggs.'

Foreman goes on to say that during 1966 he was a go-between for several more of the robbers who were 'being hassled by Tommy Butler', the head of Scotland Yard's Flying Squad. 'By then Detective Superintendent Frank Williams, whom I trusted and who had helped me in the past, was his deputy. Butler was obsessed with catching *all* the men involved . . . To stop him pestering the men, I was asked to offer him £50,000 as a bribe. Frank Williams put it to him and Butler seemingly agreed the bribe. I made a meet with Frank to take the £50,000 cash stuffed in two holdall bags to Nunhead Station in South London . . . When I walked into the station with the money, Frank Williams, looking a bit flustered, said, "Fred, I can't take it. Tommy's backed out."'

'I told him it was no big deal and I'd take it back', but a few months later 'Frank was obviously keen to get his hands on a nice Christmas present and this time arrangements were made for me to leave the money in a telephone box in Great Dover Street'. Unfortunately for Williams, Butler took the money straight to Scotland Yard where he declared the lot, not stopping to collect a further £10,000 left at a betting shop. 'Oddly enough the ones who got away weren't bothered by him any more', observes Foreman. From this remark, are we meant to believe that Williams took that £10,000 or did Foreman snaffle it instead?

Then Foreman tells how Buster Edwards, after three years on the run (mainly abroad), 'asked me to make a deal with Butler. I said I didn't trust him and that I thought he would double on him. But I promised to speak to Frank Williams. I treated Frank and Tommy Butler to a lunch at Simpsons-in-the-Strand . . . and I gave them the full treatment. Plenty of fine wine, roast beef, cheeses and vintage port . . . All Butler wanted to talk about was cowboy films . . .. Frank kept looking at me as if to say: "Don't upset him, Fred."' This scene resulted in a deal: in his trial Buster would be portrayed as a minor player and Butler would 'do whatever he could to get him a lighter sentence. We all shook hands on this.'

On that understanding Buster returned to this country and went to Foreman's pub on 19 September 2001 to surrender to Frank Williams. Foreman says, 'We sat in my lounge above the pub and got stuck into the vintage brandy . . . Frank, me and Buster spent hours chatting and got plenty of drink down us . . . Buster got up and went to the loo at one time and Frank said: "He can go if he likes, Fred. If he has changed his mind, I don't really care."' But Buster went ahead and surrendered, and he got 15 instead of 30 years. He was out in eight.

Foreman claims that even then Butler 'tried to get Frank Williams to double on us' but 'Frank was a man of his word and went along with our defence'. He ends with a back-handed compliment for this scourge of the train robbers: 'Tommy Butler, for all his faults, behaved like a gentleman around a lady, and wouldn't dream of nicking them like today's police.'

Why say that? If being 'one of the chaps' means 'hatred of and non-co-operation with authority', why is Foreman not only consorting with a top cop but paying him such a compliment? Does he know something about Butler that he doesn't dare mention? Is he sending out a signal that Butler had a particular penchant regarding the 'ladies'?

It's difficult to tell what's true in all this and what is false, but for sure Foreman has told only a tiny bit about his relationship with Butler and Williams. I'll be filling in some of the gaps in later chapters, but for now I'll say that he's only given a cover story to allay the suspicions of many underworld figures that the man who 'sweet-grassed' the Great Train Robbers was the man who shared all that wine, beef, cheese and port with their chief tormentor.

When people ask if I've ever read Foreman's book I say, 'No, I stopped reading comics when I was six.' I've only read this bit now to confront all his lies head-on. The reason he's so upset now is that his so-called reputation was blown away with his brother's bollocks.

Let's go back to the full definition of 'chaps' on the cover of Foreman's book: 'an almost mythical grouping of criminals whose ethos includes; professionalism in the pursuit of crime; loyalty to others of their kind; hatred of and non-co-operation with authority; and courage. Many aspire to membership, few qualify.'

On that yardstick Freddie Foreman doesn't qualify. He is certainly not 'one of the chaps'. And as for Respect, he knows as much about respect as I know about nuclear physics.

THIRTEEN

The Nude Murders

IN January 1965 all I knew of Fred Foreman was that he was the brother of George Foreman, he ran a pub, he was business partners with Charlie Kray and he killed people – so I'd been told – whether on contract or for pleasure. I still had no idea of his deep connections with Scotland Yard. Indeed, all I knew of his bond with Tommy Butler was that snatch of conversation with Tommy Marks minutes before the Foreman mob killed him. Straight after that I had other things to worry about – like staying alive myself and preserving my assets, especially the House of Peacocks in Beulah Hill.

Although I had been living at my mother-in-law Wag's since I'd shot George Foreman, I did spend occasional days and nights back at Beulah Hill in the hope of ambushing brother Fred. I guessed he might fire-bomb the place – the obvious thing for a coward to try – but on the other hand, I thought, since I had been to his brother's place with guns, he would probably come to mine with guns. Maybe he would bring his own killing crew plus that mob of six or seven that I'd seen with George in Cable Street, but even I wasn't crazy enough to take that many on alone. That's why I called in a lot of my own pals. For a few days they stayed in the House of Peacocks with me, 30 of them, and they all had guns. Some brought their own but I gave out handguns, shotguns, everything, to the rest.

They knew why this had to be done. Many were South Londoners and they knew far more about Freddie Foreman than I did. They took up positions all over the house. I stayed up on the minstrel gallery where I could get a good view of any intruders. I said, 'If anyone comes in that drive with a petrol bomb, shoot the bomb so it blows them up. Then they get it.'

To give the Foreman mob more of a challenge, I made my wife sit under one of the picture windows that went right down to the floor. I put a spotlight on her and I said, 'If anything gets thrown through this window, you're going to be the one that cops it', and she sat like she was told, in that big gold hessian Swedish egg chair of mine. It was a sixties design icon, the first fibreglass piece of furniture that was made. I saw a second-hand one for sale the other day. It was going for two and a half grand. I wish I'd kept mine.

We went through this procedure for several days but the Foreman mob didn't show up, so I stood everybody down and I took my wife back with me to her mother's home in Chingford. By now I was sure the police would be looking for me but they had still made no formal request for an interview, even though it was three weeks since I'd shot George Foreman and three days since Fred had shot and 'disappeared' Ginger Tommy Marks. Neither Tommy's wife Annie nor his brother Terry had told the police I was there that night because they knew we'd both been 'at it' at Attenborough's, a crime which alone could bring me five years in jail. But as soon as my name did come up – by whatever route – Scotland Yard knew my solicitor was Jimmy Fellowes so any day they could call him to arrange a meet. So far we'd heard nothing.

On Wednesday, 6 January 1965, I was over at Wag's house with her bloke Harry, my wife and my kid Denise. It was around tea-time and we were watching television. On came the news and all of a sudden there was an item about the police raiding a house in South London. And it was our house! The House of Peacocks – in Beulah Hill! I couldn't believe it, especially as it was being portrayed as a siege, as if someone inside was going to shoot the police if they came in. There was some commentary about a tip-off that Ginger Marks was being held captive in there but when the police broke in they'd found no one. It was empty. And I was sitting there saying to myself, 'Of course it was empty.' I could have told them that if they'd bothered to ask.

Next morning it was all over the newspapers: 'Police seek Ginger in the House of Peacocks' was a typical headline. The *Daily Mirror* called him a car salesman and said, 'Swarms of police raided the House of Peacocks yesterday in the search for Marks who is believed to have been shot in a London street. Since two a.m. hidden detectives had kept watch on the big detached corner house where two pet peacocks strut in the back garden. At lunchtime 50 police – some with dogs – suddenly surrounded the house. One detective

THE SURVIVOR

climbed to an upstairs window and tried to get in. Others went to the back, broke a window, opened a door and went inside. The police had been given a phone tip that Ginger Marks had been taken to the house, badly hurt. But after an hour-long search, a spokesman said, "Nothing was found to suggest that Marks had been there or is likely to go there."' The *Daily Sketch* reported that our Siamese cat 'cowered spitting in a corner' while 'revolver-carrying detectives' moved in 'after an informer said Marks was held prisoner' there, but fingerprint experts found nothing. Even so, the message was clear: whoever lived in the House of Peacocks had shot and abducted Marks.

I was mad. I figured the police must have summoned the whole of Fleet Street to Beulah Hill long before the siege phase had ended, otherwise how come there were photos of dozens of officers outside before they broke in? In my view, the raid was a Scotland Yard publicity stunt. And it was based on bollocks information because if by now the police knew the truth – that I was a pal of Ginger's, shot by the same mob that shot him – how could they think I would be holding him prisoner? Then I thought, 'Who is this "informer" with the "phone tip"?' I was long past believing anything police said about how they get 'information', but it struck me that the person most likely to say I had shot Ginger would be the man who had him shot. Perfect. Shoot Marks, then blame your brother's castrator. Get him locked up for life, then have him 'done' in jail.

I got straight in touch with my solicitor, Jimmy Fellowes, and we went to see the police. I was interviewed by some detectives but they did not take a statement, either then or when we met them again a few days later. Fellowes told the *Sunday Times* that they had 'gone to Beulah Hill not because they suspected Marks might be there but because they had fears that my client might be in danger', but I still wasn't satisfied that I wasn't a suspect. The newspapers were saying that the man in overall charge of the inquiry was Superintendent Ronald Townsend, then working out of Leman Street police station, less than a mile from where Tommy and I had been shot. I still hadn't met this Townsend but I guessed he was pleased about all this 'Siege of the House of Peacocks' crap, especially as no newspaper had dared to point out what a waste of time and money it had all been: 50 cops hanging around for, say, 14 hours was a lot of overtime.

All these stories had really upset Wag. She said, 'Jimmy, I don't mind how long you stay here – you can stay as long as you like – but I really hope we don't get any publicity. We've only just bought this house and I don't want that kind of headline.'

'Don't worry, Wag, you won't get them,' I said. 'I'll make sure this Townsend bastard doesn't do that to you.' See, she was a very nice little woman. She didn't do any harm, she was just helping me and I wasn't going to let Townsend get loads of publicity at her expense, so I went out and got a van from Joe Wilkins, my then business partner. It was a blue Herald that he used for transporting fruit machines. Then I phoned up the Leman Street HQ and I asked for Ron Townsend. He came straight on the phone and I said in a quivering voice, 'Look, I can't give you my name but I know where you will find Tommy Marks. I can't say any more 'cos I'm in fear for my life if these people find out I'm talking to Old Bill.' I made it sound convincing. I could feel him bite and I led him on. 'I've got information but I can't do it over the phone. I'll meet you but you must come alone. If you turn up with anybody in sight, the meet's off.' So he agreed to meet me alone. I said, 'Clapton Pond, just by Laura Place', and I gave him a time.

I'd chosen a spot where I could easily watch both lengths of the road to see if he was being followed. My scheme was to get him in this van and not let him out until I'd made a few things clear, so earlier that day I had removed the lever handle and the window winder from the inside passenger door. Now it could only be opened from the outside. Once Townsend had got in, he wouldn't be able to get out until I let him out.

I got to Clapton Pond well before time and waited. Up came this little Mini Minor. It was just like Noddy's car in *Noddy in Toyland*, but it wasn't Noddy. It was a huge fat fellow. It took him ages to get out, plenty of time for me to check there was no one else in the car. It was a cold night – this was January – so he had a big coat on. He looked like Oliver Hardy but far bigger – six foot two inch, 16 stone and around 50. As for me, I was wearing the same sheepskin I'd worn when me and Tommy were shot a few nights prior. With my collar up and my hat on, I walked over, got him by the elbow and I said, 'Quick! Quick! I know a lot of people round here. Get in the car before anyone sees us!'

I opened the door and he's got in. Now he's in, he can't get out. I ran round to the driver's side, I've got my .45 with me, and I said, 'Now you fucking stay where you are! I'll tell you what we're going to do, you slag. You know what you did to my house, you know the publicity you've given me. My little girl's suffering over you, I'm suffering, so's all my family. I'm taking you now to where I'm staying, and whether you like it or not, you're going to search that fucking place from top to bottom. You can dig the garden up too. You're not leaving there till I'm satisfied that you're satisfied that there's no blood, bullets and fucking Ginger Markses there!'

He has shit himself. I mean, really shit himself. He must have had a really upset stomach. I took him along a narrow track called Folly Lane, where all the gypsies used to be. There were just bare trees, with owls and a big moon that night – and he was stinking that van out. I had to open the window. You'll never believe how it upset him. When I'd left Wag's I'd kept the garage door open, so as I came up to the house, two or three doors from the Hall Lane Tavern, I drove up the ramp straight into the garage. I've got out my side, knowing he was too fat to escape past the handbrake, gear-lever and steering wheel. I've shut that door, switched on the garage light, gone to his side, opened his door and said, 'Now fucking get out! This is where I'm staying. And it's got to be put on the record that you know where I'm staying. I'm only here till I can sort myself out, but if I have any problems here, with any fucking mugs with guns, *you're* to blame. This is where I am. I'm not fucking hiding it from you. Now you get in this house.'

I took him straight in through the integral door and I called to Harry, 'Go and get the ladder out the garden.' He got it and took it up the steep stairway but it wouldn't reach to the attic, so I had to balance it on a kitchen chair. Then I stuck Townsend on it. By now he was saying, 'No! No! No!' – maybe he thought I was going to kill him in there or starve him to death – but I said, 'You're going in that fucking attic, whether you like it or not.' But he couldn't get through the hatch. He looked like Winnie the Pooh stuck in the rabbit hole. I compromised and let him put just his head in. There he was, waving the torch around, making out he was searching, and all the while the ladder was wobbling on the chair. Then for a joke I'm saying to Harry, 'Shall we let the gun off?', and he's saying, 'Please don't do that!' And the ladder's quaking, reflecting his own shudders. Then I let him come down, and now this big heavy lump – he wasn't half a big geezer – he's got dirt all over his nose and his face. He could tell that no one had been in that attic for years, and he managed to stutter, 'I . . . I . . . I'm quite satisfied.' And we got him off the ladder and down from the chair.

Just at that moment Wag has come up the stairs with a cup of tea – I can see it like yesterday – with biscuits on the saucer, and he says, 'Aah!' and goes to take it, but I said, 'No, that ain't for you! This ain't a fucking picnic. You do your fucking work. You're working, pal, you're working!' Then I took him out in the garden and I made him dig. I made him look everywhere. I took him into the main bedroom and in the wardrobe, where he did find some 9mm bullets. He was holding them in his hand, saying, 'I . . . I . . . I won't report these.' So now he's trying to be nice but this didn't mean a thing because at that time possessing ammunition was not a crime. Meanwhile I was thinking, 'See the change in these bastards: when they've got their army around them they are bullies; when you've got one on his own, he's a coward.'

I made him look everywhere else but all he found was those 13 bullets. If he'd looked properly, he would have found a few guns as well. I kept him there all night until around 5.30 in the morning when I said, 'All right. You can fuck off now.' He said, 'How am I going to get home?' I said, 'The same way as us poor bastards when you swag us down the nick. You walk or you get a fucking cab, like I have to.'

As he was leaving, I remarked on the problem he'd had over the Challenor affair, when a West End detective called Harry Challenor was caught planting evidence on innocent people. During his trial in 1964 he was deemed unfit to plead and walked out of court a free man, but three of his squad went to jail. Jimmy Fellowes had told me that Townsend had been Challenor's boss and he'd lost some pension rights over the scandal, so Townsend was told, 'This is your chance to get back your full pension: you solve this Marks mystery.' Whether this was true, I don't know, but now I felt that he was trying to redeeem himself by gaining a lot of good publicity at my expense, the expense of my house and my kid's schooling. All this crap about 'The Siege of the House of Peacocks'. Do reporters and photographers have crystal balls? Are they psychic? No, they were getting phone calls from Scotland Yard saying, 'Be there!' That's how they get their stories. And in those days coppers used to get a pay-off too, from newspapers who wanted to be first on the scene. Later I found their flashbulbs trodden into my lawn, and my poor little peacocks had been chased away. The coppers and the snappers had scared them off. Eventually I recaptured them and gave them to a children's park in Crystal Palace.

So I ended by telling Ron Townsend, 'I don't care if you fucked up over Challenor, you're not going to get the same publicity from my mother-in-law as you got from me.' That was my way of putting a block on it. Only then did I fuck him off into the street that cold dark morning. I just put him out of the door and let him walk.

You might think kidnapping a police officer is a serious offence. Too right it is. Kidnapping anyone is a terrible crime and it carries a very heavy jail sentence. I knew that well enough because the police laying siege to the House of Peacocks was like saying I had kidnapped Tommy Marks. Yet I suffered little retribution over snatching Townsend. He never dared officially report it, probably because it made him look such a twat. But the next time I saw Tommy's brother, Terry, he said, 'Fuck you! Me and my old woman was dragged out of bed at four in the morning by a group of coppers saying, "Your fucking pal Jimmy Evans has kidnapped our governor! Where's he taken him? What's he done with him?"' This must have been while I still had Townsend at Wag's house. When I'd been talking to him on the phone I had never said who I was, so how his boys put two and two together, I don't know.

I'd had to take the law into my own hands because Fred Foreman already had the law – Old Bill – in his hands.

After slaying Ginger and (as I believe) cremating him, then telling the cops I'd got Ginger in the House of Peacocks, he came back at me in a way that was devastating beyond anyone's imaginings. The scheme was so brilliant that I don't think he could have made it up on his own. He must have had help from inside the Yard.

I was still staying at Wag's on Friday, 15 January 1965, when I stepped out to phone a good pal in South London. He said, 'Jimmy, I'm glad you called. I don't suppose you get the *South London Advertiser* where you are. You ought to take a look at today's edition.'

'What's in it?' I asked.

My pal replied, 'You won't believe it if I tell you. Let's have a meet and I'll give it to you.'

We met and he showed me the front page. 'Has the House of Peacocks a link with Thames Nude Murders?' ran the main headline of an 'Exclusive' story spread across the entire page. This linked me to a series of murders so grotesque that they had filled almost as many newspaper pages as the Great Train Robbery. By the time the *South London Advertiser* got in on the act, seven women had been found dead: the first four in the shallow reaches of the Thames, between Mortlake and Hammersmith in West London, the next two on land close by in Chiswick and Acton, and the latest one just off Kensington High Street. Most were discovered nude, they had all been strangled, but none had been killed where they were found. Each corpse had been stored elsewhere before being dumped overnight for some passing dog-walker or early shift worker to stumble across the next morning. One other thing: they were all prostitutes, or so the press and police were saying.

By now the police had decided there were enough similarities in the last five killings to believe they were the work of the same crank, though they seemed to think that the first two victims, Elizabeth Figg (found in June 1959) and Gwynneth Rees (November 1963), were killed by someone else. In those days no one used the term 'serial killer' but as the body count went beyond the tally of six piled up by Jack the Ripper in 1888–89, the press nicknamed this slayer 'Jack the Stripper'. And just like the Ripper, the Stripper hadn't been caught. All these murders were unsolved. This was worrying for Scotland Yard as the Stripper was stepping up his activities. In the course of 1964 he had killed women in February (Hannah Tailford), April (Irene Lockwood and Helene Barthelemy), July (Mary Fleming) and November (Margaret McGowan). So now, in January 1965, Britain's public enemy number one was Jack the Stripper, way ahead of the few 'most wanted' Great Train Robbers who had still not been delivered up to Tommy Butler by their underworld pals.

And just at this moment when the national press was obsessed with yet another grotesque crime, the shooting and disappearance of my pal Tommy Marks, this local rag was branding me both as Tommy's abductor and as the slayer of all these prostitutes. Now I've filled you in on the background – and I didn't know much of this myself at the time – you may appreciate how bad this article was for me:

NORWOOD RIDDLE

Has the House of Peacocks a link with Thames Nude Murders?

On Tuesday an 'Advertiser' reporter passed on to a senior Scotland Yard detective information linking an Anerley man with the Beulah Hill 'House of Peacocks' raid, the disappearance of 'Ginger Marks' and the Thames Nude Murders.

The information came during three telephone conversations between the reporter and a mystery voice who was an underworld 'tipster'. [He] explained that the man in question is believed to have controlled the activities of three of the murdered prostitutes – Hannah Tailford, Margaret McGowan and Gwynneth Rees. He was detained at Kensington police station by detectives inquiring into the murders, but later released.

The name cropped up again after last week's Flying Squad raid on the 'House of Peacocks' during the massive London hunt for the missing East End car dealer, 'Ginger' Marks.

The 'grass' or 'tipster' said that the name of the man owning the 'House of Peacocks' was known to criminals as an alias of the man questioned about the nude murders. The 'grass' also said that the man had done some 'crooked' car deals with 'Ginger' Marks . . .

In a third conversation the 'grass' cast further light on what might have happened to two of the prostitutes the night they died. Gwynneth Rees died of an abortion – not as the result of a sexual assault as such; one of the other[s] died in a bath in a house in Marylebone Road before being dumped in the Thames.

The 'grass' then alleged that the man bossed a chain of brothels and call girls, and held the lease of a house in Curzon Street, Mayfair, formerly owned by the notorious Messina brothers. He gave the reporter names of two South London prostitutes, the addresses of houses in Notting Hill Gate and Bloomsbury used by prostitutes and the name of a South London public house used by an unnamed prostitute – she arranged to meet the man at the 'House of Peacocks' – all the women were controlled by the same man.

The 'grass' said the man, knowing he was known to police, had provided himself with an escape route to Dublin. The 'grass' then said that the underworld generally believed that the man was in hiding abroad. 'But,' said the 'grass', 'I know that he is living at Number . . . . Road, Anerley.' He added, 'My underworld friends tell me that "Ginger" Marks is not dead but seriously wounded.'

When I'd fought my way through this article's strange construction, I realised that of all its accusations against me, wounding and abducting Ginger Tommy was the least damaging. I was now branded as the murderer of three 'Nude Murder' victims (which meant at least five, because they were all done by the same man); as their ponce; as the 'boss' of many other call girls; as the owner of a chain of brothels; as someone so seedy that I would use my own family home to meet prostitutes that I 'control'; as a ponce so cruel that I would condemn my girls to death by forcing them to have unlawful backstreet abortions; as some kind of pervert, killing women in baths; and as a crooked car dealer to boot.

My neighbours in Beulah Hill would have no doubt who the newspaper was talking about. I wasn't named but I could be identified just from my cars, for the article also said:

One of the two cars still standing in the driveway of the 'House of

Peacocks' – the blood-red Ford Classic – belongs to the man. The other, an American convertible, is known to criminals as belonging to an associate of the man.

Wrong on both counts. That Ford Classic was the car I had bought my wife – it was the one she drove when I hid in the boot and caught her at George Foreman's pokey hole – and the convertible was my own Galaxy. But our neighbours wouldn't notice these mistakes. All they would absorb was that I was a crazed, perverted sex killer. Not content with shooting, snatching and disposing of Ginger Marks, I now stood accused of being Britain's most evil murderer of the twentieth century.

In case you believe any of this, I'll put you out of your misery. I hadn't been questioned about the Nude Murders at Kensington Police Station or anywhere else. I had nothing to do with them. I wasn't living in Anerley (which incidentally is only a mile from Beulah Hill, so not a good place to hide), nor was I abroad in Dublin or anywhere else. I was still in Chingford with Wag and my solicitor, Jimmy Fellowes, could produce me any time at any police station, if anyone at Scotland Yard bothered to ask.

I'll jump ahead a little and tell you that I sued the *South London Advertiser* over this article. They didn't have a leg to stand on and Jimmy Fellowes won a £6,000 settlement for me – nearly £180,000 today. Within a short time the newspaper went out of business. So even this nonsense ended up in my favour. But when a story is so wrong, so false in every way, it's not the newspaper's stupidity or gullibility that matters; it's the story's malicious origin, the motive of the dirty bastard who conned the rag into publishing such crap. Let's look for clues. Clearly it's someone who doesn't like me, someone bent on vengeance and whose vengeance knows no bounds. It's someone with close knowledge of the Nude Murders and maybe a fixation about them. And clearly it's someone who's an arch-manipulator. It's also someone who likes throwing in the odd line about people fleeing to Ireland (worth noting for later on). And clearly it's someone with a close personal interest in Ginger Marks but who doesn't want to say he's dead. Now, surely, if this someone wanted to really stick the knife in, so to speak, he would have said I killed Marks too. Why hold back on that when he's accusing me of far worse? But perhaps saying that Marks was dead might have hit too close to home, as if this someone had killed Marks himself.

Whoever this 'tipster' was, he had so beguiled the newspaper that it did not bother to check even the simplest detail – my whereabouts – with the

THE SURVIVOR

officer heading the Marks inquiry. If that had been done, I'm sure Superintendent Ron Townsend would have hinted he knew where I was, and it wasn't Anerley. He was never going to forget his trip to Chingford, so I wouldn't accuse him or any of his team of feeding this nonsense to the newspaper. It had to be someone in the underworld and my bet – yes, you've guessed – was Freddie Foreman.

There's a funny twist to all this. In one of those quirks of real life that no writer would dare put in a work of fiction for fear of being accused of stretching coincidence too far, each week the *South London Advertiser* carried a different saying above its front page mast-head. This week, right next to the headline 'Has the House of Peacocks a link with Thames Nude Murders?' was a quotation from Dr Samuel Johnson: 'Slander is the revenge of a coward and dissimulation is his defence.'

This was only the beginning of a long campaign against me of lies, disinformation and defamation, coupled with the physical retribution. As Wag's partner Harry had said when we first saw the TV news about the siege of the House of Peacocks, 'If the police know where you live, you can be sure the other mob know too. You'd better be careful that they don't try and blow it up.'

Two days later, a little before four in the morning on Sunday, 18 January, some people chucked a petrol bomb into the House of Peacocks. The place burst into flames and a fire engine had to put them out. The damage was limited but those scumbags had thrown their bomb through my daughter's bedroom window. She wasn't there that night, and neither was I – we were all still living at Wag's – but the bombers didn't know that. They didn't care if they killed her. They wanted to kill me, fair enough, but don't take it out on the kid. Look at the care I took not to shoot George Foreman's boy. George didn't do this – he was still in hospital – but again his brother Fred was the most obvious suspect. Not that he would have done it himself. He would have got some other mugs to do it.

But he was still one step ahead. Forty minutes after the House of Peacocks was fire-bombed, the same mob went to the premises of the *South London Advertiser* in Crystal Palace and threw two petrol bombs in its reception and advertising offices, forcing the entire staff to move elsewhere. What a stroke: bomb my home to tell me the 'comeback' is coming (or to kill my daughter, take your pick), then bomb the newspaper that's just called me a pimp, strangler and mass-murderer. Result: everyone will think I fire-bombed the newspaper in revenge but fire-bombed my own home as well to cover my tracks. But, I assure you, the first I knew of either bombing was when I woke up that Sunday and switched on the TV.

On Monday the story was all over the national newspapers. I came over quite well because Jimmy Fellowes had been active on my behalf. The *Daily Express* said, 'A vast police hunt spread through London last night for mobsters who tried to burn out the trail leading to Thomas Ginger Marks.' It said that I was a friend of Tommy's, quoting Fellowes saying that I was in hiding for my own safety. Fellowes had also spoken to the *South London Advertiser* to say they'd got the story all wrong and we'd be sueing for libel. The following Friday the same newspaper led with the story of its own fire-bombing, then proclaimed, 'We are near the truth. This can be the only explanation for the cowardly attack on our office.' Then it came out with more weird stuff, about an unnamed man who had told a reporter that he'd organised the bombing: 'We have nothing against you personally, mate, but lay off.' Then more trumpet-blowing: 'It was the *Advertiser* that first published the news that there was a link between the House of Peacocks and the Thames Nude Murders . . . We are not scared off. We will continue to probe and attempt to find the secrets of the House of Peacocks.'

As it went to press the *Advertiser* got another 'scoop': a threatening letter which was quoted in the Stop Press column but with a lot of swear words left out. 'Ginger Marks was a ——— no good ———, Him and that ——— —— Evans.' Most of it made no sense but the drift was clear enough: 'When we finally get round to it these two will wish they had never been born! Evans – he's got it coming – and even if it takes us a year we will get the ———.' The words fucking and bastard seem to fit the gaps.

I think this letter was a hoax. I mean, it didn't come from the Foreman camp. It was too crude even for them. As for the fire-bombing itself, they were well 'in the frame', because it was so cowardly. If they had really wanted to get me, they could have posted a permanent watchman across the road. I was going to the house every day to feed the birds. If they had wanted to take their chances, they could have tried to hit me any time. And now they had bombed it, they could still have had a go because I was showing up there every day to check the damage and sort out repairs. On the day of the bombing itself I had gone straight there with Joey Wilkins. It was still smouldering and through the smoke an inspector from Streatham police station, just down the hill, swaggered over and said, 'Right. Who are you?'

I said, 'It's my house.'

He said, 'Any idea who threw the bomb in?'

'You'll soon know,' I said. 'The first person you see running round here with one hand will be the one who threw it, because I'll have chopped his fucking hand off.'

This copper was looking a bit pleased with himself as he said, 'Jim, isn't it? Jim, I've found your secret hideout, your wall safe.'

'Yeah,' I said. 'That's there for cunts like you *to* find', because it was so obvious '– behind the picture of the angel-fish above the fireplace – any child could have found it if they stood on a chair. And there was nothing in it, only documents relating to the house. So I've walked in and he's followed me. I've gone straight to my fireplace and I've deliberately shown him the stone panel, then I've pressed it to reveal the secret compartment. I took out a silver box containing some money and jewellery and I said, 'See. You haven't found my secret hideout. I'm showing it to you now. And, while you're here,' I said, 'take these away.' And I handed him 2,300 rounds of ammunition. Then I left him to scrabble around inside. He found some holsters but no guns, because I had removed boxes full of them weeks before. Storing ammunition was no crime, as I've said, and, besides, I saw no point in keeping this place secret because I wasn't going to live here any more. I just gave him the ammunition in case the Foreman mob came back and threw more fire-bombs. I couldn't risk 2,300 bullets firing off all over the place, killing neighbours and bystanders and completely destroying the house which, once I had repaired it, I would be putting on sale.

But, even when you're trying to be good, you can't beat Scotland Yard at the publicity game. A few days later there was another blast of headlines at my expense. After the 'Siege' now came the 'Secret'. According to the *Sunday Mirror*, 'A cache of ammunition has been uncovered in a secret hiding place at the House of Peacocks. Detectives pressed a brick beneath the fireplace in the lounge. The brick swung open on a hinge to reveal hundreds of rounds of ammunition, three revolver holsters and gun-cleaning equipment.'

When I read this stuff I was so furious that I got on the phone and I told that copper, 'You didn't discover my hiding place. I showed it to you.'

He said, 'Oh yes I did!'

He had to say that because all his calls were being recorded, but I wanted the truth recorded too so I said, 'No you never. And you never found that ammunition. I gave that to you.'

He said, "Yes I did, I found it!'

I said, 'Are you good at finding things?'

'Yes,' he replied.

So I said, 'Well, fucking find Ginger Marks then!' and I put the phone down in disgust. See, Scotland Yard wanted publicity more than they wanted to catch Marks's killers. Looking back, I understand why. Because Freddie Foreman was as much a Yard copper as the Commissioner of the Metropolitan Police. He was one of their own.

Thank God for Jimmy Fellowes. He told the *Sunday Mirror* what I had told the police: 'There was nothing sinister about the ammunition. He has had it for about five years and it was kept for an innocent purpose.' Fellowes added that it was wrong to say I was in hiding: 'He is still going out and about, but he is just not taking any chances.' The *South London Advertiser* seized on the ammunition story, thinking, perhaps, that more bad news about me would destroy my chances of winning a libel action over its Nude Murders story. It did quote Fellowes saying that I had all those rounds for sports shooting and I only hid them to keep them out of my young daughter's way, but it still implied I had held Tommy Marks hostage, it was just that by the time the police broke in 'the cupboard was bare'. And it wasn't giving up on the 'Nude Murders', linking them with not just Tommy's fate but also the fire-bomb attacks and the shooting of George Foreman. It backtracked slightly by quoting an informant who said the link between the dead prostitutes and my house came before I had bought it. This was bollocks. When I bought the House of Peacocks there were no Nude Murders, only one 'Towpath' victim killed four years earlier and whom Scotland Yard didn't even consider one of Jack the Stripper's victims.

I wasn't losing sleep over the *South London Advertiser*. It had a small circulation and although (unknown to me) some Yard detectives were trying to frame me for the Nude Murders, Ron Townsend didn't waste time on that nonsense. He had his hands full with the Ginger Marks case which, he now knew, was all tied in with our attempt on Attenborough's and the shooting of George Foreman. The pressure was really on Townsend. By the end of January 1965 Tommy had been missing for four weeks and Fleet Street had gone crazy. Newspapers were putting forward a brand new theory every few days. Tommy was either alive but in hiding in a holiday village on the Essex coast; or he was dead, and his body had been put in a cement jacket and dumped in a water-filled Kent sandpit, or it was lying weighted at the bottom of the Thames at Chertsey, or it was concealed in the cellar of a house. The *News of the World* were trying to do Townsend's job for him, running a big feature headlined, 'Where is Ginger Marks? We offer £5,000 reward for him – dead or alive.' That was a lot of money in those days, equal to over £150,000 today.

All this time I was lying low at Wag's but always ready to be called in by Jimmy Fellowes for a formal interview with Townsend, or with Detective Inspector Fred Littlefield who was investigating the George Foreman shooting. But I was never 'in hiding'. Every day I was showing up in predictable places, such as the House of Peacocks, and I wasn't shy of the police, confronting detectives in person and on the phone, as that Streatham DI found out.

Imagine my surprise when on Tuesday, 9 February, I was at the post office in Bethnal Green Road, opposite Attenborough's, in a phone box and making a call, when I was surrounded by cops and nicked. There was no need for that – one call to Jimmy Fellowes and they could have avoided this melodrama – but as usual they wanted to put on a show and generate more headlines. The officers were arresting me over George Foreman but they were working for Townsend in his 40-strong Ginger Marks team, now based at Commercial Street. They knew I had kidnapped their governor and this was their comeback. And this way I had no solicitor to stick up for me. So when Littlefield came in to see me about George Foreman, he wasn't alone. Townsend was there too, and so was Chief Inspector Williams: the same Frank Williams who was Freddie Foreman's crooked partner in deals to split big chunks of robbery money between themselves and Tommy Butler and to turn in Great Train Robbers like Buster Edwards. Looking back, I wonder if the interview I had with Littlefield, Townsend and Williams on 9 February 1965 was one of the times when, as Foreman puts it, Frank Williams 'had helped me in the past'. Like copping train money for 18 months already

During this interview I was accused of shooting and 'disappearing' my pal Tommy Marks – when all the while Frank Williams, the partner-in-crime of the real killer, was sitting in the same room on the same interrogation committee. There was Ron Townsend saying, 'We think you killed Ginger Marks. We think you dumped him over a six foot wall, then you came back and moved him later.' What bollocks. Imagine me doing this when I'd just had one of my ribs shot away, then I'd gone to see Annie and his brother Terry to tell them he'd been shot and taken away. In that condition would I heave this 15-stone man over a wall? Today, 35 years later, I don't have to argue the point because Foreman has finally admitted he killed Tommy, but where had Townsend got this crap from? Well, if he had Frank Williams in the room, we don't have to look very far. I would guess that Williams already knew that Foreman had shot and killed Tommy. Two years later Williams would cover up for his pal again when Foreman did the same to poor Frank Mitchell in return for a fat fee from the Krays.

Of course, I knew nothing of the Williams-Foreman connection back in February 1965. All I knew was that after this encounter I was taken to Kennington police station – Fred Foreman's local nick where Williams had served for years – and charged with shooting George Foreman with intent to do him grievous bodily harm. I did not get bail and I was remanded to Brixton Prison.

I would spend the next ten years in and out of courts and in and out of jail, on the end of a vendetta orchestrated by Fred Foreman. Even though he was a serial killer, he was far more dangerous working with his partners in the police than he ever was with a gun.

FOURTEEN

Revenge of the Body Snatchers

FROM February 1965 onwards many things happened to me during long spells in jail. I have plenty of tales to tell about these years and I'll tell them in another book. Here I'll stick to events that relate to my blind struggle against the Foreman-Butler-Williams firm: blind because I could not see that a bunch of villains could be joint shareholders in a firm with some of the highest-ranking officers in Scotland Yard. If Sir Robert Peel could see the monster that he created when he set up the Metropolitan Police, he would jump up and smash his head on the lid of his coffin. The Mafia in Blue.

Banged up in Brixton as I waited to go on trial for shooting George Foreman, I was a little concerned that some of Freddie's friends might be in there too. I could deal with them, provided I knew who they were. Meanwhile I was living in a normal cell, I didn't ask for special protection and I didn't fake illness to get on the hospital wing. Far from receiving a hostile reception, I found that standing up against the Foremans on the outside had earned me a lot of 'respect' on the inside. I even picked up useful information, for this was where Hungarian George told me what had gone on in George Foreman's place during the shooting. And one day I was walking round the exercise yard with several old pals, when up came Buster Seeger. I knew him as one of the Seeger brothers, Buster and John, who were capable robbers, good on the pavement, risking their liberties. Buster's first words were, 'I'm fucking glad you did that. He's a right bastard.' It turned out that he knew George Foreman very well. 'I really hate him.,' he said and he explained why.

He said that a little while back they'd had a 'nice touch', so they laid out five grand of the proceeds – a lot of money then – for a little club down Vauxhall way. This was right near where Georgie Foreman lived but before I'd shot him there. They had got this club going and running well, when one evening Georgie turned up with a woman. As Buster was going through this story I asked him what this woman looked like, so he described her and the dress she was wearing – silver grey with a panel in the back, very unusual – and I realised she was my wife: she had the same looks and that same dress. Anyway Georgie suddenly said to Buster, 'Look, we'll give you two grand for the club.' And Buster said, 'Two grand? You must be joking. It's just cost us five grand.' So Georgie said, 'Well, this ain't your line of business. This is our game running clubs. We'll give you two grand for it.' The Seegers just laughed. They really thought he was joking.

The next week he came in again and he said, 'We'll give you a grand now.' Buster said, 'You said two grand last week.' He said, 'Yeah, that was last week. It's a grand this week. Take it or leave it.' When he had come in two men had walked in close behind. They sat down at a table near the door and as George walked out, they called Buster over and they said, 'Two Scotches. And, by the way, we'll be coming in every week for 200 quid.' Buster looked a bit upset. When they told him they were police officers, he was even more upset. So Buster was telling me that when George Foreman couldn't get his own way, these bent coppers came in as reinforcements. That was another tiny piece in my jigsaw.

For the next few months my main concern was how to get out of jail. I still faced a charge of breaking and entering Attenborough's on the night they shot Ginger Tommy Marks, and in March I was taken to the committal hearing. Inevitably Tommy's name came up. My kidnap victim, Detective Superintendent Ron Townsend, testified that I had told him, 'I only came up to have a drink with Tommy in the pub. I can't talk about what happened that night but it was nothing to do with me. I never went along to look at it. You can't put it down to me. I wasn't on the roof.' As the police had no witnesses to prove I was on it, the magistrate threw the case out.

I still faced the shooting charge. At each remand hearing my solicitor tried to get me bail. Arguing against this, Ron Townsend testified that I had told him how I had hidden myself in my wife's car and caught her at Foreman's rat-hole. He claimed I had said all this when he met me at Clapton Pond, but he said nothing about what I did to him that night. I thought that kidnapping him would have been a far stronger argument against bail – it was a serious crime in itself – but Ron couldn't bring himself to tell the court it had happened. I never did get bail. Instead the police claimed I had asked for special protection in Brixton and they had asked the governor to provide it. But I had never asked for special protection and certainly I never got it.

At the committal hearing my solicitor Jimmy Fellowes put George Foreman on the spot, testing if he would dare grass on me. According to a newspaper report he said, 'I was knocked backwards. I remember nothing else.' That wasn't too helpful. He could have said, I saw the gunman and it wasn't Evans. Fellowes got him riled on the subject of his flat and my wife. He said, 'I don't want to answer these questions.' Ordered to do so, he said, 'I had my reasons for taking the flat and Mrs Evans had her reasons for going to it. I do not know what they were.' Fellowes came back, 'Do you expect the court to believe that? Did your wife know Mrs Evans?' He said, 'No', which made the arrangement pretty clear. Fellowes then suggested that Foreman, who worked in a betting shop, might have taken the flat 'out of fear', to hide from enemies in the bookmaking racket. Foreman said he just 'wanted somewhere to be alone'. Fellowes said, 'Somewhere where your enemies could not find you.' Foreman denied that but Fellowes was laying the foundations of a defence: plenty of people might want to shoot Foreman, not just me. This was vital for me, otherwise the prosecution might win the case on the evidence of the straight couple who lived in the flat opposite Foreman's, where my wife had run in and shut the door and I had kicked it in. They had seen me there with a shotgun only a few hours before he was shotgunned. That evidence might convince a jury to convict me, unless we could show that a lot of people might have wanted to shoot this bookie.

The trial was set for April at the Old Bailey. Before then there were a lot of behind-the-scenes negotiations. I needed to know if Foreman was going to identify me. My wife was visiting me in Brixton. Two weeks before the trial she said, 'Don't worry, he won't name you.' I said, 'Of course he won't name me. He can't afford to lose face. But when he's asked, "Who shot you?", he only has to say, "I answered the door, there was a blinding flash and I woke up in hospital", and I'll get ten years, because the jury will think it can only be me. On the other hand, if he just says it wasn't me, then I'm out of it.' Then I told her, 'I don't want him to do me any favours. I'd rather do ten years without any favours. It's up to him.'

On the first day of the trial Joe Wilkins, my then business partner in the clothing game, came along to watch. Who should he see on the steps of the Old Bailey but George Foreman. Joe was shocked and asked him, 'What are you doing here?' He said, 'I've got to give evidence. I've been subpoena'd'. So Joe told him, 'Subpoena? Bollocks! Go on holiday. I'll give you the money to go. Fuck off on holiday for a couple of months'. Foreman said, 'I'll have to ask my brother'. The bloke couldn't give evidence quick enough.

So when he was called into court – the historic Number One Court where I had four trials in all – and he was asked who shot him, he said, 'I don't know, I answered the door, there was a blinding flash and I woke up in hospital'. He said exactly what I'd told her he shouldn't say. This wasn't how brother Freddie later described his behaviour: 'Even in the face of death, he honourably stuck to our code of not grassing who shot him.' No, George was leaving it open, playing on the jury's sympathy, then keeping his fingers crossed and hoping I would get a ten-year stretch on top of all my other aggravation.

Now we had to discredit him, to show how many other people might want to shoot him. My counsel, John Lloyd-Eley, cross-examined detectives about all the violence surrounding bookmaking and the enemies Foreman might have in that business. Then I said to him, 'Ask them what was on the mantelpiece at Cable Street', and the detectives admitted they had found those Christmas cards to the Great Train Robbers. Lloyd-Eley recalled Foreman who said that, yes, he had signed these cards to the likes of Gordon Goody, Tommy Wisbey and Roy James, each then in jail for the robbery. He said, 'they have all been good friends of mine'. He also admitted that he had owned the 'Walk In Club' in Lambeth with another robber, Buster Edwards, who was still on the run at the time.

This stuff didn't endear him to the jury. The robbers hadn't been especially violent but the train driver did get coshed, he never drove another train and never recovered. That incident had gone down very badly with the public, so we felt the jurors would decide that if he was friends with these people he didn't deserve their sympathy. Maybe they worked out that, if any of the robbers had fallen out with him, they could have hired a hit-man

I think the jurors might have had a bit of sympathy for me. I recall they were all men and, when they went home and were lying in bed with their wives, they might have thought, 'yeah, if my wife was playing around, I'd want to shoot the bloke', especially as they had been told that Foreman had introduced Mrs Evans to the caretaker of that block as 'my wife'. After that, most of the jurors probably thought that Foreman had it coming.

And out came the story of how I had been present when persons unknown – or still unnamed – had shot Ginger Marks. This affair came over as a tit-for-tat shooting, through which the Foreman mob had already exacted more than their share of revenge. Maybe the jury felt: this is what gangsters do to each other, so let them get on with it. And maybe I had come over as someone with a little decency. Mr Smith, whose door I kicked in when my wife had run in there, testified that I came back to apologise and offered to come back again to repair the door. He looked down at the bag I was carrying, saw the shotgun sticking out and said, 'Well, don't bring that with you.'

At one point the prosecutor had a pop at the jurors. He said, 'Some of you may snigger every time it is mentioned that Foreman was shot between the legs, but it makes me want to cross my legs in pain.' A barrister should never criticise jurors, even if they do find a man losing his bollocks amusing. I think this gave the men on the jury the hump. And they still had my simple denial: I had never been to Foreman's home and I had never shot him. As there were no witnesses it was easy for my counsel to argue that I should be acquitted. On Friday 9 April the jurors were sent out to consider their verdicts. They came back in just an hour and a half. They had found me not guilty of shooting Foreman. They even cleared me of unlawfully possessing that shotgun at Cable Street. I walked out of court a free man.

The only good thing for me about spending the previous two months in Brixton was that, while I was in there, the real Jack the Stripper had been at work again. On 16 February a woman called Bridget Esther O'Hara was found dead on the Heron Trading Estate in Acton. She had disappeared on 11 January, then her body was stored until it was dumped on the estate no earlier than 12 February. Whether this was the Stripper's sixth or eighth victim, it was clear that he wasn't me because I was locked up in Brixton. I don't think any detective on the Foreman, Marks or Attenborough's cases ever believed the pack of lies that had appeared in the *South London Advertiser*. There never had been any evidence to support its claim of a link between the House of Peacocks and the Nude Murders.

As soon as I had got over Brixton and the trial, Fellowes and I issued a writ for libel against the newspaper. Even then, it had the nerve to print a front-page story headlined, 'Evans Sues for Libel'. There was also a rather good photo of me. I think someone on that paper liked me. In an earlier issue it had described me as 'tall, dark and good-looking' – and now it would have

THE SURVIVOR

to pay me handsome retribution. As I've said, Fellowes won me a £6,000 pay-out. Far more than my costs for the Foreman trial. So these Mickey Mouse gangsters had done me a big favour. And remember that quotation the *South London Advertiser* had above its mast-head when it first published the Nude Murders allegation: 'Slander is the revenge of a coward and dissimulation is his defence'. When it announced I was taking action, the quotation read, 'Dare to be true; nothing can need a lie'. Exactly. If they had absorbed both messages, they wouldn't have had to pay up – or go out of business a few months later.

Now I had to reconstruct my life. First I had to sort out the marriage. Obviously it was over, long before she had made that plea to me in Spain: 'Can't we just stay down here forever and never go back to England again?' Soon after our return, when we were still staying at my mother-in-law Wag's place, I decided to end it all. I was just waiting for the right moment. Every morning she would go down to the kitchen, which had all-white tiles, she'd sit there with her knees up and she'd have a cup of tea. And she always smoked these bloody cigarettes with a filter tip. And she'd stand the filter tips up like soldiers. And it always annoyed me. That annoyed me more than the smoking. There was a big carving knife down there and I thought to myself, I'll wait for her to go down one morning and I'll set about her with that. I'll cut her to pieces with it. But then I thought to myself, if I do that, and I call Wag and tell her what's happened, she's going to come home and the blood's going to be all over the white tiles. That's how I could see it. I imagined all this mess down there, and that put me off. I thought, it wouldn't be fair to Wag, not after a hard day's work. I liked her. She was my friend.

But as for her daughter, I'd had enough. I think it was when suddenly she told me how she had first got involved with Foreman: he had given her suitcases full of ten-bob notes from the Great Train Robbery to change up. And just as suddenly I thought, 'Of all the people in the world that she could have got tied in with, it had to be with scumbags who were in bed with bent coppers.'

For me this was the last straw. We were still in bed and I thought we were the only people in the house. She was very small and very light and she was lying on her stomach, so I just picked her up and I threw her on the floor. And I turned her over and I knelt on top of her, and I thought, 'I'll kill you with my fucking hands.' I started punching. The first one must have broken her cheekbone. I kept hitting her in slow motion. I got to the point where I think one more blow would have killed her when, all of a sudden in the background I heard someone saying, 'I'm going now.' It was our daughter, Denise. She was just going off to school. I thought she had already left. But now her voice snapped me out of it. I stopped the punching. My wife was unconscious. We phoned for an ambulance and they took her to Whipps Cross Hospital. She had a lot of facial damage and several broken bones. When Wag came home I told her what had happened and she went to the hospital, but she didn't recognise her own daughter. She was so bruised and swollen that Wag walked right by her. She looked like the Elephant Man in drag.

When my wife told me about this a few days later she said, 'Do you know the first thing my mother said to me when she came in? "Serves you right. You deserve it."' She was always on my side, Wag. I never tried to patch things up. I just needed some time.

It was only a few weeks later that I kidnapped Ron Townsend and forced him to search the house for any sign of Ginger Marks. I took him in our bedroom and made him stand on a chair to look on top of the wardrobe. He said, 'What's all this up here? Is it cocoa?' I peered over and it really did look as if cocoa had been spilt up there. Then I realised. It was some of her blood. When I'd got her down on the floor, I had hit her so hard that it must have spurted out and landed all the way up there. I don't think Townsend caught on, otherwise he might have thought I really had done Ginger myself.

I don't tell this story with pride but equally I'm not ashamed. I was just a nasty, violent person. I did not end the marriage immediately. After I was acquitted, the three of us, with Tony Samms and his family, were all intending to live in New Zealand for a few years. I bought all the tickets for our passage there on a passenger ship. I even booked a cabin on the sundeck for my wife, my daughter and me. I still had plenty of money and I was planning to buy a petrol station between Auckland and Wellington. I was taking two Jaguars and also a huge motor caravan, sleeping eight people. This was costing £8,500, a huge amount, and I'd put down a deposit. This was going to be a big adventure and Tony, who had been to New Zealand before, was set on it.

Two days before we were due to sail, I arranged with my wife to pick her up from some place and take her back to Wag's. My little girl and I stood waiting for her in the autumn fog but she didn't turn up. We waited for about an hour, then I took the kid home. My wife never came back. She had probably gone to her sister's. Later I found out why. As she told Ann, Dave

Norman's wife, 'I'm frightened. I daren't go on that ship. I know what's going to happen. I shall disappear one night. He'll throw me overboard to the sharks.'

So I cancelled the trip. I could have said, 'I've got the tickets, so you're going. If you don't go, I'll blow your head off.' Or I could have said, 'I'll go and kill this mug now – and his brother – but you're coming with me.' And then I thought, 'Fuck it, I'm not going to bother any more. I've done what I've done, I've stood on my own two feet, I've fronted all these bastards, so that's it.' I just wiped my mouth and she was out of my life. We had been together for 17 years, since I was 17 and she was 15. But when she started messing about, she severed something that could never be put back together again

With that part of my life over, I had to sort out where I was going to live. There was no going back to the House of Peacocks. The fire-bomb had caused £5,000 of damage, only part-covered by insurance. I did it up and sold it. In the meantime I had a bolt-hole. Thinking along the lines that you never know what's around the corner, I had always kept a flat in Hackney. It was in a council block called Pitcairn House. For years I had let my wife's brother live there with his wife. Now I told him to go. He didn't want to leave but Wag put him right. She said, 'Jimmy needs a roof over his head as much as you do', so out he went. And there I was, back in Hackney, where I started.

Wag and I talked things through with Denise and we agreed that she should keep living with Wag in Chingford and stay in school there, and at the weekends she could visit me in Pitcairn House. The flat was well secured. I had two locks on the door but at weekends I would only lock one of them, to which Denise had the key. She kept her pets there, some hamsters, gerbils and finches. I would feed them in the week and she would do it on Saturday and Sunday. At this time I was a concerned parent and it was partly because I was trying to be a good father that I found myself on the end of a fit-up which, I believe, was just the start of a long campaign against me by Scotland Yard and its gangster pals.

One night in 1966 I was standing outside the Dalston Odeon, looking at the stills of the main feature, trying to decide if it was suitable for my daughter. I had nowhere else to take her at weekends. I remember the film. It was *Arabesque*, a thriller starring Gregory Peck and Sophia Loren, so this wasn't an easy decision, but eventually I thought, 'Yes, it's OK for Denise.'

All this time my Jaguar was parked outside the main door, with a fellow called Alan Hobbins in the passenger seat. Alan was working with me in a building and saw-mill business that I had set up in Lea Bridge Road. He was a good-looking boy, he looked younger than he was, which is why he had the nickname Baby Face Alan. When I came back to the Jaguar, Alan said, 'Jim, see those blokes in that car over there, watching us. I think they're police, plainclothes'. I said, 'You think so? I'll tell you if it's them or not. Let's have a look. Follow me.' We walked up behind the car, a grey Rover, and I dropped my keys at the rear end, deliberately, so I could look on the exhaust pipe and see if it had a supersonic spray on it. In those days police cars had a flexible hose running from the back tailpipe. This delivered a supersonic spray, which blew back through the exhaust to give the cars an extra boost. So I took a look up this one and I said, 'Yeah, you're right. They're coppers.' But coppers I had never seen before.

We walked to the corner, we got in the Jaguar, and the next thing I know, they've cut us up, they've stopped us. They told us they were arresting us on suspicion and took us to Dalston police station, along with the Jaguar. They kept us in there overnight, slinging me in one cell and Alan in another. I was lying on a bunk in a cell in the early hours of the morning when in came a detective. He wasn't one of the arresting officers. He had a check jacket on. He looked down at me, I looked up and I said, 'I ain't done fuck all, I ain't done anything.' And he smiled and said, 'We know that, but we'll find something for you.' So now they were building up a case against me and Alan Hobbins.

The following morning the detective inspector told me, 'We're going to search your home.' I couldn't stop them because they had taken my keys, but why they wanted to search my home I didn't know. Now I had to tell them about the keys. I said that there were two locks and I stressed, 'Please do me favour, please do not lock the bottom lock. I leave that unlocked so my daughter, who has the key to the top lock only, can feed her hamsters and finches. If she doesn't get in to feed them while I'm in here, they'll die.' See, I was thinking about my kid. She'd already had a fire-bomb thrown through her bedroom window, She was a little girl who had done no harm to anybody, least of all these police.

OK. They seemed to be listening and they agreed to do this. Then they searched my home. Meanwhile they put Hobbins and me up before a magistrate and we're charged with conspiring to rob the Dalston Odeon. Imagine: I was only there trying to decide whether to let my daughter see a film. On the basis of what the police told him, the magistrate refused us bail. We got it ten days later. I think Wag and Denise collected me from the nick. We went straight to my home, only to find that the police had locked both locks, so no one else could get in, not even Denise. At this point I told Wag, 'Don't let Denise come in with me, I'll go in on my own.'

When I went in I saw that they had pulled everything off the walls, they had thrown papers all over the place, they had shat in my toilet, stuck a bunch of flowers down it, they hadn't flushed it and they'd stunk the flat out because there were no windows you could open, only air vents. All the plants were dead, because they couldn't be watered. And all my little girl's pets were dead: the little birds in the cage, the hamsters, the gerbils. Everything, was dead.

This is what the public don't know about. This is something that they would not imagine the police can do. These are your upright pillars of society. Yes, I was a villain but I had my civil rights like everyone else. They were abused and so were my daughter's.

When we go to trial – and they've put me back in Number One Court at the Old Bailey just for this minor charge – we're confronted by the biggest amount of fiction I had ever heard. For a start the police didn't say they had arrested us outside the cinema. They said that we had legged it – run away on foot – and they'd had to chase us for miles. Even though they were in that souped-up supersprayed Rover, they still had to drive for ten minutes before they caught us. So our defence had measured all the distances and my counsel, John Lloyd-Eley again, proved that this was rubbish. If that was so, they would have caught us in seconds, not minutes.

Then they said that there was a third man in this conspiracy, some giant they'd had a terrible fight with in the middle of Kingsland Road. So John Lloyd-Eley said, 'Where are all your witnesses?' and they said, 'Well we haven't got any.' A terrible fight with a third man? In the middle of the rush hour, in an arterial road with lots of buses going by? And they haven't got even one witness?

The prize exhibit was what they said was a huge mallet that we were going to smash on the head of the middle-aged cinema manager, before robbing him . And then the judge – a Freemason called Edward Clarke – picked up this mallet and started waving it around his head, as if to tell the jury how evil I was to conceive such a scheme. But where had they got this mallet from? From the tool-kit in the boot of my car. It came with my beautiful 3.8 silver-blue Jaguar. This had stainless steel wire wheels and you needed this so-called mallet, which was in fact a fibre hammer, to knock off the wing nut so you could change or repair the tyre. I had to get a senior Jaguar representative all the way from Coventry to testify that the hammer was part of the tool-kit in all new Jaguars, to counter the judge's performance.

Another thing they found in the boot was a sheet of gauze. The police had cut this into three pieces and claimed we were going to use these as masks. The prosecuting barrister, who had a huge head, told me to stick one of these cut-outs on my face, so I did but it fell off. He told me to do it again but it was so big it wouldn't stay on. When he told me a third time and it fell off again, I said, 'Well, it may fit your fucking big head, but it won't fit mine!'

I don't know where these ideas came from, but without them the police had no case. When they arrested us I didn't have the hammer in my hand, it was still in the boot where it belonged. I had no mask or gloves on and neither did Alan. All they had was me looking at the photos outside the cinema, like any other responsible parent might have done. Luckily for us, the jury saw through all this rubbish and found us not guilty. At least the police hadn't picked the jury.

Free again, I was standing on the steps of the Old Bailey when out came some of the jurors. I went over and said, 'I'd like to thank you for finding us not guilty. Without you, I would have got ten years over absolutely nothing.' They went, 'Don't thank us, mate. We knew you were innocent from the first day of the trial.'

But the police hadn't finished with me. On my car key-ring they had found an empty .45 cartridge. They had whipped that up into another crime, so now I faced an immediate second trial with a new jury before this same Judge Clarke. My defence was that the empty cartridge was an ornament, which I had made myself. I had boxes of these cartridges. I used to drill holes in them and empty out the explosive, then put a ring in them and give them to my pals. They were a little symbol of mine. I had even given one to my solicitor, Jimmy Fellowes. During the case he held it up and said he kept his car keys on it too. Judge Clarke went mad and said, 'You put that away, Mr Fellowes, or you'll be standing in the dock as well.'

The police claimed they had done forensic tests which proved that the primer was still active and it could blind somebody. This was such rubbish that I told the judge, 'If you're going to do me for that, you'd better get that torpedo they use as a collecting box out of Waterloo Station.' My protest did me no good. I was convicted. Clarke sentenced me to six months in prison or a £200 fine with no time to pay. That was a lot of money but I paid it straight away. The police had won a tiny victory but what a waste of tax-payers' money. Some weeks later I got a call telling me to come and take my car. This beautiful Jaguar was in a dreadful state. The seats had been ripped out and all the tyres were punctured. So I asked this copper, 'Is it in your way?' He said, 'Yes', so I said, 'Well you keep it. I don't want it now your people have been all over it.'

By now it was dawning on me that I was being framed: not just by the local CID trying to get a scalp but by some central command. How else could I explain the effort they'd put into creating this case against me. What finally made it click together was a conversation I had with John Lloyd-Eley. He had a very serious look on his face and he said, 'Jimmy, please take my advice. Sell up, get rid of everything you've got, and go as far away from this country as possible.' I said, 'Why should I do that? I'm not running away from anybody.' He said, 'Because we do not know what Freddie Foreman has had his friend, Tom Butler, put on your criminal record.'

When Lloyd-Eley talked about my criminal record he didn't mean a simple chart of my charges, convictions and sentences. He meant the full-blooded intelligence record that the police maintain on all professional criminals. Each file contains frank and often unprovable comments from detectives about the villain in question. These may be based on a kind of fact, like saying, this person was seen in this pub with another named criminal. Or they may be mere conjecture, like saying, I know this person is Jack the Stripper – or he was on the Great Train Robbery or he killed Ginger Marks – only we can't prove it. All these comments are kept in the files – which back in the 1960s were compiled in card index form – for the benefit of any other officers who might have an interest in these characters later on.

Nowadays if officers want to inspect a suspect's criminal intelligence file they must log their name and explain why they need to see it, but in the 1960s the system was still dangerously informal. As everything else about Scotland Yard was bent, I'm sure that any villain with money or connections could have got anything written on my record. It's also possible that John Lloyd-Eley had already seen my record himself. Barristers often see material that solicitors aren't allowed to see, on the strict rule that they don't disclose its contents to anyone else. In this Dalston Odeon case Judge Clarke might have seen it too, before he waved that mallet at the jury or when he sentenced me for that piffling key-ring offence. Also Lloyd-Eley used to prosecute, as well as defend. He would become a QC in 1970 and later a part-time judge. Such a trusted man might have seen lots of stuff on me that he couldn't tell me about. After defending me in the George Foreman case, he might well have had my record thrust in his face in an effort to dissuade him from representing me again.

This was the first time I had ever heard anything about Foreman having such power over Butler that he could have got him to join his vendetta against me. Yes, Tommy Marks had told me what Dukey Osbourne said about Foreman, Butler and the train robbers. And I knew from people like Buster Seeger that they had other coppers working for them. But I hadn't realised that Butler could frame me, anywhere in London, at Foreman's request. And this time my source wasn't a villain, he was a member of the 'Establishment'. Whatever Lloyd-Eley knew, he must have had very strong reasons for telling me to leave the country straight away.

It was about this time also, I believe, that George Foreman's wife got rid of him, and he moved in with my soon-to-be ex-wife, but I didn't care. When she didn't show up the night Denise and I waited for her in the fog, in my mind she was dead. Now it was easier for Dave Norman's wife Ann to tell me what she had heard from her about all the friends the Foremans had in the police. So now I had a lot more pieces for the jigsaw. The truth had hit me at last: Butler must have written something so terrible on my record that every police station in London, every CID unit, believed I was some kind of Public Enemy Number One. Did Butler write that I had killed and disposed of Tommy Marks, rather than his own informant and lunch pal Freddie Foreman? Or that I was Jack the Stripper? Whatever he had put on my file, it was giving me a hell of a hard time.

After I was found not guilty on the Dalston Odeon charge, I tried to get redress through my local MP whose surname, coincidentally, was Butler. I made an appointment but he still kept me waiting for three hours, and even then he wouldn't let me speak. He said, 'I know what you've come to see me about and I'm not interested. I know what you're going to say but I can't help you in any way. I can't do anything about it. Goodbye.' And that was that. That's how far these people would go when they wanted to give somebody hassle and aggravation. The police had even got to my MP.

But, as the old saying goes, you never know what's just around the next corner. In the last 18 months I had been through a lot of troubles – a marriage destroyed, a close pal murdered and me shot, a spell in jail, four trials (two of which could have got me ten years) and a newspaper branding me a serial sex killer – but I had survived. And as I've always said, anything that's ever happened to me in my life has happened for the best – even that bolt from the blue with Foreman and my ex-wife. If that hadn't happened I would never have moved back to Hackney. And if I hadn't moved back to Hackney, I wouldn't have been driving past Victoria Park in my builder's van and seen this lovely young woman pushing a pram.

As soon as I saw her, I thought, 'What a beautiful face – and the best pair of legs I've ever seen in my life.' God made us all different, men and women. Some have faces like angels, other have faces like anvils. This one had a face like an angel. In Hackney, of all places. She was like a rose among the thorns, an orchid in an allotment field. I was smitten.

I could swing in those days. Remember what the *South London Press* had said about me – 'tall, handsome and good-looking'. I could pull, do you know what I mean? If I wanted it, I could pull it. But if I hadn't stopped and got into conversation with this young woman, she would not have become my present wife. At the time Annick was just 22. That was ten years younger than my ex-wife. She was French. And what a change: chalk and fromage! And here's another twist too good for fiction, her father was a judge. Today Annick and I have been together for 35 years. Through all the fiascos, through all Foreman's mischief with his bent coppers, we have survived. Not one regret.

When we met, Annick was living in Hackney because she had married an Englishman and they had set up home there. She now had an eight-month-old daughter, Geraldine, but that marriage was over and when I met her she was in the process of getting a divorce. So was I. And now I had just walked free from the Dalston Odeon fit-up, I thought I could get to know Annick rather than the walls of some prison cell.

I wasn't spared for long.

THE SURVIVOR

FIFTEEN

The Robbery That Never Was

ONE evening in May 1967 I walked into the Eden Roc Club, in Leicester Square, owned by my then partner Joe Wilkins. I was sitting with his brother John and a few other people when suddenly Joe ran through the club into the basement. Then a stream of men chased through after him so I ran down to see what was going on. One of these blokes pointed at me and told another, 'That's him, isn't it?' The second bloke looked down into the floor and nodded a yes but he never looked at me. I found out later that his name was Bannan and the man who had fingered me was George Chandler, a detective inspector. Chandler arrested me, took me to Bow Street and charged me with armed robbery with violence. Here we go again, I thought.

A little while later they brought in a pal called Lofty Mason. Lofty was six foot five and 18-and-a-half-stone. I had first met him on the ships in 1952 but I only got to know him again in 1965 when I was running my building and saw-mill business in Lea Bridge Road. At that time we were installing a bar in Winston's Club. I happened to run into Lofty and I said, 'Why don't you come up and work with us?' So he packed in his job as a window-cleaner and started working at Winston's and at other clubs run by Joe Wilkins, including the Eden Roc. This particular night Lofty had only come into the Eden Roc because he was driving past and saw a load of police outside. He stopped and went in. He was immediately arrested, taken to Bow Street and charged with the same offence as me. We were both kept in the cells overnight and in the morning we were hauled before the Bow Street magistrate next door and charged with a lot more offences. I still had no idea what this was all about but now Lofty explained that one night the previous week there had been some trouble in the Eden Roc with this bloke Bannan. Since then Bannan and the CID had come up with a story that when he was in the club he had been stabbed, his throat and wrist had been slashed, his false teeth had been knocked out and his watch had been stolen. I wasn't there that night – I was with Annick – but this fact didn't stand in their way.

After hearing this violent saga, the magistrate packed us straight off to Brixton prison where Lofty told me what had really happened. He said that around 11 that night he had been minding the Eden Roc, sitting in the office watching the TV, when in came three blokes. They called over some hostesses – it was that kind of club – they ordered a lot of brandy, got pretty well drunk and ran up quite a bill. Two of the blokes ran out without paying, leaving Bannan to pick up the entire tab. Then Bannan tried to do a runner but he was very drunk. He ran through some curtains, fell over down some stairs and the doorman brought him back.

Lofty then took him into the waiters' room where, with the club manager, he asked Bannan about this unpaid bill of around £42. 'My friends will pay,' he said. 'But they've gone,' said Lofty. And the manager said, 'If you can't pay it with cash, do you have a cheque?' 'Yes, I'll pay by cheque,' said Bannan. It turned out that he had no cheques on him so the manager gave him a club cheque to sign, with the normal requirement that Bannan put his personal bank details on it. Someone was just going off to check these details when suddenly up piped Bannan, 'No, I've written a false address.' So then, with Bannan's agreement, Lofty took his watch in lieu of payment. The watch was given a ticket with his name on and it was lodged in the club safe. Bannan was given a receipt and a copy was also put in the safe. Bannan was told that when he came back to settle the bill he would get his watch back. And out he went into the night.

A short while later a constable found Bannan, sick and distressed, on the street. He was taken to Charing Cross Hospital, claiming he had been beaten up, stabbed and robbed of his watch. He gave the police a statement, describing the man who knifed him and took his watch as six foot three inches and 17-and-a-half-stone. This was supposed to be me. I was the one he picked out without even looking one week later. If he had taken one look, he would have seen that I am not six foot three and I did not weigh 17-and-a-half-stone. I am no more than five foot ten and at that time I weighed 11 stone. So five inches shorter and six stone lighter.

Lofty was also charged with stealing the watch, along with taking £5 off Bannan, stabbing him in the throat and stealing his false teeth, which I was accused of hitting with a steak mallet. Let's cut to the trial itself and start with those false teeth. A state-registered nurse, on duty that night, appeared for the prosecution but testified that when Bannan turned up she gave him a basin to be sick in. In among his vomit were his false teeth. So they hadn't been stolen by Lofty or smashed by me. He'd spewed them out in hospital.

As for his claim that Lofty had stabbed him in the throat, the hospital doctor said he had no stab wounds anywhere. Nor had the doctor or the nurse stitched any other wounds because he did not have any. All he needed was a plaster on the wrist to cover a graze he inflicted on himself when he fell down the stairs as he ran away, which the doorman confirmed. Then there was the lock-knife that Inspector Chandler had produced at four in the morning in Bow Street, after the raid on Lofty's home. 'Seen that before?' asked Chandler. Lofty said, 'Yes, it's my son's.' This was true – it was a present from a pal of Lofty's who stupidly thought it was suitable for a six-year-old – and in court Lofty came back, 'I'm 18-and-a-half stone and six foot five. What would I need a knife for? I just brought him in, he was drunk, he was sick all over the place and he fell downstairs.'

The nurse said Bannan had nothing wrong, only a few scratches on his wrists. These were consistent with him getting disorderly with a hostess who testified that he had been pawing her. She didn't like it and she might have scratched him with her nails as she resisted his approaches. The nurse said: 'I don't know why he was brought in. We were busy that night.'

As for his claim that I had cut him up, not only did he bear no stab wounds, I was those five inches shorter and six stones lighter than his alleged attacker. And I could prove I wasn't there. Annick came and testified that I was with her that night. She told the court, 'My father was a judge and I'm not here to tell lies. We were together that night.' Even Lofty said I wasn't there, though he admitted being there himself.

The watch was produced in court with the proof that it had been kept in the safe for him to collect if and when he settled the bill. We had the receipt and Lofty had even kept the cheque which Bannan had signed before he admitted giving false bank details. That signature matched the signature on his police statements, a fact which should have told the jury that his statements could not be relied on. If he had lied on the cheque – and the proof was incontrovertible – why believe what he told the police or the court? And how could anyone believe I had stolen his watch when it had never been stolen?

And that £5 which Bannan said Lofty had stolen? That was all Bannan had in his pocket to settle the £42 bill. If anyone was thieving from anybody, it was Bannan for not paying the remaining £37, not Lofty for taking that fiver. He never did pay that bill. Nor did his two companions whom the police never produced or even identified, as far as we could discover.

On Thursday, 6 July 1967, when all the evidence had been heard, Judge John Maude gave us both bail. He told us that in the evening he was having a 'jolly-up' with his friend, Sir Francis Chichester, the round-the-world yachtsman who was being knighted on Friday. Maude would not be sitting that day 'and there is no reason why these two gentlemen should suffer', he said, so he added it to our weekend off and said he would see us on Monday, when he would send out the jury to consider their verdicts. As we had been locked up in Brixton ever since our arrest, we took this to mean he thought the case was so weak we would be acquitted. The police were upset but he stuck to his decision.

When we came back on the Monday, the jury spent three hours discussing the case and then found us both guilty. Maude seemed shocked. He kind of apologised by saying to both me and Lofty, 'Unfortunately, you have been found guilty of armed robbery with violence, so I have no alternative but to give you a custodial sentence. But I'm going to give you the minimum of 12 months for robbery while armed, and three months for grievous bodily harm, to be served concurrently. And I urge you to appeal immediately. I have no doubt that the Court of Appeal will seriously consider quashing the convictions.'

So I did appeal but it wasn't until I had almost served my time that I got a hearing. Then, far from throwing out the conviction, the judges talked of my 'audacity' in appealing when I had been given the minimum sentence. They said, 'If it was within our power we would make the sentence eight years.' I thought, 'Who cares about minimums? I'm not appealing against sentence. I'm appealing against conviction. If I'm innocent, why should I be grateful for a 12-month? If I've done nothing, I shouldn't go to jail at all.'

Annick was shocked that I was sent down for something I had not done. She had always believed that England had the best justice system in the world. How could it go this wrong? Anyhow, with the time we'd spent on remand and a little discount for good behaviour, Lofty and I were both let out on 2 February 1968.

So where does this fit in with my belief that I was the target of a vendetta by you-know-who?

Again a lot of time, effort and tax-payers' money was invested in this job, and the shadow of Tom Butler wasn't far away. As soon as I was arrested I thought, 'This is Dalston Odeon 2' They hadn't locked me away on Dalston

Odeon 1, so they had to try again. I had not followed John Lloyd-Eley's stern warning to leave the country over what Freddie Foreman had got Butler to put on my criminal record, because I did not believe even Foreman could sink so low, but I had taken a close look at any photos of Butler in the newspapers. There had been a lot of them that year because he'd arrested several more Great Train Robbers, such as Jimmy White and Buster Edwards, so I knew what he looked like. With his huge Mr Punch nose, no one could miss him.

The morning after we were arrested at the Eden Roc Club and stuck in Bow Street overnight, we were being put in a van bound for Brixton in the station yard. I happened to look up and who should I see looking down at me from an upstairs window but Tommy Butler himself! It was definitely him – the nose, the eyes, the balding head. As Lofty Mason remembers, all of a sudden I pulled myself up on to the roof of the van and shouted, 'Butler, you bastard! Another fit-up!'

They hauled me down from the van and off we went to Brixton, but Butler's presence there only confirmed what Lloyd-Eley had told me. And during our trial he loomed up again. It had started in the Old Bailey but after a few days they needed our court for something else. There was too much going on at the Bailey – the so-called torture trial of Charlie Richardson and his associates was over-running – so we were shifted to the Guildhall. One day I looked round the courtroom and I saw Tommy Butler sitting there. He was watching my trial. This silly case about a drunk and his watch in a nightclub. Hardly the trial of the century. I wasn't the only one who was surprised to see Butler. The officers running this case were surprised too. Even the beat PCs who had found Bannan drunk on the street were saying, 'What's Butler doing here? Why isn't he back at the Bailey at the Richardson trial?' He was spending all day with us when the trial of South London's biggest gangsters – as the press would have it – was the best show in town. It wasn't Butler's case, but neither was ours.

But did Butler have some indirect role in our case? Right up until the Great Train Robbery in August 1963, Butler had been the Chief Superintendent in charge of all detectives in the Metropolitan Police's Number One District. This covered the West End, Soho and the whole of West London. And when he became head of the Flying Squad soon after the train job, he could keep tabs on any gangland activity in London, including thuggery in West End clubs.

Chandler was an interesting character. Despite the fact that I bore no resemblance to the giant described by Bannan, he obviously convinced himself I was guilty and did his constabulary duty. A few years later he ran into trouble over the fact that he and his wife owned two houses, more than most coppers could achieve on their salaries at the time. One house was registered in his wife's name and they had let it out to a Soho pornographer. When this arrangement leaked out, it was great news for the tabloid press but bad news for Chandler, especially as the year was 1974 when the Met's new Commissioner, Sir Robert Mark, was leading a war against corruption in Scotland Yard's specialist detective squads. Chandler was suspended during a huge vice probe and his finances were investigated. He was transferred from plainclothes CID work in the West End to lighter duties in uniform in the 'sticks' – the outer suburb of Kingston – while he underwent three operations for an ulcer, which he put down to stress.

Chandler told the *Sunday Mirror* that a few years earlier, when he had been investigating the dirty book trade, he had arrested a pornographer and got him jailed for three months: 'He thought I had been fair to him, despite having done my duty. He was grateful in the way criminals sometimes are. When I was in poor health and off work with my ulcer this man was kind to me. The opportunity came to let our other house to this man's wife. It was a straight tenancy deal which did not breach police regulations. I have never taken bribes, I have never taken holidays with criminals, I have given my heart and soul to police work. My record over the years speaks for itself.' The following year Chandler retired early from the Metropolitan Police. Twenty-six years later he is still drawing a pension.

For a copper to have a convicted pornographer living in a house owned by his wife didn't look good in the years when a dozen Yard detectives were sent to jail for taking bribes from pornographers.

When I came out of jail in February 1968, I had to get back on my feet and dedicate some time to my daughter and also to Annick who by that time was my wife, though we were not yet formally married. I needed to settle down, sort myself out and take a break. We bought a caravan to take on holidays and life began to look sweet again. I was hoping for a clear run.

Then things took a turn for Reggie, Ronnie and Charlie Kray and also for me.

SIXTEEN

The Cyanide Briefcase

ON 7 May 1968, at six in the morning, Ronnie and Reggie Kray were arrested by Detective Superintendent Nipper Read and his squad over the murder of Jack 'the Hat' McVitie. A lot of other people were picked up, although not Freddie Foreman who had played the key role of 'disappearing' McVitie's body. His turn would come in October.

Just two days before these arrests, Reggie Kray and I fell out in Winston's when he tried to introduce me to that detective from West End Central. Now Reggie was in West End Central himself, in the cells waiting to be charged.

I had never been involved in any heavy matters with the Krays – no murders, GBHs or frauds – so their arrests didn't immediately affect me. I had come out of jail myself only three months earlier, I was having a kind of honeymoon spell with Annick, I had a nice lump of money put away and I was feeling pretty good.

All of a sudden I was hearing, 'Nipper Read wants to see you', 'Nipper Read's making enquiries', 'Nipper Read's been round the house'. This changed things. I didn't want to be caught up in his war with the Krays. I'd had enough aggravation from the police, I didn't want him on my back as well. And when I heard rumours that Read had got hold of the barmaid at the Blind Beggar (where Ronnie shot George Cornell in March 1966) and she was going to testify, I decided Annick and I should go abroad. I'd just done a real armed robbery and with that cash I figured we could stay away for at least six months. By then Read should have dealt with the Krays or given up. But for now I had to go.

We went to France, moved on, Italy, moved on, Switzerland, Germany, Austria. We were all over Europe. We had a nice time but we'd spent all the cash. The six months had passed, I'm still on the missing list and yet the big Kray trial still hasn't started. Every day I'm phoning up and good pals are telling me, 'Don't come back yet, not yet, they've been round, they're still making enquiries, Read's team. They've got to see you. They want to talk to you.'

I'm thinking 'Why should Read be any different from the rest of these Scotland Yard slags?' When you've been fitted up you trust them less and less, until you automatically think, 'Fuck me, it's another fit-up.' Eventually I phoned up my solicitor, Jimmy Fellowes – his number was engraved on my mind – and he said, 'Come back. You'll have to see Read. I don't know what he wants to talk to you about but don't worry, we'll be there with you.'

So I arranged with Fellowes to come back, but because I thought Read might snatch me, I didn't tell anyone how I'd be coming back. And when I was back, I kept out of sight until Fellowes fixed a meeting in his offices in Walthamstow between me and Read. I knew Read would come along four-handed so I told Fellowes, whom I could confide in, 'Jimmy, I'll climb over that ten-foot wall at the back of your offices at eight in the morning, so make sure someone's there to let me in.' So I did climb over and I sat in his back office from eight until they turned up just after ten. I was right! They had been sitting out the front for a long time, waiting for me to pull up. When Nipper Read saw me, he had a strange look on his face and he said, 'How did you get in here?'

I laughed and said, 'I've got my own key.'

So he said, 'Now look. My superiors told me that I would be wasting my time with you, but I've got to speak to anyone and everyone who's ever had anything at all to do with the Krays.'

So I said, 'Well, you've got the bird behind the counter now at the Beggar. Ain't you got enough?'

He said, 'We've got enough to get them 100 years.'

I said, 'Well, what have you been driving me fucking mad for? It's cost me a fortune keeping out of the way. I don't know anything, and even if I did, I wouldn't be able to help you people.'

He said, 'What's your sentiments on the Krays?'

I said, 'They aren't my type of people, they wouldn't come and do the things I can do, and I wouldn't do the things they do. But one thing we do have in common: they don't like you fucking people any more than I do. Because I've been framed and framed time and again by the law.'

He said, 'That's just where you're wrong. You've got no idea of the amount of damage the Krays have done to other people.'

I said, 'I know your game. You'll discredit them to me just like you'll discredit me to other people. That's how you people act.'

He said, 'No, I don't care to do that because we've got them, but I had you on the list and I have to speak to you.'

I said, 'If you're like some of your colleagues, when I walk out of here, you're going to be waiting for me and you're going to fit me up again, because, as far as I can see, you are all one parcel.'

He said, 'No, it's not my game. If you don't feel you can help me now, you'll never hear from me any more. Not unless I have a reason to come and see you.' Then he said, 'Oh by the way, have a look at that', and he threw a light-brown briefcase on my lap and said, 'Open it!'

Somehow I had already heard about this briefcase so I said, 'No, no. I've read that comic.'

But Read insisted and he said, 'That was made to kill you with, on the orders of the Twins on behalf of Freddie Foreman. And you don't want to help us with them! They had someone make it so it could be used to kill you.' As I was still refusing to open it, he went into the briefcase and demonstrated a syringe device which was meant to spring out and inject me with cyanide. Then he pulled out a group photograph that had been taken at Winston's one night when I was there. It was a familiar line-up – Reggie Kray, Albert Donoghue and other so-called 'faces' – but in the top right-hand corner one face had been cut out: mine! Then Read said, 'They gave your picture to the man who was going to kill you with this briefcase, so he knew what you looked like. Now won't you help us?'

'Well,' I said, 'this is all very interesting, but I don't know anything about the case or the photo. And I can't help you with the Twins.'

So he said, 'Yes, my superiors said I'd be wasting my time with you and they were right.' And off he went.

Nipper Read was straight with me. He was one copper who never tried to abuse my civil liberties. He carried on with his job, he did the Krays but he left me alone. I never heard any more from him.

But what about this briefcase? Obviously I was interested but it was only later that I found out the strength of what Read had told me. While Annick and I were abroad, in July 1968, there had been a committal hearing at Bow

Street about this thing and a plot to kill someone else with a gun or a crossbow or by putting gelignite in his car. That sounded so ridiculous that Reggie Kray leapt up and asked the magistrate, 'Excuse me, sir, is James Bond going to give evidence?' As for the cyanide briefcase plot, my name was not mentioned but as I read through the case papers now I see that the intended victim was definitely me.

The main witness to this plot was an American called Alan Bruce Cooper who had got tied in quite late with the Krays and may have been an FBI agent provocateur. He told the court that in September or October 1966 Charlie Kray had taken him to meet Reggie and Ronnie in the Crown and Anchor at Whitechapel. 'They asked if I could arrange for one of my friends to knock somebody off' but 'nothing was said as to who was to be knocked off or how', only that 'it should not be done in a normal manner with a gun or a knife or anything that could be put down to the Kray firm. The fee for killing the man would be £1,000.' Later Cooper said he was told to go to Winston's nightclub off Bond Street to be shown his target. Then he had a meeting in the White House hotel with two people, a Scotsman called Paul Elvey and Squire Waterman, who brought the case along and showed him how it worked. In the court Cooper repeated the demonstration. 'The hypodermic was to be filled up with a poison [hydrogen cyanide], placed in two clips; a needle pointed out through a hole in the bottom of the end of the case. Two springs were placed on the hypodermic; a plug with a sort of safety pin was put in the top of the springs to retain them in their stretched-out position. The safety pin was attached to a piece of cord which protruded at the top end of the case, underneath the handle. There is a ring on the end of the cord. When the ring was pulled and the pin came out, the springs were released, the hypodermic was plunged, the stuff came out of the needle.' Into the leg of the victim, that is.

Cooper testified that he and Elvey showed the case to Reggie Kray and Tommy Cowley (Reggie's driver, who was with him in Winston's the night we had that row). 'They seemed quite impressed,' said Cooper. Next, 'very late one night', he was called down to Winston's, where Cowley 'pointed out the intended victim'. He was told his name but couldn't remember it now. 'Cowley said the man was a "minder" at the club and was there frequently. He said something about him being on bail; his case was coming up at the Old Bailey and this was a very good place to find him as he would have to report there every day for the trial.' Cooper then went to the Bailey with Elvey, who was going to do the killing. He 'showed

Elvey the man as he came into the court'. They went twice 'but on neither occasion was any attack carried out. I later told the Twins what Elvey had told me, which was, that it was impossible to do it there as there were too many people, plus too many policemen around the court. Their remark was to leave it out for the moment and that is what happened. I did nothing further about it.'

It all fits together: Winston's, the role played by Cowley, an Old Bailey trial. It had to be me because I did have a trial there in the middle of 1967: the one about Bannan's watch and the 400. At least it started at the Bailey and then shifted to the Guildhall. But I never got bail while it was at the Bailey. That may be why the attack never took place: they saw me in court but I was brought in from Brixton prison, so they had no chance of doing me on the steps or in the street.

The cyanide briefcase charge against the Krays – 'conspiracy to murder an unknown person at the Old Bailey in 1967' – never came to trial. The Bow Street magistrate threw it out, saying, 'I have gone through the evidence with a fine-tooth comb. To me it is so confused and too slim to commit before a jury.' But why would the Krays have wanted me dead? We had no quarrel, just the odd argument. The truth came out in 1995 in Albert Donoghue's book, *The Krays' Lieutenant*. In one chapter he reveals how the Krays plotted to have me killed, but not on their own behalf. He says they were only doing Freddie Foreman a favour. This favour would have become a stark obligation after 23 December 1966 when Foreman killed Frank 'Mad Axeman' Mitchell for the Krays. He got £1,000 for his troubles but they would require his services in the future (to dispose of Jack 'the Hat' McVitie). As Donoghue explains, 'After Mitchell's murder, Ronnie and Reggie met Freddie more often, in his pub or in our East End joints or in various West End clubs. I was at several of these meetings when Jim Evans was discussed, and the Twins offered to do him on our territory.'

Donoghue goes on to explain how Ronnie then gave Alan Bruce Cooper 'the contract to kill Jim Evans'. He also confirms what Read had told me about how I was to be identified. 'So to get his face on a photo – hear this for an act of treachery – me and Reggie went to Winston's club one evening when we knew Evans was going to be there so we got a picture taken showing Jim Evans alongside me, Reggie Kray and an MP called Reader Harris, all chums together. This photo not only gave us Evans' face so the hit-man could identify him but it would also come in handy if the police moved against us after Evans died, because it would show we were such good friends with him.'

After they failed to kill me with the briefcase at the Old Bailey, they tried again at Winston's. When that failed, they gave up on the briefcase and switched to sending Donoghue off to Hackney Town Hall to check the voters' lists to find out where I lived, then Alan Bruce Cooper was going to shoot me as I opened the door. Sounds familiar. But this never happened. 'Nothing Mr ABC did for the Krays ever worked,' says Donoghue, but he adds that the Krays were still helping Foreman to kill me when I had that row with Reggie in Winston's.

'The plot to kill Jim Evans was never called off. We were still meant to be looking for him right till the end. In the first few days of May Ronnie Kray gave me a piece of paper with a car number on it: TVX 482E. He said, "Take that over to Freddie, tell him that's Evans' car. It's a white Zephyr or Zodiac. He'll be able to check it through a car dealer." '

Donoghue never delivered that piece of paper because the Krays were arrested a couple of days later. I'm sure he's telling the truth – it all fits into the jigsaw – but I think that the Krays were leading Foreman on. I don't think they were ever serious about killing me. If they had been, they could have killed me many times over.

For instance, after I'd shot George Foreman, Charlie could have suckered me into a meet, but instead he warned me, 'Keep a low profile, Jim. They're looking for you four-handed.' So there was no loyalty there. Then Reggie could have done me the night the Foreman mob shot Tommy Marks and I went to their house in Vallance Road. If the Krays were such good friends of Fred's and they wanted to oblige him, why didn't they do me then? I was out the way. I had no gun. They could have gone boomf – just one shot – as I turned round or stabbed me in the eye. There was none of that. OK, the father was upstairs and maybe the old mum was asleep, but in their little dark scullery that night they never did to me what they did to Jack the Hat.

They could have got me to go to Winston's or any other place, on any pretext, and I would have gone and they could have killed me. Reggie used to ring me up and say, 'Gonna come up Winston's tonight? I want to talk to you about something' or 'Jim! You coming out tonight?' And I would say, 'Yeah, I'll be up there.' We would never give a time because it would always be just prior to midnight until the early hours. That's how they got me up there for that photo. But why bother to get me photographed when they could have shot me, there and then? Winston's was in a lovely dark turning, just off Bond Street with lots of cars parked up so I would have suspected nothing. I'd have left the club to walk to my car. They could've gone bosh,

bosh, and driven off. Why say, 'Fred, we got a photo, we've got someone who's going to do him', when they only had to say, 'He's going to be there tonight', then Fred could ceremonially execute me in front of the entire Kray gang? Then he would have made a real name for himself.

Once I had a meet with Reggie at Winston's and he told me they had a scheme to do business with people running a long firm fraud from a warehouse in Mile End Road. Maybe the Krays wanted to extort a share of the profits. Then he said, 'Jim, I wonder if you could do me a favour. When we went round, these people said that you're minding them, you're getting a bit of dough out of them already.'

I went mad. I said, 'I don't mind anyone, only myself. I don't blag anybody and I don't like people sticking my fucking name up. I'll tell you what I'll do, Reg. I'll come down there with you tomorrow and I'll say, "Look! You've got nothing to do with me. I don't even know you, you're not giving me any fucking money. What are you sticking my name up for?" And I'll bosh them.'

'No', he said, trying to calm me. 'No, it's all right, Jimmy. I only wanted to know. As long as we know, Jim, we know what to do.'

He had to argue me out of going there, but if he had wanted to do Foreman a favour, he would have encouraged me to go there. What more could he have done for Foreman than say, 'I've got Evans coming to the warehouse tomorrow. Come over yourself. You and your mob can do him there'? And I'd have gone over and he could have been waiting in the warehouse. Sure, I would have been tooled up – I never went anywhere without a gun, especially after what happened to Tommy Marks – but I wouldn't have suspected an ambush, because I never had distrust in Reggie. But on this occasion I had such a temper, I'd have gone in there to have a row, not expecting any scumbags. It would have been easy. Boom! Boom! A couple of .22s in my nut. Next stop, Foreman's crematorium.

So, if any of the Krays really wanted to oblige him, they could have delivered me up any time with a ribbon tied round me, but Reggie never showed any interest in setting me up. They were just kidding Foreman: pretending to show willing but never really doing anything. It might have intrigued Ronnie to put Alan Bruce Cooper and his little team of assassins to the test with that cyanide briefcase, but not to help Foreman.

Around this time I heard Foreman himself was trying to do something similar. One day I was in a car with a bloke called Green, who had previously worked with Charlie Richardson. And Green said, 'A while back Freddie Foreman and his little mob wanted me to get you in my shop in Crystal

Palace, so they could be waiting in the back room. Foreman told me to get you in there on some pretext.'

I said, 'So what did you tell him?'

He said, 'I told him, no.'

I said, 'You should have told him, yes, then told me, and I'd have got there a bit earlier, and done to them what they were planning to do to me.'

Even all that stuff about getting Donoghue to run around checking the voters' lists for my address, that was just to kid Foreman they were doing something. The same goes for that car number, which was correct. I still have a photo of that car with the number on it. But Foreman didn't have to get my address through a car dealer. The Krays knew it already. They had my phone number and in those days it was easy to get operators to give you an address from a reverse directory: where numbers are listed first and addresses next. You could get it in two minutes. Foreman's own dear pal, Mickey Regan, knew my phone number and my address because I gave them to him when I told him to visit at home in Pitcairn House, Mare Street, Hackney. And the police knew it. They were always coming round to charge me over driving offences so Foreman could have got it through them.

According to his book, he 'tracked' me to a block of flats in Hackney, concealed himself on a flat roof overlooking the entrance and 'sat there night after night' with a rifle waiting for me to come home. This couldn't have been Pitcairn House because there was only a single-storey block of garages near its entrance. This had a flat roof but it was overlooked by Pitcairn House, so anyone lying there with a rifle would have been seen by dozens of residents in this eight-storey block as they looked over the walkways. You couldn't help looking over them. I was living on the top floor so I would have seen him myself. I was always looking out for creeps like him. He would have found it far easier to have hid in the bushes and shoot me as I parked in the street nearby. He says that one dawn he came face-to-face with me as he drove from the flats and I was driving back. 'It was him. And he got me in an instant. His eyes were everywhere. He was like a hunted animal. He knew he had escaped death by inches and it was only a matter of time before his luck ran out.' All bollocks. This never happened. He was never there. If he had been, he would have turned his car round and come after me. That's what I would have done. If he had been there, I would have shot him. But that's Freddie the Fib.

It was all a masquerade. He was putting these stories around: first he didn't know where I lived so could the Krays get my address; then when he'd got the address, he was lying on roofs with high-powered rifles. Either way, he didn't want the 'chaps' to think he hadn't done anything, because he's losing prestige and credibility all the time. Someone's shot his brother's bollocks off and he's doing nothing about it. So he's telling the Krays, 'But I am. I'm looking for him. Help me find him.' So they say, 'Yeah, we'll help you, Fred', but all the time they're telling themselves, 'Fuck you, Fred. We know where he is, but we ain't telling you. We don't want to get involved.'

But of course he was getting at me through his police connections. He's said that he had a 'working relationship' with Frank Williams and Tom Butler. If I had a working relationship with a top cop, one of the smallest favours he could perform is give me another villain's home address. Williams and Butler were visiting Foreman's poxy pub, doing deals over train robbery money and working out the deal for Buster Edwards – and probably smothering up Foreman's murders. So wouldn't it be the easiest thing for them to say, 'You want Evans's address? Yeah, we'll make a phone call, we'll get it for you now.' Then beep beep, here you are! He didn't need that masquerade with the Twins. After all, he was a copper himself.

But all these schemes to kill me, real or fake, fell away when the Krays were arrested in May 1968, then I went missing with Annick and Foreman himself waited helplessly as Read – one Yard man he didn't have on his payroll – closed in on him over the McVitie and Mitchell murders. In October he was charged over McVitie and packed off to Brixton, though a few months later he got bail when no other major player did. After a long trial alongside all three Krays, he was convicted and given ten years. Only then was he charged, with the Krays again, over Frank Mitchell. I should repeat that Mitchell was a very big, very strong, sometimes violent but simple man who had been sprung from Dartmoor prison because the Krays wanted him as muscle in a possible war with the Richardson gang. He was kept in hiding for 11 days but when he started issuing threats against the Krays, because they hadn't come to see him, they decided to have him killed. On 23 December 1966 he was told he was going to the country to spend Christmas with Ronnie, and put in a van containing the same team that had killed Tommy Marks: Freddie Foreman, Alf Gerard and a bloke called Callaghan. Foreman and Gerard then shot him point-blank and off he went to the crematorium or (if you believe Foreman) the English Channel.

The Mitchell trial started in April 1969. The strongest evidence came from two co-conspirators. One was Albert Donoghue who, on the night of the murder, led the excited Mitchell from the flat into the van where he was promptly killed. The other was Harry Hopwood who said that, earlier that day, Charlie Kray had used his flat for a meeting with Foreman. He described him as about 35, five foot eight or nine and stocky, and said he had overheard him talking about an incinerator to Charlie Kray. Hopwood was almost respectable – he had been best man at the Krays' parents' wedding – but he was still a tainted witness. So it was no great surprise that, when the trial ended a month later, Foreman was acquitted.

Foreman has now admitted killing Mitchell, as well as Marks, but in the trial he revealed a lot about his police connections. First he spun a ludicrous story that Donoghue was telling cruel vicious lies about him killing Mitchell because he had refused to pay Donoghue protection money. He claimed that Donoghue's partner in this racket was Ronnie Hart: the Krays' cousin who had testified against them and Foreman in the McVitie murder trial.

Foreman said that in 1967 he had met Donoghue's first request for £25. He refused a second demand for £50 but Donoghue bullied him into parting with £25 instead. But when Donoghue and Hart came back a few weeks later he refused to pay anything and told them, 'I don't want you in the pub, I want you to drink up and get out. Go on, get moving.' Confronted by only one other man, they 'shrugged their shoulders and made towards the door'. They never came back.

Under cross-examination, Foreman said of Donoghue, 'Not only was he nipping me, he said that if I needed anybody hurt, he would do that. I said, "I don't have any trouble in the pub. There is a police station across the road", and police officers frequent my public house and there is never any trouble – they can bear that out.'

Then the prosecutor asked, 'Did you go to the police about it?' He answered, 'I spoke to police officers who frequented my public house. Superintendent Frank Williams was a regular customer, and Thomas Butler, and I asked them to frequent my public house more regularly. I didn't want to be an informer and inform on people, but I liked their presence there.'

Foreman then said that around autumn 1967, 'during one evening when I was having a drink with Williams, I said I was expecting some trouble from certain people. I told him, "I don't want to mention who they are." He asked me, "Who was it?" and if I wanted anybody arrested or anything like that, or any charges made. I didn't. I can't do that sort of thing. It's more than I dare do. I didn't give him any names. As I told him, I am not a police informer, though I have friends in the police. I have friends in the criminal world.' Foreman said, 'The police and criminal world in London is like a village, and you get to hear things and whispers, and I was told that there was going to be a petrol bomb thrown in my house. I was going to get my legs blown off by Donoghue and Hart.' He admitted he had never told Williams about the bomb threat, he just asked him 'to come in a bit more often to keep these people away', and he did come in on a couple of weekends.

But when Foreman testified that this bomb was due to go off late at night, the prosecutor Kenneth Jones asked, 'What good would police officers having a drink in your pub during opening hours do about that?' And if Williams had been a 'fairly regular customer' for years, 'there would have been nothing fresh about seeing him having a drink in your public house'. Then Jones ridiculed the idea that seeing Williams would stop 'determined men' from pitching a bomb in his pub late at night, especially as Foreman had never told Williams he was expecting one.

Foreman retorted, 'I am not a police informer. I can put my head down when I go to sleep at night. I have nothing on my conscience. I don't know if you can sleep at night, Mr Jones, with the witnesses you have put before the court, telling lies.'

All this talk by a gangster like Foreman about being so close to a high-ranking Yard detective who even offered to arrest and charge people for him drove the Prosecution to drag the superintendent into court to rebut Foreman. When Frank Williams turned up, he testified that he had known Foreman for years and that during 1967 he was in the Prince of Wales 'once a week' or sometimes once every three weeks, but Foreman had never mentioned anything about expecting trouble and never asked him to show his face more often to deter troublemakers. Foreman's counsel tried to pick something from this wreckage, pressing Williams to admit the Prince of Wales was a well-run house but in a very rough area where there could be trouble. He also said that if a publican ran to the police, it certainly wouldn't help him with the clientele.

At the end of all that, Foreman was lucky to get off, you might think. Except that throughout his defence he had not only committed perjury, he had got a lot of other witnesses to lie too, in a vast conspiracy to mislead the jury into thinking he couldn't have murdered Frank Mitchell because that night he was visiting his wife in hospital. And his claim that Donoghue and Hart had tried to extort from him was a big lie too. As Donoghue says, if you were a member of the Kray gang, South London was 'Indian Country': you went there on pain of death. Besides, would anyone from anywhere dare try to extort the Underworld Undertaker?

At last Foreman's links with Williams – and Tom Butler too – had been given a public airing. Williams had been little help to Foreman in court, but behind the scenes he was working like crazy for Foreman, spurred on not only by bribes derived from some of the Great Train Robbers. He had also been doing Foreman a huge service over the Mitchell murder. Just at the time when Foreman claimed Donoghue was shaking him down, the *Sunday Mirror* had published the first convincing report that Mitchell was dead. The story, written by the highly reliable Norman Lucas, appeared on 29 October 1967 under the headline, 'Axeman May Have Been Murdered', and it confirmed rumours circulating since soon after Mitchell's escape that his minders may have killed him.

The story and the rumours were true but in Scotland Yard they were furiously denied. According to Yard files, released to the public only a couple of years ago, the Mitchell case was being minded by a chief inspector in the Flying Squad, E.G. Harris. On 31 October he sent a note to his commander attacking Lucas's story and saying it had come from John Quill, landlord of the Barley Mow pub in the East End. Harris wrote, 'Quill is distantly related to the Kray twins and I have no doubt that at their instigation this rumour was commenced, purely with the object of causing the cessation of police inquiries into the Mitchell escape.' He then continued most curiously, 'Detective Superintendent Williams and I have received information from entirely separate sources that Mitchell is in Eire, and this is undoubtedly correct. We are constantly in touch with the Garda Siochana [Irish Police] respecting him.' In a grumpy final paragraph Harris added that 'the article was printed in spite of the fact the newspaper knew the police believed the contrary to be the truth'.

These same files show that, by the time this note was written, there had been many sightings of Mitchell in Britain and abroad, all false or mistaken. Only two claimed he was in Ireland. The first, dated 19 April 1967, was a telegram for the attention of Tommy Butler, from a female Yard detective, saying that Mitchell was being taken to Dun Laoghaire, near Dublin. The second, dated 22 April, was based on a prison officer's account of overhearing some inmates saying that Mitchell had been taken to Abbeyfeale in County Limerick. Nothing in the files shows that the Yard was 'constantly in touch' with the Irish police. There is only one piece of correspondence with the Garda, and it's a knock-back. Following up the prison officer's report, Tommy Butler, who was Harris's immediate boss, had recommended that the Garda be asked to try and find Mitchell who, according to a 'usually reliable source, was in Eire and spending a great deal of his time in Abbeyfeale'.

On 23 May back came a terse note from the chief superintendent in County Limerick: 'Enquiries have established that Mitchell is not resident in Abbeyfeale. He has never visited that locality, as far as the Gardai are aware.' So all this undoubtedly correct stuff about Mitchell being in Ireland – based in part on Frank Williams's information – was not correct at all. So who was Williams's source for this bum steer? Why was he even bothering himself about Mitchell when he was still meant to be catching any Great Train Robbers who were still on the loose?

Just imagine we are back in October 1967. As Williams himself admits, he is a regular drinker in Foreman's pub. According to Foreman, Williams is corruptly involved with him over the Great Train Robbery – and other matters, we may assume, as the pair have known each other for years. Foreman has murdered Mitchell in December 1966 and then burned or cremated his body. Now his close pal, Williams, tells his Yard bosses that Mitchell is alive and living in Ireland – a claim which is not only untrue, it goes against the reports in the Yard's own files. So the Yard attacks the only newspaper that ten months after Foreman has killed Mitchell has dared to run a story calling this a murder.

If Williams was drinking in Fred Foreman's pub in December 1964, he must have known all about me, Jim Evans, shooting brother George as soon as it happened. And didn't Williams sit in on my trial for this when it wasn't even his case? So, still drinking in the pub in January 1965, he must also have known that Foreman had killed Marks. Maybe he knew about that before it happened. Maybe he supplied the Q car number or even a warrant card to ensure Foreman and Co could cross London without being stopped and asked to explain why a dead man was in the back of the car. So when, two years later, Mitchell disappears, why does Williams falsify the record by claiming he is in Ireland? To cover the tracks of his drinking pal and partner-in-corruption: Freddie Foreman, serial killer. Simple, really.

And what of Tommy Butler, that other frequent visitor to the Prince of Wales? He too is involved in the Great Train Robbery corruption, if we believe anything Foreman says. And he is in overall charge of the Mitchell case, as head of the Flying Squad. Indeed in January 1967 Butler writes an aggressive memorandum stating, 'Mitchell is a ruthless, violent criminal who is now enjoying freedom at the expense of those who can be frightened into supplying the financial support for it.'

But as he writes those words, Butler is himself enjoying the financial support of the man who has already murdered Mitchell. He is not just visiting Foreman's pub, he is being wined and dined by him at Simpsons-in-the-Strand, and for over three years he has been involved in dodgy dealings over the Great Train Robbers and their money, through Frank Williams.

Butler was not called to appear in the Mitchell trial. He had retired four months earlier. He would soon be seriously ill and he would die a year later. Friends of Butler might say that his reputation should not be trashed just because a villain like Foreman has claimed he was corrupt 30 years later. But Butler never publicly denied Foreman's claim that he 'frequented' his pub or that he was 'asked to frequent it more regularly' to combat the fake Donoghue protection racket. Maybe he found Foreman's claim that he 'didn't want to be an informer and inform on people' too outrageous to cope with. Not an informer? Who was he kidding?

So why, back in 1969, didn't other villains take a close look at how Foreman was justifying his relationship with the men who were nicking all his Great Train Robber buddies?

The trouble was that a lot of South London villains would go to Foreman whenever they had a problem with the police. My old alarm man, Alan Maguire, whose relatives were quite well in with Foreman, told me, 'I was in the Prince of Wales one day and a geezer come running in all panicking and saying, "Fred! Fred! I've got a fucking right problem. I'm in trouble." "What's happened?" said Fred. The bloke said, "We've just nicked a lorry-load of stuff and pulled a shooter out on an Old Bill, and I've had to leave it." So Foreman said, "Hang on," and he got on the telephone and he was saying, "Tom, I've got a little problem here. Yeah. Yeah. OK." Then he turned to the bloke and said, "Go and move the lorry. Take it away and you can go home tonight." It was Butler he was talking to.'

But if anybody ever challenged Foreman about how he could do business with Butler and Co, he used to brush them aside, saying, 'I run a pub and the police come in. I can't fuck 'em off, they're useful. If my pals get in trouble, I can get them out of trouble.' He would disguise it that way. But if he could get his pals out of trouble, he could also get his enemies into trouble. Remember what he said about Williams asking if he 'wanted anybody arrested or anything like that, or any charges made'.

For arrests, charges and especially 'anything like that', I was top of Foreman's list.

SEVENTEEN

Performance

AT the start of 1969 things seemed to be looking up again. Annick and I were getting on fine. I had got Nipper Read off my back, blanked him on the cyanide briefcase and had no repercussions. I wouldn't wish jail on anybody, but Fred Foreman would soon be given ten years for getting rid of Jack McVitie. I was putting my business life together and there hadn't been any fit-ups for a while.

One sunny afternoon I was sitting outside a coffee bar in the King's Road, Chelsea, when all of a sudden up pulled a little grey Alfa-Romeo with the hood down and someone shouted, 'Jimmy! Jimmy! Come here a minute!'

It was Robert Fraser, a fellow who had been in Wormwood Scrubs when Lofty Mason and I were there (thanks to Detective Inspector George Chandler). Robert Fraser was no relation to the pathetic Frankie. He was a college-boy type who owned an art gallery that he'd named after himself, and he was inside because he took a fall for the Rolling Stones. They had been picked up for possessing drugs, only for personal use but in those days even that was a very serious offence. Obviously the Stones were a great catch for the drugs squad but just when it looked like Mick Jagger and co might go to jail, Robert Fraser held his hands up, said the drugs were his and got six months.

I liked him for that. I thought, 'Yeah, he can't be bad. Whatever he got out of it I don't know but while we were in the Scrubs we got a little bit friendly, which was lucky for him because he upset some very violent people.

See, he wouldn't honour his debts. For all his college education, he was a bit fly. For instance, during periods of free association when all the cell doors were open, he'd be playing chess with another prisoner. So I'd be standing in his cell doorway watching and I'd see him deliberately knock the board so one or two pieces would fall on the floor. And while the other player was bending down to pick them up, Robert would be moving the other pieces about on the board so he could win the game. He just had to cheat.

There was a Scotsman in the Scrubs with us. We called him Chick. He was a redband – a trusty – and he was doing life for murder. Chick made himself busy with Robert because he knew there was money somewhere in Robert's background, not just because of the Rolling Stones but also because of the type of people who came to visit him. Chick showed Robert he was ready to do things and could get into all sorts of places other prisoners couldn't reach, so Robert said, 'If you can get me any steaks, milk, eggs and things out of the kitchen, I can make sure some money is sent round to your family.'

This was just what Chick wanted to hear because he was in for life and would do anything to help support his family outside, so he told Robert, 'Yeah, I can get you some stuff', and he did. So now Robert was living in the lap of luxury, even though he was in jail, and for the next couple of months he had an easy life.

But he hadn't kept his word. No money was reaching Chick's nearest and dearest. They didn't get a penny. Robert knocked them, didn't he!

Despite this, I liked him. I don't know why.

So one day Chick and I were walking back from a visit – we'd both had relatives come to see us – and his visitors must have just told him they'd got nothing from Robert Fraser: 'I'll kill him, I'll fucking kill him!' said Chick, 'The bastard! I've got nothing to lose, I've got nothing to lose.'

So I said, 'Well you have got something to lose, Chick, because, if you have a crack at him, I'll have a crack at you. Leave him alone.'

And that worked, because later Chick told him, 'It's only 'cos of Jimmy, or I'd have fucking killed you.'

Naturally, after this, Robert liked me even more. I can't remember which of us left the Scrubs first but that day when he spotted me in Kings Road, he hailed me like a long-lost brother. I went to the car and he said, 'Would you like to earn five grand?'

I said, 'No, not really' – just joking around, as usual – but he insisted, 'Jump in! Jump in!' So I left the capuccino, got in the car and he said, 'I want to introduce you to some people. They're making a film called *Performance*. Mick Jagger's gonna be in it, it's gonna be his debut, there's a girl called

Anita Pallenberg, and James Fox is going to play the leading part. It's a gangster film and perhaps you could help with it.'

So I said, 'Yeah, I'll come and meet them', and he drove to Cromwell Road where we went up to the apartment of a character called David Litvinoff, who was a writer. While I was there they phoned the film's co-director, Donald Cammell, so he came round and so did the actor, James Fox. Fraser had already told them about me and how I used to take care of him inside, so we all got talking. I was into fitness at the time. I'd just come out after a year spent mostly in the Scrubs gym and I was very fit. I couldn't keep still for a moment and in no time I was lying on the floor doing press-ups with James Fox.

So I helped them with the film. I lent James a few suits and they asked me things like, 'Where do you keep a gun?' So I showed them the hip-pocket that I had stitched into each of these suits. It was made of shammy leather and that's where I used to keep a little Derringer or a little .22 or a revolver. They used that idea in the film. Then they asked, 'Where would you keep a gun in the house?' I said, 'I always stick one in the laundry-basket in the bathroom among the towels', and in the film there's a scene where Chas, the character played by James Fox, is being bashed up, and he's fallen into the bathroom, where he reaches up to the laundry basket and he cops for the tool.

All the time I was with them, Donald Cammell was still shaping Chas's character. So one day he said, 'We want Chas to be a little bit bisexual.'

'Why?' I asked him.

''Cos a lot of gangsters are bisexual; Ronnie Kray's bisexual'.

I said, 'Name another one! Name one more. Because I know everybody who's at it. I know all the bank robbers, I know all the safe-blowers, I know all the cranks – and there's only Ronnie that I can say is like that.'

That's true. Ronnie Kray was the only gangster, robber or thief I ever knew who was homosexual. On the other hand, David Litvinoff was a bit like that. He even had a scar on his face that I think he got from Ronnie.

Robert Fraser knew I wasn't homosexual. He knew I wouldn't even let the screws strip search me. Once after I'd been to a visit in the Scrubs they tried to give me a 'dry bath' – when they strip you off and search every crack in your body. So I told them, 'You fucking come near me and I'll stick that truncheon right up your fucking arseholes.'

I advised this crowd for a few weeks. They offered to pay me but I wouldn't take any money. Eventually James Fox took me to the Pheasantry in King's Road, with Litvinoff, and in the basement there was some painting going on. And James said, 'This is one of the Queen's artists', and he went up to him and said, 'Please give Jimmy a nice water-colour. Something to do with animals.' So this bloke gave me a painting of some jays. I've still got it. It's signed by Basil Ede.

Nowadays, I'm told, *Performance* is a cult movie. That may be but practically everyone connected with it came to a sticky end. Donald Cammell shot himself between the eyes, just like the Chas character does in the film. David Litvinoff died of an overdose. As for Robert Fraser, a few years later I phoned his home. His mother answered. She said, 'He's not here, he's not very well.' The next thing, I heard he had died from AIDS. Then there was Johnny Bindon, the actor-gangster who appeared in the film. He also died quite young. Some people say he had cancer. Others say he had AIDS too.

That proves my point again. James Fox, Mick Jagger and me, we're all survivors – only I'm in much better shape.

THE SURVIVOR

EIGHTEEN

Swiss Cottage Incident

ABOUT this time I was contacted by a detective called Harry Mooney who, according to a middleman, was saying that a newspaper would pay me £100,000 if I told the story of what happened the night Tommy Marks was shot. His disappearance was still being called 'the crime of the century' – committed by 'the slime of the century' – so this Mooney might have been right. At the time I was pally with Charlie Reader, who thought there was money in it too, and a meeting was set up. But before we went, I told Charlie, 'I'm not interested in any 100 grand. I want to be left alone.'

Charlie said, 'You're mad. You'll get all that money for telling that story because no one else can tell it.'

So I said to him, 'OK. I'll come with you, but it will be rigged up. They'll be taping us. You wait and see.'

So we met in this pub, opposite Kensal Rise cemetery, and Mooney came straight up. He said, 'Sit down, sit down,' and he pushed the others aside and sat right on top of me, too close for my comfort. And he said, 'How are you, Jim?' I'd never seen him before in my life and I thought he was too eager. Then he said, 'What happened that night? I know the editor of a big newspaper. I can get you £100,000.' Then he said, 'It was Freddie Foreman, Alf Gerard, Callaghan,' and he named the fourth bloke and said, 'They were the ones in the car, weren't they? Tell me who was in the car.'

I said, 'I don't know who was in the fucking car. I'm not interested in any stories. I'm not interested in any 100 grand.' Then I said, 'Wait a minute,' and

I got up and walked to the side door. There was a grey car out there and someone sitting in the back seat with headphones on. I walked over and I saw that he had a tape-recording machine on his lap. In those days tape-recording machines were big things. So I put my head round the side door and I said to Charlie, 'Come here a minute.' He came out and I said, 'Have a look.'

He said, 'Fuck me, you're right. Come on, let's go.' And we went. We just left Harry Mooney in the pub.

I don't know how he knew these people's names. I didn't give him any names. I had never named anybody to the police. But he was naming them, which means Scotland Yard knew very well who had done Marks. So was a war going on inside the Yard between the straight ones who wanted to convict Foreman (I assume Mooney, who was clearly an honest cop, belonged to this faction and tried to record me in the line of duty) and those who were protecting him: the Butler camp? As Butler himself had just retired, I guess Foreman's main protector was now Frank Williams – though who knows if he made other friends in the Home Office or MI5 or MI6 in return for services rendered? There must be a reason why they went to so much trouble to put me in prison. They never put as much effort into nailing known IRA men as they did into getting me jailed.

The Mooney incident was a few hours' interrogation of my business activities which were now largely legitimate. In 1969 a straight pal of mine called Martin Stockman introduced me to the assistant manager of a branch of Williams and Glyn's bank. This banker was very keen to lend almost anyone £500, which was quite a lot of money. He would also give you a credit card and you could borrow even more money against your assets. The assets we pledged were the titles to some properties which were yielding a few quid in rent. Meanwhile I was paying back the 500 quid loan at 25 quid a week. I also introduced maybe three people to this banker and they took out loans too. It was all legitimate and everyone gave their right names except me. I borrowed in another name, not because I intended to commit a crime, but I just wanted to keep a low profile. Because of all the hassle I had been getting from the police, I didn't want my name on any financial documents. Searching for another name one day, I looked at my watch and saw the initials 'JE' inscribed on the back, so I got the loan in the name of James Edwards. But I gave the bank an authentic address. With a fictitious address, I would have been in trouble, but this way I could receive my statements and deal with any other paperwork, whatever I called myself.

I hadn't committed any crime. You can write a book under the name of

Joe Bloggs, you can use any name, that's no offence. And if you open up an account with an address where you really can be contacted, what have you done wrong? I was using an address belonging to Johnny Wilkins, Joe's brother, with his permission, like he had used mine in the past. I was paying the money back, I had all my accounts and statements, I wasn't defrauding the bank nor did I plan to do so. What I did not know was that the assistant manager had been overlooked for promotion and a younger man had got the manager's job. This may be why he started handing out money like there was no tomorrow, though he was not acting dishonourably or improperly. Then the police fraud squad found out what he was doing, checked out my name and address, found they did not match, worked out who I really was, saw that I had recommended other borrowers and decided I had put together a cunning conspiracy to defraud the bank. All bollocks, but I still had no idea there was even an investigation.

Annick and I both happened to be out when they came 50-handed in their cars and waited for the 'off' below Pitcairn House. I must have walked right past them and up our stairway without noticing them, or them recognising me. Then I heard Annick coming in too. I looked through the letterbox and saw she was frightened. I opened the door and she said, 'Run. Run. They're here! They're coming for you. They're waiting to arrest you. Run!'

So I walked out and down four flights, then I knocked on a door. I didn't know the guy but he let me in. When I told him the police were after me for no reason, he said he knew what the bastards were like and he let me climb over his balcony on the outside of the building. Then he held my wrists and said, 'Don't break your leg.' I dropped some 20 feet onto the grass verge below, then I ran for it. All this time the coppers were waiting for me on the other side. When I was clean away I contacted my pal Posh Ken. He took me to his mother's, and I stayed there while I found out that they wanted me over Williams and Glyn's.

The detective running this inquiry was a Sergeant Dunn. When he eventually got hold of me – I'll explain how later – he said, 'We're going to make this a bigger case than the Krays. All 32 of you!' The other 31 were borrowers like me. None had done any wrong, and I only knew three of them. Dunn, clearly a straight and zealous detective, saw me as the mastermind behind a vast fraud. And so I was charged.

When the case came to court, the Prosecution was forced to admit that Williams and Glyn's hadn't lost any money and it could not prove any intent to defraud. Then we presented my case. Johnny Wilkins testified that, for all

THE SURVIVOR

legal purposes, the address I had given was genuine. And I made as much as I could out of the fact that Dunn (whom I called 'Dung' throughout to upset him) had come to my home mob-handed and chased me all over the place. When the judge had heard all the evidence, he said, 'I cannot see that this man has committed any crime. I don't know what he'd doing here. Why is he in court?' Then the representative of Williams and Glyn's said that the bank didn't want to bring this matter to trial, only the police. At that the judge threw out the case and said, 'He's discharged.' The 31 other people were cleared too. But they would never have been charged if I had not been on the list of borrowers, under whatever name.

But although the judge had discharged me, I was not a free man. While I had been on my toes trying to keep away from Dunn, I was captured on another matter. That's the only way Dunn ever got hold of me. He found me in Brixton prison when I was on remand for something far worse.

After I had slipped out of Pitcairn House to get away from Dunn and Co, and I had found out that it was just this Williams and Glyn's business, I thought: 'If I can keep away for a year or so, it will fizzle out because that's all it is ever going to do – there was no crime – and in the meantime I'll keep a low profile.' Obviously, this meant I couldn't go back to Pitcairn House. I've always liked my home life but once again this was screwed up. I felt sorry for Annick. She had no family over here, just her daughter and now my daughter. In the meantime the police were really bearing down on us, wasting vast resources and funds.

Now I needed somewhere else to live and a pal in the clothing business called Natt Best found me a little apartment a few miles west of Hackney, in Belsize Road, close to Swiss Cottage. Nobody knew about this place but Natt and he didn't tell a soul. Obviously the fraud squad would be following Annick so she could never visit me there. Instead, on weekdays when she had finished work she would sometimes drive from Hackney in her Ford and leave it in the Swiss Cottage carpark. Then she would slip into the Underground station, take a train to central London, I would meet her for the evening and then I'd drop her back to her car. After that I would return to the apartment.

This had been going on for quite a few months when, on a summer evening, 28 July 1972, Annick left work as usual. She drove to Swiss Cottage, we met in the West End and I took her to a little Italian restaurant in Tottenham Court Road. A normal night out. When I dropped her back at Swiss Cottage at ten past eleven, only a few cars were still around, mostly on the edge of the carpark. In the central area, where Annick had parked, there was just one other car. In fact it was right on top of her car, only six feet away. It couldn't have been parked any closer. Then I saw a man and what looked like a woman inside, embracing. But they were giving such an unconvincing performance that I realised they were Old Bill. If a couple wanted to have a cuddle in a carpark they wouldn't choose to park next to the only other car. They would use the perimeter where there were trees. 'Get out quick,' I told Annick. 'It's the police.' She got out to go to her car, while I spun round my three-litre Capri and drove to the exit. There I paused and looked back to see if she was driving off too. Suddenly I heard a scream. I could see that Annick's car had nosed out of its parking place and then stopped. It looked as if she had stalled but I couldn't see properly because all the lights had been turned off, not just in the carpark but in the nearby street. This wasn't a power failure. It must have been done deliberately on the orders of the police.

But the diffused lighting from the broad Finchley Road close by allowed me to see a group of men crowding around Annick's car and trapping her there. My instant thought was that these were the same people who did Tommy Marks, but without Fred Foreman because he was in jail. I reversed my car fast and I hit one of them, knocking him up in the air. The next thing my door's being yanked open and I'm being yanked out and kicked and punched. As I found out later, they weren't Foreman's mob or the police but five drunken Scotsmen who had been thrown out of the Swiss Cottage pub 20 minutes earlier for causing a nuisance. So now I was getting kicked and punched from behind. Fists were flying all over the place. But with that bit of light from Finchley Road, and my own excellent eyesight, I could see that one of my attackers was wearing a pale pink shirt and a pair of light-coloured fawn trousers.

I was getting one hell of a beating. Later a police sergeant examined me and said that I had bruises and abrasions consistent with being kicked and punched. I eventually fought these drunks off, spinning the pink-shirted bloke round and thrusting him at his mates as they got ready to have another go at me. I waited to make sure Annick was able to drive away. As she left I could see the bloke in the pink shirt was leaning against a Volkswagen. I caught sight of a tiny patch about the size of an old penny, on his fawn trousers. Then I drove off. I overtook Annick and she followed me to my little flat in Belsize Road.

The next day we saw a newspaper saying that a man had been murdered in the Swiss Cottage carpark. When I read that, I was convinced this was some sort of set-up. We drove 200 miles straight down to Devon, where Annick's daughter, Geraldine, was on holiday with my mother and her partner Albert. I grabbed hold of the latest newspapers which identified the dead man as a 21-year-old Scotsman named William Fernie. Was he the man in the pink shirt and fawn trousers I wondered, even though I knew that I had not killed anybody. There were just these five yobs, making obscene gestures and rude suggestions to a young woman – my wife – whose car they had surrounded. She screamed. She's a very sensible person, so she must have screamed for a reason. Then they attacked me and I retaliated with as much force as I needed to escape with my life. That did not include killing anybody.

But now this was a hot murder inquiry and somehow – I don't know how – they immediately located us all in Devon. We were sitting in a restaurant, they came smashing through the door, they grabbed hold of me, frightening the life out of Geraldine, and carted us all down to the local police station. They released the others, kept hold of Annick and me, and then stripped Annick, stuck her in a cell and gave her a dirty old tramp's blanket to wrap around her body. And she hadn't done anything wrong, except be with me. Then they stuck me in another cell, leaving the door open, so coppers would take turns sitting in a chair blowing smoke into my cell. One thing that's definitely on my criminal record is that I am a non-smoker and I detest other people smoking when I'm around. So I figured this was deliberate.

They charged me and brought me back to London. The detective in overall charge was Chief Superintendent Reg Davis, who headed the CID in the area including Swiss Cottage. In 1977, when he had risen to the rank of Deputy Assistant Commissioner, Davis would be named in connection with a South London villain called Charlie Taylor who had owned a hotel in Streatham called the Leigham Court. Taylor was arrested on charges of taking part in a counterfeiting conspiracy, and then confessed that he had close relationships with Reg Davis and – even more staggering – Assistant Commissioner for Crime Jock Wilson, who was the head of all London's detectives. Following these revelations Davis resigned from the Metropolitan Police. His boss Wilson was bumped sideways into becoming head of London traffic cops. As for Charlie Taylor, he collapsed and died at Waterloo Station in the middle of his trial.

My experience of Davis started while we were still in Devon. He humiliated me at the local police station by insisting I remove all my smart clothes and making me wear a pair of trousers and a shirt made for someone of six feet six. I had to stay like that all the way on the train back to London. After that, nothing surprised me. I knew I was back in the mincer.

Back in London, I was charged with murder. I stood trial eight months later when all the police evidence was put before yet another Old Bailey jury. Fundamental to the case was identification. I was not denying that I had been in the carpark that night. The issue was whether I had stabbed William Fernie to death. When I was put up on an identification parade, nobody was picking me out. I had taken care to change my shirt just before each new witness came to look at the line-up, to defeat the possibility that I might be picked out just on what I was wearing at that parade. Suddenly I was told there was one more witness: a girl who, they said, had followed the Scotsmen into the carpark, though I had not seen her there. Later she was described as the girlfriend of the dead man. I said to Davis that I wanted to put on a different shirt, instead of the one I now had on, which was blue. He refused. She picked me out. Later, when she gave evidence, she identified the dead man's attacker as 'the man in the blue shirt'. That's all she could remember: what I was wearing at the ID parade, not what I was wearing on the night. Originally she had said that she couldn't see anything that night because it was too dark. She was the police's last hope. If she hadn't picked me out there wasn't going to be a trial.

They had found no blood on my clothes, even though they had taken every item of clothing from my home. If I had done what they were claiming, Fernie's blood would have shot out all over me. And there was no blood on my car either. They produced pictures which showed a long, thick trail of blood across the ground – like a river – which my Capri would have had to cross for me to drive away. But even though it had brand-new tyres and it was impounded the very next day for forensic tests, they could not find any trace of blood in the tread, undercarriage or anywhere else. It hadn't been raining. Nothing was washed away on the trip to Devon. But the scientists found no blood, when I'm supposed to have driven across that torrent. They had a photo of the Volkswagen and several other cars which looked as if someone had thrown buckets of paint over them. I didn't know one person could have that much blood. Even if a knife had hit a main artery, there was no way that so much blood would gush out.

There was also the shirt that the dead man was supposed to have worn that night. But when they pulled it out from a large brown envelope, it wasn't the pale pink shirt that I saw on the man standing against the Volkswagen. It was a navy blue and red floral shirt instead.

Then they produced the most horrible exhibit of all: a photograph showing a large slash right across this man's chest, and right across his heart, with big stitches, as if he had been stabbed through the heart with a knife with a two-inch-wide blade, like a Gurkha knife or a Bowie knife. I had never done that. This must have happened after I had driven off.

After I saw all the photos of this corpse, I had a recurring nightmare: I kept imagining an ambulance with a body in it. But the people around it weren't treating this body. They were stabbing it.

When I was first questioned back in London at a police station I was asked, 'Have you ever owned a clasp-knife?'

I said, 'Yes, there's one indoors at Pitcairn House. If you ask Annick, she'll give it to you.' They knocked on the door and Annick handed them a French knife which she used in the kitchen. It had a white bone handle and a two-inch blade.

But in court one officer testified, 'We went to Evans's flat and we found this clasp-knife hidden underneath the knife drawer.'

Annick jumped up and said, 'You liars. You didn't find it hidden under the drawer. I gave it to you!'

Then my barrister, Barry Payton, asked the forensic expert if there was any blood in the hinge of this knife. They said they had found traces of starch, beetroot juice, anything relating to the kitchen, but they admitted that they had not found any blood. Instead, they swore that, although I hadn't removed any of these kitchen traces, I could have removed every trace of this man's blood. Like I'm a scientist so skilled that I could leave other stuff but just remove the blood.

The prosecution never explained how the police came to arrest me. They said they had got the number of Annick's car but not who had spotted it. And they never mentioned the two Old Bill wrapped in a fake embrace in the car next to Annick's. They were definitely detectives on surveillance, so I knew at the time that they were bound to take my number because I had been the object of a surveillance exercise ever since I had dodged the fraud squad at Pitcairn House many months before. And they already knew Annick's number because they had been following her for weeks. So, however mad I was at all those thugs bullying my wife, I wasn't going to kill anybody in front of coppers sitting right there, on the spot, in that car. But they were never mentioned, even though they had witnessed the whole thing.

In court there was no doubt that Annick had been in fear of her life. She told the judge, 'I don't know what I would have done if Jimmy hadn't come back.' These men were drunk and out of control, as the landlord of the Swiss Cottage pub confirmed when he gave evidence. But instead of being portrayed as a knight in shining armour, throughout the trial I was being treated like Public Enemy Number One all over again. Each day I was transported from Brixton to the Old Bailey in a special van with Wormwood Scrubs police cars in front and behind and motorcycle outriders. Inside the van my prison guards started talking about Freddie Foreman. They were saying, 'One of our blokes in Wormwood Scrubs was getting punched up and Freddie jumped in and rescued him.'

I said, 'Fucking scumbag. Don't mention his name in my presence.'

Then they told me, 'By Christ, we're making more of a business taking you to court than we did with the Krays.'

During the trial Barry Payton came down to the cells underneath the Bailey and told me that the judge had said that this is a case of murder or nothing. I told him he had to get me off because I still had 14 charges hanging over me for the Williams and Glyn's thing. I said, 'If you don't, I'm never going to see daylight again.'

So he said, 'There's no chance of you being found guilty of murder. Murder is premeditated and this was spur of the moment. Whatever's happened, you've not committed a murder.' And as the case was drawing to a close and the jury was sent out, Barry said, 'You cannot be found guilty. We've got a restaurant booked for tonight and we're ordering your favourite wine.'

He was right. The jury found me not guilty of murder. So there was I, standing in the dock and just thinking I'm going to walk out of court a free man again, when suddenly the judge said to the jury, 'You found him not guilty of murder but how do you find him on manslaughter?'

So they all went out and came back and said, 'Guilty.' When I had been told it was 'murder or nothing' . . . So much for British justice.

Well, it was a Friday night and I guess I was caught in that Friday trap when jurors can easily rush to judgment because they want to get the whole thing over before the weekend. And as they had just acquitted me of murder, maybe they felt the police needed a consolation prize.

The worst was yet to come. I wasn't given the kind of two-year sentence for manslaughter that a man would usually get for killing someone in an unpremeditated fight in defence of his wife. If a policeman or a parking warden had come to Annick's rescue, he would have got a medal. Instead the judge sent me down for seven years – yes, seven – because this conviction triggered a reference back to my previous conviction over that man Bannan's watch at the Eden Roc Club, when I was also wrongly convicted of using a knife. When the judge looked at this grim record, maybe he had to give me a seven.

I was sent back to my cell beneath the court. In came Barry Payton. He slung his wig on the floor and said, 'I can't believe this. All through this trial I have been banging my head against a brick wall.'

I would be banging my head on brick walls for years to come – in prison.

I don't even think William Fernie died, but if he did die it was not at my hands. I still can't work out how he got that huge knife slash across his chest and heart. I didn't do it. I wish I could speak to the ambulance staff who took him to the Royal Free Hospital that night, or the doctors who examined him there. I also wonder about the long delay before his death certificate was issued. While we prepared my defence we kept on asking for a copy but we didn't get one for six or eight months. If only I could make contact with William Fernie's family. Together we might be able to answer a lot of questions.

THE SURVIVOR

NINETEEN

Endgame: The Ginger Marks Trial

AS soon as I was convicted of the Swiss Cottage incident I was transferred from Brixton, which houses only men awaiting trial, to Wandsworth where convicts with heavy records are kept for a couple of months before they are transferred to an equally heavy jail. Because my last two convictions were for serious knife attacks, I was a Category A prisoner, and that governed where the authorities would send me next. There were quite a few possibilities: Long Lartin, Gartree, Maidstone, Albany, Parkhurst among them.

While I was in Wandsworth, pals of mine were keeping Annick informed about where any members of the Foreman mob were locked up. She learned that Fred Foreman was in Wormwood Scrubs, halfway through his ten years for McVitie, while Alf Gerard, his partner in a murder, was locked up for something else, but where?

Then someone told her that Gerard was in Albany on the Isle of Wight and added, 'We hope they don't transfer Jimmy there because he'll do terrible damage to Gerard if he gets the chance.' When she next visited me, I told her the same thing and added, 'Fuck him.' This disturbed her so, without telling me, she wrote to the prison service people in the Home Office asking them not to send me to Albany because someone who had murdered a friend of mine and tried to kill me was already there. Annick did not give any names, but there was no need. Such requests come up quite often and usually the officials do what's asked, otherwise the Home Secretary could have a bad time if any more murders are caused by the stupidity of putting dire enemies in the same jail. But no, they sent me to Albany anyway, as if they had decided the opposite of what my wife had asked them to do. I knew nothing of Annick's efforts at this time, but when I found out I thought, 'This must be down to Fred Foreman'. I know he had people in the Home Office looking after him, so they must have seen this letter and thought, 'Yeah, good idea, we'll send Evans there, he'll do something crazy, then we can give him another ten years.'

So a day before I left Wandsworth, a pal of Joe Wilkins called Roy Hilder said to me, 'You know Gerard's there?'

I said, 'Yeah, I'll break his fucking back.'

Hilder went, 'He ain't half a big lump.'

I said, 'What fucking difference does it make? He's a big mug. He may be game in the middle of the night when he's got guns and you've only got a comb in your pocket, like I had when he shot Marks. Let's see what he's like when he ain't got guns.'

The moment I got into Albany they put me in A wing, where I ran into a couple of brothers I knew from the East End. No, they weren't the Kray Twins but I can't say who they were because a third brother was the Great Train Robber who coshed Jack Mills, the train driver. Mills never drove a train again and never recovered from the beating, but the man who gave it to him was never arrested. He got clean away. This must have upset some of the other robbers, as they got 30 years – twice what they might have expected – because of public revulsion at Mills's suffering. I knew this bloke quite well. He used to come to my clothing factory.

In Albany his two brothers' cells were on either side of mine and on my first day there, they told me, 'If you hurry, you'll see him every night.'

'See who?' I said.

'Gerard. He's in B wing,' said one, 'and every night at about eight o'clock he goes to the dispensary, 'cos he's got some condition, and he gets his medicine.'

'Thanks,' I said. Then I told the duty screw, 'I've had a very, very bad migraine. I've been travelling all day. I had to leave Wandsworth early, then I had to go on the ferry. So can I go and get some pills?' And he let me go down to the dispensary.

Albany was a maximum-security prison. It still is but back in 1973 it was brand spanking new, electric sliding doors and everything. Throughout every wing there were cameras, so it was hard work if you wanted to give another prisoner a hiding. So while I was waiting by the dispensary, along came Alf Gerard. I'm standing against the wall, and as he walked by I said, 'You got anything you want to fucking say to me?'

He went, 'What?'

I said, 'You heard me. Have you got anything you want to fucking say to me?'

He said, 'I don't even know you, I don't want to talk to you.'

I said, 'Well, if you don't know me, how come you were bottling me off that night with those other fucking monkeys? The night we were doing a bit of business, and you shot my pal Tommy and dragged him away, so his wife's never been able to give him a proper funeral.'

He kind of grunted and said, 'I don't have anything to do with those slags any more. I don't like those two slags.'

I said, 'Who are you talking about?'

He said, 'The Foremans.'

So I said, 'But just now you said you don't know me, so how do you know who I was talking about?' He couldn't come up with an answer, so I went on, 'Now, some people in the Home Office have sent me down here deliberately. I'm here for a reason. They either want you to kill me or me to kill you. I haven't asked to come here. I've been put here. Now, we're right under a camera here, so tomorrow you get out on that exercise yard and we'll finish this conversation there.'

And he went, 'Yeah, OK,' and he shuffled off.

Now the brothers had already told me that this lumpy Gerard bloke was out there on the exercise yard every day, running around the football field, growling at and bullying all the youngest inmates, saying, 'We blow people's fucking heads off. We do this. We bury people.'

So I walked back into my wing and I got hold of a bloke I knew who had a job working in the gardens next to the exercise yard, and I said, 'Have you got anything down there? I've got to do something tomorrow.'

He went, 'Yeah, I've got a big blade.'

So I said, 'I'll get there as soon as I can. I want you to give it to me.'

So the next day after I've fronted him, Gerard did not leave his cell. There was I waiting for him out in the exercise yard, but he never came out. He stayed in his cell for weeks. Some other blokes in B wing told me he was in there for five weeks. And maybe he was right to hide away because I was looking at all the usual prison tricks – boiling water, scissors – and always trying to bump into him, but that almost never happened because we were in different wings and he was avoiding me.

When he did finally creep out of B wing, he tried to get at me another way. He pulled rank on these two brothers by telling them how close he was to their train robber brother. Gerard acted as if this gave him a licence to dictate to them. It happened that both brothers had the duty of serving up meals on the hot plates to all the prisoners. This pair would dish me out my food. So one day one of the brothers told me that Alf Gerard had approached him and said, 'If we get you a bit of gear in here, put it in his grub.' This fellow was telling me that the Foreman mob were trying to poison my food.

This brother told Gerard, 'Why would we want to do that to Jimmy? He's never done you people any harm. He's never named you to the police, never made any statements.'

The Gerard said, 'But he's the only one who's ever witnessed one of our murders. He could get us 30 years.' This was true. After the failure of the Mitchell trial (which Gerard and Callaghan had missed because they were in hiding in Australia), I was the only person who could send them down for life, meaning life – like what happened to the Kray Twins. No one had seen their other murders because the Underworld Undertakers usually killed in private.

So then the two brothers told me Gerard was getting them a dose of cyanide for me. 'What? Cyanide again?' I said. 'They failed with the cyanide briefcase so now it's cyanide soup.'

When they dared to tell him they wouldn't do it, he really laid it on them: 'Gerard reckons we owe them a favour because they've done our brother a big favour. He's saying, "You've got to do it because of him. He's on our firm. He's one of us."'

Well, if killing me was the return favour, the original favour must have been very big indeed. There's one possibility that's so obvious it's a certainty. Foreman must have done a deal with Butler and Williams not to arrest the third brother: the man who clubbed Jack Mills into early retirement and premature death. The pay-off would have been most of his share of the robbery: around £90,000. Cheap at the price. Better to give it all up than spend the next 30 years in jail.

As for the cyanide, the two brothers did not give in to Gerard's pressure, so I survived yet again.

But while I was facing plots to kill me in jail, I was still getting heat from the police. Although Foreman had Butler and Williams in his pocket, he never had any of the straight cops in Scotland Yard, like Nipper Read or Harry Mooney, whom I'd encountered at that pub in Harlesden, or that fellow Dunn who tried to put the squeeze on me when I was in Brixton. All three were straight and decent cops. One minute Dunn was telling me that his Williams and Glyn's conspiracy against me was going to be 'bigger than the Krays', the next he switched subjects: 'What happened with Marks? What happened with Ginger?' He was so insistent, I could see he felt that solving the Marks mystery would be a feather in his cap.

Public pressure on the police was getting bigger. It was now eight years since Tommy went wising, yet stories were still coming out about him in the newspapers. There were reports that boy scouts had found his body in a rock crevice in Sussex, then he was meant to be concreted in a tower holding up a flyover, then someone claimed he was put in a car that was crushed to the size of a packet of cornflakes, then police in Kent were digging up a gangland cemetery containing both Marks and Mitchell. Of course, none of these stories was true.

One person who came a bit closer to finding Tommy was a Dutch clairvoyant that Annie Marks visited back in April 1965. Gerard Croiset told her that Tommy was dead and had been dumped in water. He marked up a map and then gave Annie five things to look out for. After a few days she located a spot which matched the lot: on the Thames foreshore at Woolwich. Just four days later a male corpse was found a few hundred yards upstream at Greenwich. It had been in the river for weeks and the police said it was unrecognisable. It had been embedded in mud, so it was also impossible to tell the original colour of the man's jacket and trousers. The police decided it wasn't Tommy, but if they had been able to DNA the body then, as they can today, they might have proved it was him after all. Funny. Foreman now claims he threw Marks in the sea.

But the story that may have been nearest the truth appeared in the *News of the World* in 1966. I wish I knew Peter Earle's source: 'Police tied in work on Ginger's disappearance with investigations into the Great Train Robbery. Ginger knew nothing of the robbery, but it is believed that he was mixed up with the disposal of train robbery money in South London, and that he was "executed" for something which he may have said. His body? Burned.'

By the time I was in Albany the Home Office had got so pissed off with the Marks case that some official seems to have told Scotland Yard, 'We don't care who you nick, nick anybody. Let's have a trial, the verdict doesn't matter, and then we're shot of it. Then all those moaners will shut up.' And suddenly Harry Mooney's back on my case. Raised to the rank of chief superintendent, he appeared in newspaper reports like this one in the *Evening Standard*: 'Harry Mooney has recently interviewed a man in jail who is known to have been with Marks on the night . . . Detectives are hopeful that he will give them the vital evidence they need . . . The suspected killer of Marks is himself in jail serving a long sentence.'

Thank you very much. As the entire underworld knows already, I'm the only bloke who was with Tommy that night. Now this newspaper has fingered me – as a grass – when in fact I have not seen Mooney since I walked out on him in that pub in Harlesden. He's never interviewed me in or out of jail.

So now on the one shoulder I had coppers like Mooney and Dunn trying to get me to name Foreman and his crew in open court, and on the other I had Foreman's coppers having a crack at me too. Either way I was up to my neck in a barrel of crap. That's why I was still saying nothing. But at the same time I'm lying in my cell at night, thinking – and believe me, during those prison nights you have a lot of time to think – and I figure, I'm in a bad, bad situation and I've got to get out of it, especially now Foreman's coppers are aiming to nick me for killing Tommy myself. That could happen any day because the two brothers with me in A wing were saying that Gerard was twisting the story round, saying I had killed Tommy, not Gerard and Foreman.

I knew that a story was going around the underworld that Tommy had gone on the missing list 'because he gave Jimmy some crap gear and Jimmy lost a fortune on it'. That story was true, except that I didn't put Tommy on the missing list. The full story is worth a book in itself, but here it is in brief. I had asked Tommy to take care of my stocks of gelignite. Without telling me, he used up all my current stock, trying to do safe jobs of his own. When I asked him for some jelly for a job of mine, he panicked and gave me stuff he'd got from someone else, even though this person had told him it was no use because all the nitro-glycerine had gone out of it (after a while gelignite degenerates). I went off to do this job – which was going to give me my biggest pay-day ever – but when I tried to blow the safe, this jelly just went bang! The safe stayed shut even though I'd blown the same model several times before, so we went home empty-handed. I was very angry but it was only after Tommy was taken by those bastards that I was told the crap gear was down to him. He was on the missing list long before I found that out.

But rumours like that can stick, and I knew that Foreman and Gerard

THE SURVIVOR

would make sure this one reached the ears of whoever had taken Butler's place as their chief minder. I was also getting messages sent in through pals that came to visit. They said, 'You know you ain't going to walk out of this.'

I said, 'I'm just doing my bird.'

They said, 'No, but it ain't going to be the end of it. They'll wait until the last knockings, you'll be walking out of the prison gates and then they'll slap another charge on you: Ginger Marks. They'll say you were the last one on the scene, there's never been any trace of him, so it's down to you.' And they might have been right because the Hossein brothers had just been convicted for murdering Mrs McKay, even though they had fed her body to pigs. Till then it was almost impossible to be done for murder without a body. Nipper Read was only able to send the Krays down without Jack McVitie's body because there were several witnesses to the murder itself. Mind you, I would have been in a far worse state if they had left Ginger there that night. That was their big mistake. Imagine if he had been found dead on the street, with a dozen bullet holes as well as the .22 cartridge, and I'm on the spot, and Annie Marks says I was with him that night, and I'm known as a shooter – especially after that ammunition 'find' at the House of Peacocks. With all that against me, and the body, I would probably have gone down. What was that old Perry Mason line? Motive, method, opportunity – I had them all.

But throughout 1974 I was getting more bad news from legitimate pals whom I'd met through my straight businesses like the clothing factory and the saw-mill. These people had their own connections with the police and they were trying to help me but they were being told, 'Sorry, can't help. We're going to do him for Marks.' I had a friend who was one of England's leading freemasons so he knew a lot of top detectives through his lodge, and that was the feedback he was getting. So now, either I was going to get 30 years for Tommy or I'd be joining him very soon due to cyanide soup or some other recipe. Gerard didn't want to front me himself. He wanted other people to do his dirty work. A big bully.

Talk about seeing no light at the end of the tunnel. My recurring nightmare was even worse. Most nights I was dreaming I was in a subterranean passage; I turned round and a big gorilla was coming for me with a big mace and chain; I looked back the other way and there was a big bear roaring towards me; I was piggy in the middle. You don't need to be Sigmund Freud to see that these beasts represented the mobs that were climbing all over me. On one shoulder there was Foreman's mob, on the other shoulder, Scotland Yard. One lot's trying to get me to testify, one lot's trying to lock me up and kill me.

I had to get them all off my back. I had to come up with a scheme. The only way I could do that was by giving them all what they wanted: a trial. But it would be a trial in which no one would be convicted. It was going to be the real killers. So one day I asked for a meeting with the governor of Albany and I told him, 'I wish to report a murder.' He must have realised which murder I meant because there was a note about it in my prison record. But I stipulated, 'I don't want any police from London, no one from Scotland Yard. I want to see provincial officers, from a county force.'

Six months passed with me hearing from nobody. Six months before they got their fingers out of their assholes. With anyone else it would have been, 'What?' and Old Bill would be down to the island straight away, but nothing was happening. The Marks case had been slung back on the shelf.

And now I was getting pressure from underworld messengers who had heard rumours and thought I was turning Queen's Evidence at last. One of these men was Fred Foreman's pal, Micky Regan. He had been with me in Wandsworth where we'd had a talk. He was trying to be friendly and he said, 'I might be partners with Foreman in his business, but I'm not partners with him in his problems.' Micky has a very good name. He would never have condoned his partner's attempt to frame me for Marks's murder or the other things.

Now Micky had followed me to Albany and he was in B wing with Gerard. One day we were out on the exercise yard and he stopped me and he said, 'Jim. You're going to give them a bit of a hand with that, aren't you?'

I said, 'What! Like the hand Georgie Foreman gave me?'

So he said, 'Aah, but Georgie didn't say it was *you*, did he?'

And I replied, 'He didn't say it *wasn't* me, either. Why didn't he do what Joe Wilkins told him to do when he offered to pay for him to fuck off on holiday? That's what I did when the Krays were nicked. I was on my toes for six months. He could have done the same, but instead he whimpered that he'd been subpoena'd, so he could look the "chaps" in the eye and say, "I've gotta go." And as for slipping off abroad he said, "I'll have to ask my brother." He couldn't give evidence quick enough. They all wanted me to go down. And now you want me to give them a hand?' (I wasn't going to give even Micky any hint of my scheme.)

I was also getting visits from people on the outside, passing messages from Ronnie Knight, Barbara Windsor's husband. He was also in business with Micky Regan in the A&R Club in Charing Cross Road. My visitors were saying, 'Ronnie's asking how much would you want to say it was four niggers in the car that night, when they pulled on you and Tommy Marks?'

I said, 'How much does he think my house was worth when I had that petrol bomb put in it? And did George Foreman say it was a nigger that knocked on his door and shot him?' You may not like the language but those were the words we used.

Then I heard from a visitor with pals in Wormwood Scrubs with Freddie Foreman (his family didn't have to go to the Isle of Wight to see him). He told me Foreman was telling everyone, 'Jimmy Evans hasn't got the guts to stand up in court and give evidence.' See, if his pals don't give evidence, it's because I don't have any guts. When I heard this, I was even more convinced I had to give evidence just to frighten the bastard.

Suddenly I got a visit from a detective superintendent called Bob Chalk. But instead of meeting me in a special room, like on a solicitor's visit, he and his colleague saw me in the normal visits room with all the other cons and their friends and relatives. There were 200 other people there and they could all smell coppers a mile off. This was a bad start. Then I found out he wasn't a provincial officer from a county force, he was from Scotland Yard. So he steamed in, voicing his legitimate misgivings. 'We know you're going to waste our time. I have had a look through your records and you won't help us.'

I said, 'No, I want to go to trial. I shall name everyone in the car the night they killed Tommy and I'll testify against them in open court.'

He pulled several fat files out of his case, slapped them on the table — they were a foot high — and he said, 'That's your entire criminal record. I haven't had time to read it all, just a bit of it on the way down. For all these years you've refused to say what happened with Marks, so what's new? What's your game? You're up to something.'

I said, 'Listen. If you don't want to look into this murder, then fuck off and leave it. I'm only doing the right thing.'

So he replied, 'All I can say is, there's something going on here. You've got a reason to do what you're doing.' Which was right. I did have a reason.

And now, at last, there was action. Whatever Chalk told his bosses in Scotland Yard or the Director of Public Prosecutions, they leapt at this chance to have a Ginger Marks trial. I was immediately shipped out of Albany and into Lewes prison in Sussex, where they stuck me in solitary confinement. I would spend the next 15 months in solitary, except for my trips to court. After a while I could have asked to come out of solitary but I thought I was better off in there. I liked my own company.

So now Chalk and Co went and charged the four people that I named as being in the car the night Tommy Marks disappeared. They nicked Callaghan. They nicked Gerard, who had finished his previous sentence. They charged Foreman, who was still in the Scrubs. And they nicked the fourth man.

It was at this point that I revealed my scheme to just three people: Annick and two legitimate pals, Martin Stockman and Nat Best. I told them that this trial would go ahead. The entire case against Foreman and Co would be presented, I would give all my evidence, but right at the end I would tell the jury that I committed perjury ten years earlier in a previous trial. This way, I figured, the trial must collapse, because the judge has to tell the jury that in law I cannot be believed and he must dismiss all the charges. Then all four of these animals would be free forever from the fear of going to jail over Tommy. I was going to get them to trial, then get them *off* the trial. Provided this would be on a jury trial, the Foreman gang could never be retried for what they did to Tommy. In England under the double jeopardy principle you cannot be tried for the same offence (though some politicians today have other plans). I figured that if I did all this I wouldn't be any threat to them. I'd no longer be the only one who, as Gerard said, 'could get us 30 years'. I would grass them but 'ungrass' them at the same time. Far better than they deserved, of course, seeing that they were full-time informers themselves. So I wasn't going to mark their card, give them any advance warning. They would have to stew in fear of spending the rest of the century in jail until I had had my day in court.

That day came in October 1975, ten years and almost ten months after Tommy Marks disappeared. I wasn't the only prosecution witness. There were statements from Dave Norman that he had seen their red Austin 1100 and heard a shot, and from a prisoner called Baker, who said that Alf Gerard had told him, 'I will make you a lump of bacon, like I did that cunt Marks'. The prosecution had also hoped to call one of the two brothers that Gerard had asked to poison my food. He had also spent months in Lewes in solitary confinement after agreeing to testify, but he chickened out, telling me he couldn't do this, for the sake of his third brother, the Great Train Robber who had clubbed Jack Mills and got clean away, thanks to Foreman, Butler and Williams. I hadn't asked him to give evidence. He wanted to himself.

In his opening statement, the prosecutor John Mathew told the story of the night they had shot Marks, based largely on my account. He also threw in a few choice reactions from the defendants when the police questioned them about my allegations. Gerard had said, 'That no-good maniac has been shooting his mouth off,' and Foreman, 'Oh, not again. That bastard Evans is grassing. One of these days I will shut him up for good.' When the police had asked Callaghan what they had done with the body, he replied, 'I daren't tell you that.'

When I gave evidence I looked directly at Foreman. He was sitting there, looking like a little Tibetan monk, imploring me with his eyes to let them all out of it. But I told the full story – from the Georgie Foreman shooting through to how they shot Tommy, they shot me, they took his body away and I haven't seen him since. I was in the witness box for days as Callaghan's barrister, Lewis Hawser, did his best to put me on trial – like Foreman's police pals had been trying to do for years. He kept firing the same questions at me: 'Where is Tommy Marks? What did you do with Tommy Marks? You know who it was. You know who shot him. Where is Marks?' He was trying very hard to put it down to me when the fuckers who had really done it were sitting up there, all smug, in that huge dock in Court Number One – where I myself had sat in four trials. But now I'm in the witness box instead, and I'm defending my life.

So when Hawser kept on asking me, 'Where is Marks?' I was on the verge of pointing at Foreman and saying, 'Don't ask me, ask him, ask Foreman. He's finishing off ten years for disposing of Jack "the Hat" McVitie's body. Ginger's probably keeping Jack company.' I was getting very, very close to saying that but I didn't because, if I had, the judge would have had to declare a mistrial because of the rule that a defendant's previous convictions must not be revealed to the jury – especially a conviction for doing much the same to McVitie as Foreman now stood accused of doing to Marks. If they had heard that he had a strange habit of disposing of people's bodies, the jurors would have convicted him in five minutes.

Of course I wanted a mistrial but I wanted to bring it about in my own way. So, at the end of all my evidence I asked the judge, Mr Justice Donaldson, 'Do you mind if I address the jury, sir?'

He said, 'You may.' (What else could he say? I was the main witness.)

I got straight to the point: 'Ladies and gentlemen of the jury, I would like to tell you something. I think you should know that I committed perjury here in this very same court ten years ago.'

Lewis Hawser jumped up and nearly hit the ceiling. 'When was that? When was that?' Till now he hasn't made out such a great case for the defence, but suddenly he thinks it's off.

So I said, 'I stood trial here for shooting Freddie Foreman's brother, George, ten years ago. I had shot him but I said on oath that I hadn't. That's perjury. And as a result I was found not guilty.'

So now Hawser knows for sure the trial's over and everybody's off. Because what was left of the prosecution case? They never had a body. The jury knew already that I was serving a prison sentence, so I had a bad character, and I was also due for parole, which meant I had an incentive to do the Crown a favour. And now I, the only eye-witness, have admitted perjury. So there was absolutely nothing left. How can they convict even these four pieces of shit on the word of a serving jailbird who is a self-confessed liar? Reasonable doubt? You betcha!

So Judge Donaldson called a halt to the proceedings. He pointed out that this crime was ten years old and yet, 'The first time Mr Evans condescended to say it was these defendants who were in the car was last year.' He added, 'You have heard Mr Evans in the witness box. Is it not quite clear that, as far as he is concerned, perjury just does not count?' Then he seemed to make an announcement to the entire nation: 'Let no one think from anything I have said that this case was not brought properly by the prosecution. It was clearly a case which had to be very fully investigated before a jury. That has now been done.'

When he directed the jury to acquit and the foreman stood up and said 'not guilty' on all counts, there was clapping in the public gallery. Suddenly it was all over.

So everyone should have been happy. The Home Office should have been happy because they had finally dealt with the Ginger Marks affair. Convictions or not, for them it was over. Scotland Yard should also have been happy because they wouldn't have to waste any more money on it. At today's prices, over ten years, millions had been spent on solving this mystery – which was all down to Foreman taking the body away to burn, bury or sink. OK, maybe Superintendent Bob Chalk wasn't happy but at least he now knew what my game was. The press should also have been happy. Ten years bashing away at the same old story gets tedious, even if it was the 'crime of the century'.

As for the slime of the century, Freddie Foreman, he should have been happy too. There would be no more Marks trials. And as Gerard had told those two brothers, there weren't any other living witnesses who could get them 30 years. Gerard would walk free immediately, though he wouldn't live a lot longer. Callaghan was also free. He lived another 25 years but never said what happened that night. He just shut up. Foreman too would be out soon because, with remission, he had finally finished his sentence for disposing of Jack the Hat. Twenty-one years later he finally came clean by admitting that he had killed Tommy Marks after all. Even this was a fib, because Tommy was shot with .22 automatics, not the .38 that Foreman claims he was using. So it must have been Gerard and the fourth man.

And what about me? I went straight back to Lewes prison and completed 15 months in solitary. In theory, I could have been up in court again for committing perjury in the George Foreman trial. After all, I had just admitted this on oath in the Old Bailey. But maybe they thought that the confession on oath of a self-confessed perjurer couldn't be regarded as evidence, even against himself. But I had still taken a big chance.

Now I really was no longer a threat. They may still have wanted to kill me, but they didn't *have* to kill me. I wanted the authorities to have their trial, but at the same time I didn't let them have any bodies. I had grassed the murderers but ungrassed them by deliberately letting them get off. Just as I had planned in my cell at night, nobody got bird. And both camps in Scotland Yard gave up persecuting me. I was no longer any use to any of them. My plan had worked. I had survived.

I served a total of five years and three months for the Swiss Cottage incident and came out in October 1977. I have kept a clean sheet since. As for my home life, when I was sent down for that killing I never did and Annick came to visit me, I said, 'Look, I'm going to be in here for a long time, so I won't blame you if you don't want to wait. I'd like you to be there for me when I come out but I'll understand if you want to make a new life for yourself.'

And Annick said, 'I don't care how long it takes. I'll wait for you.' She did wait and we're still together 35 years since we first met. We have survived.

Looking back as far as I can go, when I was a child that light at the end of the tunnel of life was just a little pin-prick. All of a sudden, now I'm 70, it's the size of a manhole, and I know it's only a matter of time before I'll be slipping through it. When that day comes I guarantee you this. Of all the things I've done, I'll have only this one regret: that I can't do the whole thing all over again. Every single second. All those days and hours and minutes in solitary confinement. All my 22 appearances at the Old Bailey.

All those scumbags. All the times with slates in my head and bullets smashing the rib off my spine. All that aggravation with my ex-old woman. I wouldn't change one single freckle.

There's just one other thing.

TWENTY

Tom the Stripper?

IN the 1960s there were four long-running London crime sagas: the Great Train Robbery; the rise and fall of the Krays and the Richardsons; the disappearance of Ginger Marks; and the Nude or Towpath Murders.

The first three were all gangland stories and all bound up with each other. The Nude Murders might seem unconnected: six or eight prostitute murders committed by some freak weirdo, a serial killer in the tradition of Jack the Ripper and the Boston Strangler. But they were connected, through me for a start. When the *South London Advertiser* published its rubbish linking the Nude Murders to the House of Peacocks, they got tied in not just with me and the ginger Marks story but with the whole London gangland scene – cops as well as robbers.

But were they already tied in? How had my name come up? Who had fed that story to the newspaper? And why?

The Nude Murders smear is still in my criminal intelligence file at Scotland Yard. The *South London Advertiser* said it passed all its information to a 'senior Yard detective' on 12 January 1965. Forever after, my file would state at this time I was suspected of being Jack the Stripper. And very close to the same date there must be another entry saying I was the prime suspect for killing Ginger. That would have justified Ron Townsend's siege of the House of Peacocks on 6 January – four days after Ginger went missing – when he should have been targeting the real killer-in-chief, Fred Foreman. Why was my home raided and not the Prince of Wales pub? Because some other copper had fed Townsend a whisper from his trusted snout. It could have been Tom Butler or Frank Williams. As Williams was present when Townsend interviewed me after my arrest on 9 February, and as he was joined at the hip to Foreman, it's almost certain that whoever put me in the frame for Marks put me in the frame for the Nude Murders. The Yard's records should still show which copper wrote down what lies about me.

I wasn't the only man falsely accused. The previous year a tennis club caretaker called Kenneth Archibald was charged with murdering one of the women after he walked into Notting Hill police station and volunteered a confession. But the confession was false, the fantasy of a lonely old soldier who was depressed and wanted a bit of attention. Scotland Yard were so desperate that they didn't tell him, 'Don't waste our time – go away.' They locked him up for 56 days, then put on a six-day show trial at the Old Bailey when the jury found him not guilty. He should never have been charged, let alone tried, but the police never had the grace to admit it. Instead Chief Superintendent John du Rose, who later took over the whole inquiry, said, 'We had no reason to believe that Archibald had anything to do with the murder, but he had to be charged and a jury had to decide the case because he had repeated his false confession twice before eventually retracting it.' So Scotland Yard would put a man on trial for murder knowing he had nothing to do with it. What a scandal and what a waste of public money.

After the discovery of the Stripper's final victim – Bridie O'Hara, on 16 February 1965 – police raided a lock-up garage and found a gun. They claimed it was stolen and charged the garage owner but this was only a holding charge. The Stripper angle was immediately leaked to the *Daily Mirror*, whose crime reporter, Tom Tullett, was an ex-Yard detective. The following morning the story was the *Mirror*'s front-page lead: 'Nude No. 6 – Murder Squad Interview Man'. Tullett did his duty, saying, 'The Yard's top murder detective was certain that the killer would soon be hunted down . . . John du Rose – who broke his holiday to lead the hunt – expects the final link in the puzzle to fall into place in the next 24 hours.'

As Tullett reported, the garage owner's home was raided and detectives carried off 'a bundle of women's clothing'. The bloke later explained what happened. 'They said they had come to see me about the nudes. I couldn't help but laugh.' But it wasn't a joke. They carted him off to the murder hunt HQ at Shepherd's Bush, where they took hairs from his neck and a sample of his blood. Next day a magistrate refused to protect his identity so his name, William Chissell, was blasted all over the press. He was locked up for a week until the same magistrate threw the case out because the police had no evidence that the gun was stolen. Chissell said it wasn't even in the garage before they arrived. He was innocent, legitimate and married with kids.

Du Rose's sudden arrival on the squad had started a frenzy of activity. The same weekend they locked up Chissell, they named one Anthony John Holland as someone they wanted to see 'to assist inquiries'. The *Sunday Mirror* filled its front page with 'Nude Murder Hunt, Yard Seeks Man's Help', and a photo of detectives arresting a full-size waxwork of an Indian woman. The reporter added that though the wanted man 'may possess valuable information', there was 'no suggestion that Mr Holland is in any way involved in the killings'. Too right. Within days Holland disappeared from the headlines, just like Chissell, their names trashed.

Mine too, of course. But at least the real Ripper had done me a favour. When he dumped his final corpse I was in Brixton prison. This forced Scotland Yard to take my name off the list of suspects. In October 1965 they suddenly stopped looking for him. Despite having 200 detectives and 100 uniformed coppers on his team, plus the 300-strong Special Patrol Group on tap – and after interviewing 120,000 men – John du Rose gave up altogether. The *People* branded 'his expensive bid to catch the murderer a failure', but back-tracked by saying that every night du Rose had ordered a 'mammoth check' on the numbers of all cars seen moving in West London between seven in the evening and six in the morning. When the next murder occurred, the police would call on every driver whose number was taken at the time of the killing. 'Du Rose was confident that the murderer would be caught in the net', but the plan failed 'due to one gruesome fact – the sex maniac has never struck again'.

And that was that. No more females were found dead, naked and strangled in West London. The press lost interest and the search for the Stripper faded from public consciousness. It was as if everyone thought: what does it matter, they were only whores, strippers and good-time girls? The case files were left open. Even today all these killings are still officially unsolved.

In earlier years du Rose's reputation for solving murders quickly won him the nickname 'Four Day Johnny'. But he should have been renamed 'Four Year Johnny' after this failure because suddenly, four years after the Nude Murders squad was shut down, out came a story claiming that du Rose had caught Jack the Stripper after all. In 1969 an article inspired by him appeared in the People, claiming that 'the search for the killer is over': Jack the Stripper 'will never be brought to trial. He is dead. He committed suicide just a few hours before detectives . . . were to swoop on his home to arrest him'. So why has Scotland Yard 'allowed the world to assume that they failed in their search'?

> Because of a remarkable act of fairness and humanity that perhaps could only happen in this country, Jack the Stripper was just John, a quiet 'respectable man' in his forties, living in a quiet 'respectable' London suburb. To this day his wife and children do not know the secret of their loving, devoted father. They believe that his suicide was caused by worry and overwork.
>
> The police have accepted the role of 'failures' rather than allow that family to suspect that for years they were living with the most insanely perverted sex-killer of this century . . . In the fairness of British justice they can never accuse a man who cannot now defend himself.

The evidence was 'overwhelming', said this article, most significantly in that after 'John' committed suicide, no further murders occurred: 'When family man John "X" died, sex murderer Jack the Stripper died too.'

Because the *People* had changed any details which might have revealed the Stripper's identity to his family, no readers could judge if the evidence was 'overwhelming' or not. The article did say that 'traces of acetate used in paint-spraying' had been found in all the Stripper's victims. Police scientists then established that at least two of the bodies had been kept in a factory where paint was used. 'John "X" had access to that factory – alone and undisturbed. He must have known the net was closing when he learned that detectives had made a minute inspection of the garage where he kept his car. He did not wait for them to come for him. He killed himself and the nude murders came to an end.'

The *People* listed a lot of things that had allegedly occurred during the man's childhood and war service which 'all added up to a classic case of the repressed, brooding, sex criminal'. He was brought up in a 'gloomy household governed by "extreme puritanism"'; 'he was often beaten by his father for "pleasure-seeking" or forbidden "self-love"'; his mother was 'a thin-lipped humourless woman who nagged the father a lot'. Then the newspaper turned to a psychiatrist to pump out the usual stuff about why such a man might go to a prostitute, but 'once the woman had given him physical satisfaction, he would feel compelled to revenge himself on her for making him "sin"'.

No evidence was produced to back up this stuff, nothing to prove that John 'X' wasn't a figment of some copper's imagination. The article also contradicted itself. It claimed that checks on this man's movements over six years 'established that every one of the nude bodies could have been dumped on nights when John "X" was away from home'. The police could only have gathered such detailed information with the help of this man's wife, so how come she didn't realise they thought he was Jack the Stripper? If your husband commits suicide, you wouldn't expect to be asked if he was at home in a particular week six years earlier. Wouldn't you ask the police why they want to know?

An even vaguer account appeared in du Rose's autobiography, *Murder Was My Business*, published in 1971. He said that the conclusive paint shop connection emerged only when the Stripper's last victim was found on a factory estate right next to a paint spray shop. But then he says, 'it transpired eventually that the paint shop was purely incidental to the killing. It did not lead us to the killer, though he must have had some association with the estate.' In the meantime du Rose claimed he had reduced the suspects from twenty to three, but 'within a month of the murder the man I wanted to arrest took his own life. Without a shadow of a doubt the weight of our investigation and the enquiries that we had made about him led to the killer committing suicide . . . Faced with his death no positive evidence was available to prove or disprove our belief that he was the man we had been seeking. Because he was never arrested, or stood trial, he must be considered innocent and will therefore not be named . . . Without doubt, the killer's wife and relatives could have known nothing of the double-life of the man who was normal by day and Jack the Stripper by night. And their feelings count . . .'

So their feelings count, but not the feelings of the relatives of all the women he murdered. Or the feelings of the innocent men named as suspects by Scotland Yard. How could they be publicly fingered as serial sex-killers but the man himself cannot be named? Even today – and even if they are long dead – they can only be properly cleared when Jack the Stripper's true identity is revealed. The police have no right to sit on this information. Who was du Rose to make the decision to suppress what had cost the taxpayer millions to discover? And since when has Scotland Yard cared about anyone's feelings? Do the relatives of serial killers have special privileges?

Anyhow, what du Rose said in his book conflicts with what he told the *Sunday Times*. In June 1965 reporter Cal McCrystal quoted him as saying 'we are getting near', in a piece headlined, 'Police close in on the Nudes Murderer'. But this was three months *after* the date du Rose gave in his book for the suicide of his prime suspect. So did he make it all up? Did he invent the 'suicide paint stripper' to justify the Yard's failure to catch the real Stripper? Or even to protect that person and his reputation.

It's odd that none of the detectives who worked alongside du Rose ever publicly supported his account, but none of them dismissed it as nonsense either. It seems no other Nude Murders investigator has ever said a word. It's as if there has been a conspiracy of silence all these years. There's something funny going on here, as if this entire tale is a smokescreen to conceal a far worse truth.

In 1974 the *Daily Mirror* crime reporter Brian Mc Connell wrote a book, *Found Naked and Dead*, in which he transformed the John 'X' of the *People* article into 'Big John'. He told the same basic story but added a magic ingredient. Big John had been a policeman, a uniformed copper on the beat. But when he tried to become a detective he was turned down, on the grounds that 'he was too aggressive, too tactless on occasion, too plain-spoken at other times to investigate something complicated'. According to McConnell, Big John brooded on this setback. He took to complaining bitterly about a constable's duties: 'The subject of his most bitter, ferocious complaints was the nightly round-up of prostitutes. This mockery of the law, this gross wastage of a policeman's time, this endless procedure without hope of reforming the offenders, played on his mind.' Then, 'suddenly he left the police force'. He took a job as a guard with a security firm which hired him out to different factories. 'This enabled him to change his routine; his beat was wherever his firm sent him.' With no fixed place of work he could vary his movements to pick up prostitutes – all under five feet two – and kill them. He took his final victim, Bridie O'Hara, to the factory estate at Acton where had had access as a security guard. He kept the body in an electrical transformer station for a night or two, then dumped it a few feet away.

Big John went home. When his wife was out he wrote a note: 'I cannot go on . . .' He locked himself in the kitchen, fixed a tube to the coal gas supply, and killed himself. 'The inquest was not reported. There was no reason for a criminal investigation into the death of Big John. No one connected with the nude murders had any reason to probe his suicide' – until a constable went to check why his car number had been logged so often during those night-time checks. He made no confession: 'to safeguard the whole family face, he remained silent even in death'.

And yet, as McConnell says, 'in the absence of a confession, and a well-annotated declaration of guilt, there must be a degree of assumption'. That's one way of saying there was still no evidence that Big John was Jack the Stripper. And not every informed observer agreed.

Back in 1972 an article had been published in the *Sun* which directly challenged du Rose's version. The writer was another veteran crime reporter, Owen Summers, and the article was entitled 'Was the Maniac Killer a Cop?' He didn't mince his words. He said that it was wrong to assume du Rose's man was the Stripper simply because the murders ceased after he had killed himself. Rejecting that theory, Summers said that the real murderer did not kill himself, but has 'halted his killing spree only because he knew that a police net would surely have caught him if he had struck again. How? Because he may well have been a policeman, perhaps retired, who knew the area better than most men, and could have been in touch all along with the progress of the murder hunt.'

Summers went on: 'One thing is in no doubt. The killings were committed by a man with an unusually intimate knowledge of the area. The women, strangled, or asphyxiated, and stripped after death, were found in alleyways and little-frequented spots near the banks of the Thames. Who would know these out-of-the-way corners? A milkman? A postman? A taxi-driver? . . . Or a policeman?'

The policeman theory seemed even more attractive when Summers destroyed the du Rose version with these facts: his suicide suspect had been working in Scotland when at least one of the killings occurred; nothing in his car linked him with any of the dead women; none of their possessions were found in his South London home. There was no conclusive evidence linking him (or the premises he visited) with the paint markings found on four of the murdered women.

According to Summers, the real Stripper may have stopped killing specifically because he had found out about du Rose's scheme to 'set up an ambush involving hundreds of police. It would surely have trapped the killer had he made another move. Could the murderer have been aware of du Rose's secret plan? A policeman? This theory which no one wished to believe, grew in the calculations of many officers tracking the unknown killer. A chilling fact emerged . . . Each of the women was dumped in a different police sub-division – invisible boundaries which very few members of the public would know. Was it coincidence? Or was the killer trying to hamper the investigations of his own colleagues?'

Summers then came out with a devastating line about one direction those investigations had taken: 'Inquiries into the private lives of some officers still rest on secret files at Scotland Yard.'

He didn't name any policeman as Jack the Stripper. With around 24,000 male coppers in London, there were a lot to choose from. But, after all my trouble, especially being nominated as Jack the Stripper myself – and remembering what John Lloyd-Eley had told me: 'We do not know what Freddie Foreman has had his friend, Tom Butler, put on your criminal record' – you might forgive me if I explore one possibility. Might the policeman who was Jack the Stripper have been Tom Butler?

Bear with me as I go through a few facts.

Tom Butler knew Freddie Foreman well. He frequented Foreman's pub. Foreman said so in court while Butler was alive and Butler never challenged him. Recently Foreman has claimed he worked with Butler and Frank Williams as a middleman for the Great Train Robbers. Now this book should have made it clear that these relationships were corrupt and that Foreman was a valued and continual informer for both Williams and Butler. It's also clear that Foreman was a serial killer himself. That's not just my view. After 30 years in denial, Foreman himself has admitted to killing Ginger Marks and Frank Mitchell, and disposing of Jack 'the Hat' McVitie. But long before any of those murders his mob was called the Underworld Undertakers because lots of other South London villains knew that Foreman had killed other people already. Frank Williams covered up for Foreman over Ginger Marks (fingering me instead) and he blatantly misled his bosses over Frank Mitchell. If he knew Foreman was at best a double-killer, maybe Butler knew too. Maybe that didn't worry him.

Owen Summers believed the killer may have been a copper who 'could have been in touch all along with the progress of the murder hunt' and 'halted his killing spree only because he knew that a police net would surely have caught him if he had struck again'. Detective Chief Superintendent Butler certainly fell into that category. In July 1963, just before the Great Train Robbery, he switched from being deputy head of the Flying Squad to heading the CID throughout the Metropolitan Police No 1 District. This stretched from the West End and Soho right the way along the river to Richmond: the district that included all the places where the Stripper's victims worked as prostitutes and where five of the eight were found dead (the other three were found just outside the district in Ealing and Acton – two of them only yards across the dividing line).

Tom Butler also knew everyone on the special Scotland Yard committee or 'murder board' set up to catch the killer. When it met on 27 April 1964, it consisted of most of the Yard's top detectives plus the CID chiefs in the divisions where the bodies were found. The surprising thing is that Butler himself was not on the 'murder board'. By then he was chasing any Great Train Robbers still at large, but there was a bit of a lull at this time. All the original robbery defendants had been dealt with and their appeals would not be heard for months. And as head of the Flying Squad he could have made a valuable contribution to this board, because the killings might well have been directly linked to gangland. Many prostitutes are controlled or ponced off by gangsters. Also Butler was generally acclaimed as the Yard's greatest detective – and his preoccupation with the Great Train Robbers didn't stop him writing memos on the fate of Frank Mitchell in 1967.

Though Butler wasn't at this meeting, his closest colleague was – Chief Inspector Peter Vibart. They went back a long way. When Butler died in 1970 the *Daily Telegraph* said that when he and Vibart teamed up in the 1950s 'they became known in the underworld as the "terrible twins", they hunted and smashed Soho gangs and in 1958 they went to Cyprus where EOKA terrorism was at its height to examine British interrogation methods'. The obituary didn't mention an escapade in June 1956 when they went to Dublin to bring Bertie 'Battles' Rossi and Billy Blythe back to London to face trial for a knife and cosh attack on the deposed gangland boss, Jack 'Spot' Comer. A Dublin magistrate rejected the warrants on which Rossi and Blythe were to be handed to the Yard men and he ordered their release. To get round this, Butler and Vibart snatched Rossi and Blythe off the street, smuggled them out of the Irish Republic into Belfast and flew them back to London. But later admitted that he and Vibart had thwarted the will of the Irish court but this didn't worry the judge at the Old Bailey. He gave Rossi four years and Blythe five, even though they were only in court because Butler and Vibart kidnapped them from a friendly foreign country.

Nipper Read later wrote that Butler 'had the greatest rapport' with Vibart, so it seems to me that whatever Butler wanted to know about the 'murder board' he would have found out. Unless, of course, Vibart was one of those 'certain senior police officers' who, according to Owen Summers, believed Jack the Stripper was a cop.

As I check out the sequence of events during the mid-1960s – listing the big things that happened in my own life alongside Butler's hunt for the Great Train Robbers and the dates when Jack the Stripper struck – I recall that it was in December 1964 that Johnny Tilley gave me the key to Butler's safe so I could steal that £36,000 of train robbers' money that Butler hadn't declared. As I explained in Chapter Eight, Johnny Tilley had got the key from Butler's deputy, Superintendent Bob Anderson, but when he told me to 'get it done quickly', I became suspicious.

> I said, 'Why? What's the rush? If Butler doesn't know that someone's planning to nick it off him, he'll just keep the 36 grand there . . .'
> 'No,' said Johnny, 'there's something going on. They're keeping an eye on Butler', and he indicated some sort of observation, not over his handling of the Great Train Robbery round-up but over some other aspect of his behaviour, maybe something in his private life. Anderson may have seen some papers he shouldn't have seen, and that's how he knew Butler was in some sort of trouble . . . So this is the proposition: Butler might get lifted any time, so the money had to be nicked 'quickly' or not at all.

Is it possible that Anderson told Johnny to tell me to nick the 36 grand quickly because Butler was about to get lifted for the Nude Murders? Not so unlikely, perhaps, because it was only a week earlier, on 25 November, that Jack the Stripper had struck again, dumping the body of Margaret McGowan in a car park just off Kensington High Street. And not so unlikely when that was yet another week when a Sunday newspaper ran a front-page lead headlined 'Net tightens on nude killer'.

Hold on, you may be thinking: this stuff is so circumstantial that it's just a wild theory tied in with a few coincidences, all put together by a villain bent on revenge. But the coincidences keep piling up. Look at Summers' line that the Stripper may well have been a policeman who 'knew the area better than most men', and that he must have had 'an unusually intimate knowledge of the area' because most of the women 'were found in alleyways and little-frequented spots near the banks of the Thames'.

This description fitted Tom Butler like a glove. According to the *News of the World*, he was 'born in the back streets of London's Shepherd's Bush', very near the central point for all these murders. He joined the police in 1934 and served in the East End but also as a sergeant in Paddington – where lots of prostitutes worked – before joining the Flying Squad.

And where did Butler live? In Washington Road, Barnes – less than half a mile from the River Thames, practically right on the towpath. Even more of a coincidence, Washington Road is within a finger of land that has the meandering Thames on three sides. And Washington Road is less than a mile from where the first four of the eight nude murder victims were found.

Again, you might say, how terrible to accuse a dead policeman of being Jack the Stripper, when he can't sue and his children will be shocked at the mere idea. But Tom Butler never married. He had no children. He had lived in the same house from 1934 right up until his death in 1970, for the last 33 years alone with his mother, Rose. When he died aged 57 from lung cancer, she was over 90 and survived him.

Strangely enough, at the end of April 1964 an article appeared in the *Daily Express* saying that all London police had been ordered to trace 'The Solicitor' – 'a mystery man who has appeared on the fringe' of all five murders that had occurred by then. A senior detective had compared statements made by a lot of prostitutes during the investigation. They all referred to a man who said he was a solicitor with independent means. 'The police had a sheet of pale blue writing paper on which the man listed what he always required of the women, always for the same fee: £40 . . . He has mentioned that he is unmarried and lives with his mother. He is small and balding, aged between 45 and 50, and prefers the company of small women. None of the dead nudes was taller than five feet one.'

Sounds like a 'dead ringer' for Tommy Butler: balding, not tall ('slight' is how some newspapers describe him), 46 when the first victim died, 51 when this article was written.

All right, you may be saying, but this is a long way from proving Butler was Jack the Stripper. Was he really the sort of man who would go out at night and kill women? Surely he couldn't have done that sort of thing when he was in charge of dozens of officers, perpetually in the company of men who are, by nature and training, deeply suspicious?

Several famous detectives have written memoirs in which they describe their colleague Tommy Butler in none too flattering terms. In his book *Nipper*, Nipper Read says that 'people had enormous affection for Tommy because, on the face of it, he was such a lovely man. He had a good sense of humour and a nice attitude. The police and detection were his only obsessions.' Then Read changes course: 'But in one way Tommy Butler was the worst detective I've ever come across. He was so secretive. He was a great investigator . . . but really opening up and having a conference saying, "Listen, chaps, this is what it's all about", would have been as alien as cutting his throat. He was obsessed by security. He would never tell his men what was happening where or when . . . Occasionally he would join his team for a drink, but it was only occasionally. He was a very private man and no one was every really close to him. Unmarried, he lived with his mother, but home was really the CID office . . . he spent every evening typing in his room upstairs at Paddington. Downstairs we could hear the tapping of the machine. No one knew what he was doing.'

In *Slipper of the Yard* another famous detective, Jack Slipper, who worked with Butler on the Great Train Robbery inquiry, also recalls him as a dedicated, traditional detective, but his pattern of working did not fit in well with other people's. 'Often you'd see him at night, with his sleeves rolled up, typing out his own reports . . . the night was his best time. He never came in early in the morning, but if he did it was best to keep out of his way. Often, if you passed him in the morning he'd walk right by you, or he might just growl at you.' Jack Slipper then really opens up about the 'Grey Fox', as he was nicknamed. 'He had quite a few odd habits, but one in particular was the way he liked to go home at night. Late in the evening, he'd sometimes go down to the Red Lion, a pub just near the Yard, for a drink before going home . . . He wasn't much of a drinker, and by Squad standards you could say he didn't really drink at all! He didn't smoke either but he would drop into the pub occasionally to be sociable . . . Then, if he'd sent his driver off earlier, he'd take a lift with whoever was last on duty. He was a single man and he lived in with his mother in a little house near Hammersmith Bridge . . . Tommy would always insist on being dropped off away from the house. It didn't matter whether you'd known him for a few weeks or 15 years. He would never go home with another policeman or be seen being dropped off in a police car. He never said why, but he'd walk the last half mile, even if it was raining, just to keep the squad car away from his home.'

Slipper comes out with an interesting aside on Detective Inspector Frank Williams: 'a very quiet man who was always deep in thought. His speciality was dealing with informants and I don't think I've ever come across anyone who was better at it.' I agree with all that. One of Williams's best informants was Freddie Foreman.

If you read between the lines of Williams's own book on the train robbers, *No Fixed Address*, it's clear that Foreman was the middleman in deals relating to the robbery. Williams says that his 'knowledge of those involved, stemming from service as a junior officer in South London, was to become so valuable that I would be able . . . to convince one of the robbers [Buster Edwards] to surrender himself and persuade others to return some of the stolen money'.

Williams's view of Tommy Butler was far more hostile than Nipper Read's or Jack Slipper's. He said that Butler was 'over-secretive, played everything close to his chest, was autocratic and delegated work reluctantly and only sparingly . . . This attitude was completely one-way. He was continually pressing me to keep in close touch with my informants and contacts.' Then Williams comes up with a most odd statement. He says he went to Butler to discuss an offer to surrender a further £30,000 but Butler was sceptical. 'I do not know why he . . . was so reluctant to seize on any opportunity of catching one of them or of getting more of the stolen cash back.'

He also comments on one of Butler's weirdest habits: 'He became so obsessed that as time went on he even spent his holidays on the beaches touring the South of France, parading up and down with binoculars and photographs, scanning the sun-bathing crowds through the glasses in the hope of spotting one of the missing robbers (he particularly favoured the view that they were on the Riviera).'

In fact, Butler's trips to Riviera beaches got him into serious trouble. The sight of a balding, hawk-nosed Englishman spending hours with his binoculars focused on crowds of scantily clad bathers inevitably aroused suspicions. So much so that police at Juan-les-Pins arrested him as a Peeping Tom. He only escaped being put on trial by producing his Scotland Yard warrant card. As he neared retirement, several newspapers referred to this incident, but only as proof of his obsessive dedication to capturing the likes of Bruce Reynolds (who really did spend time at Saint Tropez). But on this evidence who can be sure that Butler wasn't a Peeping Tom, a pervert, a dirty old man who might resort to using prostitutes to release his sexual urges and then feel so guilt-ridden that he could go as far as strangling them? A man who, even after a late night's work, would never be dropped off at home, who always preferred to be left by Hammersmith Bridge, right by the river and the towpath where the first four murder victims were found?

It's all circumstantial, of course, but when you read about the psychological profiling techniques that police use nowadays – as reproduced in *Cracker*, *Prime Suspect* and so many other TV crime dramas – then all the facts laid out here would certainly earn Tommy Butler at least a heavy grilling and a night in the cells. There's also a point at which Butler certainly would have been questioned: when police interviewed 120,000 men caught up in the car number check. It's possible that Butler didn't own a car but he certainly drove – up and down to Aylesbury during the Great Train Robbery inquiry in a rented Mini, like a maniac, according to Jack Slipper. And surely he would have had a car of his own, if only to drive his old mother around at weekends. But, of course, if he did happen to get caught up in that car number check, it's likely that someone on the Nude murders team made the specific decision not to question him.

Let's recap. Butler lived within a mile of where four of the bodies were found, within two miles of two others, and within three miles of the other two. He had been born and he grew up in the heart of this territory. As a young copper he had pounded its streets. As a painstaking and brilliant detective, he would have known all the tricks needed to defeat other detectives, most of them far less gifted than he was. As head of CID for that whole Thames-side area, and later as head of the Flying Squad, he would have known every twist of the Nude Murders inquiry, every night's allocation of manpower, where any road blocks might be. He could ask any questions and see any reports because he was a copper above suspicion. That way he would have been able to anticipate and thwart his colleagues' every move.

His psychological profile has all the necessary hallmarks: unmarried, had always lived with his mother, ultra-obsessive in his work, a loner, found it difficult to socialise, nocturnal in habit, childlike in some ways (westerns were his favourite films), sexually repressed. He had a steady 'lady friend' but never married. And he was arrested for being a Peeping Tom. One other thing. I'm not privy to his diaries or career records, but it seems that when each of the murders took place, he could have been in London – not off on one of his long-distance trips to catch a train robber.

Add all this together and there was far more reason to suspect Butler of being Jack the Stripper than Kenneth Archibald, the fool they put on trial just because he'd made a fantasy confession. And far, far more than me – the owner of the House of Peacocks – whatever my criminal record. To give a 21st-century comparison, there is more evidence for believing that Tom Butler was Jack the Stripper than for believing Barry George killed Jill

Dando. Wasn't Barry George demonised as an obsessive loner? Every bit of evidence against him was circumstantial – including how close he lived to the murder scene – and yet he's been jailed for life.

People might say that all this overlooks the practicalities. That Butler couldn't possibly have picked up all these girls, taken them somewhere to have sex, strangled them, stored their bodies for days and then dumped each one so quietly that nobody ever saw him do it. That's probably true. But how do we know that Jack the Stripper was only one man? Why has everyone always assumed that he was working alone? Why couldn't he have been working with someone else? Isn't that far more likely? Or several other people? Some cult, a circle of people who practised ritual slaughter? Anything is possible. Yet it seems that all the detectives on the case automatically assumed that the killings were done by a single man.

We do know of one other serial killer at work in London in the 1960s. Fred Foreman. What's more, according to Albert Donoghue and Micky Englefield, he didn't just kill people, he took out their brains and measured them – like he did with Frank Mitchell. As Donoghue told the Old Bailey, 'they must have cut the body up because Foreman described Mitchell's heart as ripped and burst, and he cupped his hands and said, "It is surprising how small his brain was for a big man like that."'

Maybe that's the kind of thing Butler really had in common with Foreman. By now it's pretty clear that Williams took cash bribes from Foreman out of the Great Train Robbers' money, bribes that Butler may have known about and shared. But it seems Butler wasn't interested in money. He lived a very humble life, so some nights he could easily have spared £40 for prostitutes, just like 'the Solicitor' with independent means. Pay-offs from Foreman would have come in handy for that. Crime can bring the oddest people together. Don't forget: the gangster Ronnie Kray and the politician Lord Boothby used to share the same very young men.

If you still think all this is farfetched, you may be right. But on 15 February 1965 I woke up to find that I was accused of being Jack the Stripper. That newspaper had linked me – the owner of the House of Peacocks – to the Nude Murders. The only people with an interest in planting that story were Fred Foreman and his mob. But why would Foreman have chosen those crimes to smear me with? Maybe because he knew a lot about them himself. He used his police pals to plant the idea that I had killed Ginger Marks when he had done it himself. So perhaps he smeared me as Jack the Stripper to take the heat of his pal Tommy Butler, to get them off the hook and destroy me at the same time.

Remember the old saying: birds of a feather flock together.

Oh, and here's an offer.

I shall give any policeman, serving or retired, £50,000 if he can come forward with proof that I have ever helped the police in any way at all. I've done them a lot of harm and they'd done me a lot of harm, but I've never helped them. Freddie Foreman has called me a grass but the truth is that he's the grass.

There are two kinds of people in the world of crime. You've got your contenders and you've got your pretenders. Freddie Foreman was a pretender, the kind of person who overestimates himself and underestimates everybody else. But I'm still around. I ain't going anywhere. So, if you don't like what I've said about you in this book, you have two choices: sue me or see me.

THE SURVIVOR

POSTSCRIPT

The Secret State of Scotland Yard

By Martin Short

IN April 2001 I wrote to the Records Management Branch of the Metropolitan Police requesting the release of all records concerning the Hammersmith 'Nude Murders' and the murder of Thomas 'Ginger' Marks. All these crimes are still formally 'unsolved' so Scotland Yard's original files and papers should still exist and I felt it was time for them to be opened up for public scrutiny through the Public Record Office.

Under the 'Thirty Year Rule' a lot of material from the same era of London gangland is already open, including highly revelatory papers from the investigation into the murder of Frank Mitchell, which is also 'unsolved'. The final Nude Murder was committed 22 months before the Mitchell slaying. Ginger Marks had been killed even earlier – by Freddie Foreman, who has since owned up to killing Mitchell. Surely, I reasoned, if the process governing the release of such archives has any logic, the files on all these nine murders should have been made public before the Mitchell files.

That would make sense, and yet, even as I was making my request, I felt it was doomed to fail.

It took one year and three months for the Metropolitan Police to make a decision. Even then, it came to me in a letter mysteriously addressed to a Mr Seabrook. I wish this Mr Seabrook well and sympathise with him as he may well have received a letter in the name of Mr Short.

My pessimism was justified, for when this response finally arrived, it boiled down to a complete rejection. Here are its main points.

• It will not be possible to release either of the records you have requested at this time. The rationale behind this decision is based on the necessity to ensure that any possible future prosecutions, no matter how unlikely such eventualities might seem, are not compromised by the release of the records into the public domain. In view of this it will be necessary to keep the records closed at least until such time as any hypothetical suspect for the crimes would be past the age where prosecution is an option, usually 85 years of age.

• Unfortunately, in order to comply with this policy it has been necessary to increase the closure period in the case of the 'Ginger' Marks record [previously 2017]. With regard to the 'Nude' murders records, it allows us no scope to reduce the existing closure date. You will appreciate the need to balance the right of the public to access records with the requirement to protect the confidentiality of information that one day might be used in a prosecution.

• In addition, there are a number of personal sensitivity issues that further impacts on when we can release [these records] for public inspection. In the case of 'Ginger' Marks, there is personally sensitive information concerning the mental health of named individuals, the sexuality of another named individual and unsubstantiated criminal allegations of a serious nature, the release of any of which risks causing substantial distress. There are other instances of personally sensitive information.

• With regard to the 'Nude' murders, there is, once again, a host of 'personal sensitivity issues relating to named individuals'. [They] revolve around the sexual activities of named persons and the identities of prostitutes. In order to protect these named individuals we are obliged to withhold this information for a period of time commensurate with a life expectancy of 100 years.

• In order to comply with the above prerequisites it is necessary to increase closure of the 'Ginger' Marks record until 2037 and retain the existing closure period in respect of the 'Nude' murders record which varies between 2065 and 2086.

So, far from gaining access to the Ginger Marks papers by my request, I had merely provoked the system into hiding them for another 20 years – when I (if still alive) will be 93 and Jimmy Evans 106. As for the crimes of Jack the Stripper, both of us will have been dead for decades before the public can know whether Scotland Yard had any idea who he was (or they were).

These decisions are ridiculous. In the case of Ginger Marks, Freddie Foreman has now publicly boasted that he shot him dead, therefore keeping the files closed – indeed prolonging their closure from 2017 until 2037 – brings the entire system into disrepute. This decision appears to protect no-one except the murderer, Foreman, and his two main accomplices, Callaghan and Gerard, both of whom are dead.

The official response states that decisions not to release papers are taken so as not to compromise 'any possible future prosecutions, no matter how unlikely such eventualities might seem'. But no such prosecution will ever take place over Marks, for back in 1975 Foreman was acquitted of this murder, therefore he enjoys the protection of the 'double jeopardy' principle: he cannot be tried twice for the same offence. And even if that ancient civil liberty is swept away in forthcoming legal reforms, Foreman can still evade trial by simply denying his own confession. As he has made it merely in a book and on television, in law it does not amount to conclusive proof of his guilt. He has not sworn it on oath so he cannot even be charged with perjury for having testified in court that he did not kill Marks. During that trial the only eye-witness, Jimmy Evans, himself confessed to having committed perjury ten years earlier during his trial for shooting Freddie Foreman's brother, George. For all these reasons Freddie will never be tried again for killing Ginger Marks.

Besides, he has also confessed to killing Frank Mitchell – another murder for which he has been acquitted – yet the police and prosecution papers for that crime are already open at the Public Record Office. Where is the logic in that? Does this mean Scotland Yard still has a theoretical notion that Foreman may still be prosecuted for killing Marks but not for killing Mitchell?

You don't have to be a conspiracy theorist to suspect that, while the Records Management staff operate with integrity, other people in Scotland Yard have dishonourable reasons for sealing the Marks files until 2037: perhaps to suppress materials indicating that Freddie Foreman was a police informer and to protect the reputation of his Yard handlers, Frank Williams and Tommy Butler, who, by shielding Foreman, were accessories after the fact of Marks's murder.

Similarly, the decision to suppress the Nude Murder files until 2065 or even 2086 can have nothing to do with possible future prosecutions, for none will ever occur: not 40 years on from these dreadful crimes. As for the defence that these files raise 'personally sensitivity issues relating to the sexual activities of named persons and the identities of prostitutes', this is stating the obvious. All the victims were known prostitutes therefore the files must contain information and/or speculation on the sexual activities of any suspect.

And if there is a need to protect named individuals for a period 'commensurate with a life expectancy of 100 years', those same records surely state these people's ages and even their dates of birth when they fell under suspicion. Thus today Metropolitan Police archivists would have no difficulty in calculating when the suspects would reach 100. If we assume that the killer(s) had to be at least 20 years old at the time of the last killing none would be 100 later than 2045. Indeed, by checking nationwide registrations of deaths, they would rapidly discover that many of these suspects are already dead. For instance, by 2002, any suspect who was already 40 in 1964, when five of the murders were committed, would have reached at least 78. This is an unlikely age for anyone cursed with such a mania. Besides, in the intervening 38 years that person would surely have killed again, unless he had died himself.

In short, there can be little doubt that 'Jack the Stripper' – whether he acted alone or with others – is long dead, therefore the continuing suppression of these files in their entirety is unnecessary. If innocent people were logged as suspects, people such as Jimmy Evans, the files can be weeded to protect them or their reputations. Not that Jimmy wants his name weeded out – on the contrary, he wants to know who nominated him for this grotesque role – but it is surely not beyond the skills of Scotland Yard's archivists to exclude materials which would cause gratuitous distress to the manifestly innocent or their surviving relatives.

Again, the suspicion arises that these files are being suppressed not to safeguard the integrity of a future trial or to protect the innocent but to shield the reputation of Scotland Yard itself. When this book came out in hardback, the Yard appeared to be shocked by the revelation that its own most famous detective of the day, Tommy Butler, was a prime suspect for the Nude Murders. Anonymous press officers were quoted as saying, 'We never comment on speculation in a book': not the resounding denial they would have issued if the claim was untrue. As Jimmy Evans comments, 'If we had said some ordinary bloke was Jack the Stripper, they would have investigated him straightaway. As we say it was a copper, they've done nothing. They always protect their own.'

THE SOHO DON
Gangland's Greatest Untold Story
Michael Connor

ISBN 1 84018 599 6
October
£15.99 (hardback)
234 x 156mm
224pp
1 x 8pp colour & b/w

The Soho Don is the explosive biography of a shy, well-spoken South London boy from a respectable family who became a shadowy but powerful figure in the Soho underworld.

The protection business drew Billy Howard into a lucrative world of nightclubs and gambling on the back of the post-Second World War black market trade. A former boxer in the army, he was capable of meting out punishment to villains who stepped out of line and instilled terror in those prepared to speak out against him. *The Soho Don* illustrates the extent of Howard's influence in the Soho of the 1950s and '60s before detailing his subsequent slide from power and, finally, his pathetic death in 1984.

Michael Connor is a writer and journalist and has contributed to numerous publications including *The Guardian, GQ, Catering and Hotelkeeper* and *Now*.

IN SEARCH OF PIRATES
A Modern-Day Odyssey in the South China Sea
Robert Stuart

ISBN 1 84018 569 4
Now available
£15.99 (hardback)
234 x 156mm
224pp
1x 8pp colour

'Pirates have come a long way since the days of the cutlass
and galleon. Now they use high-speed launches, AK47s –
and they're making the South China Sea the most dangerous
place in the world for shipping . . .'

Instances of piracy have risen dramatically in the South
China Sea in recent years. The hundreds of ships
which pass through the narrow straits of Malacca and
Singapore often prove an irresistible temptation to the
poverty-stricken inhabitants of the coastal villages –
and the anonymous bosses in Singapore who
coordinate the pirate gangs. In search of the story
behind the statistics, Robert Stuart spent three years
tirelessly tracking down some of the most ruthless and
dangerous criminals in South Asia. In this true
modern-day tale of romance on the high seas he
presents a vivid account of his quest and gives a
fascinating insight into present-day piracy.

Robert Stuart divides his time between freelance
journalism and television.

GANGSTER

The Inside Story on John Gilligan, his Drugs Empire & the Murder of Journalist Veronica Guerin

John Mooney

ISBN 1 903813 02 6
Now available
£7.99 (paperback)
198 x 129mm
208pp

In 1996 the Irish journalist Veronica Guerin was assassinated because of her unwanted investigations into organised crime. *Gangster* is the story of her murder and of the man charged with her killing. Chronicling Gilligan's underworld regime and including interviews with police, anti-drugs activists, paramilitary organisations and more, this unnerving book portrays a culture that silences freedom of speech by killing.

John Mooney is an investigative journalist and works as a consultant for newspaper and television companies.

MILESTONES IN MURDER
Defining Moments in Ulster's Terror War
Hugh Jordan

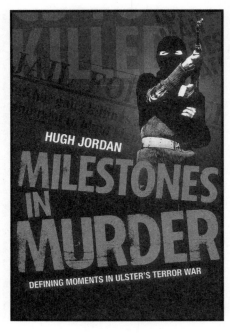

ISBN 1 84018 640 2
October
£9.99 (paperback)
234 x 156mm
224pp
1 x 8pp colour & b/w

Beginning with the death of legendary IRA figure Sean South of Garryowen on New Year's Day 1957, *Milestones in Murder* details the background to what we have now come to call 'the Troubles' in Northern Ireland and paints vivid portraits of the major players in the conflict. It examines the killings which marked new lows in the republican/loyalist terror war and discloses aspects of certain killings that have remained unknown until now. *Milestones in Murder* is an extensive, revealing and gripping account of the crimes that have been committed during the long-running conflict in Northern Ireland.

Hugh Jordan has worked for over ten years as a senior crime reporter with the *Sunday World* – Ireland's biggest-selling Sunday newspaper. He has been responsible for breaking some of the biggest exposés in the country, naming top drug dealers and paramilitary godfathers.

BOTH SIDES OF THE FENCE
A Life Undercover
David Corbett

ISBN 1 84018 195 8
October
£9.99 (paperback)
234 x 156mm
208pp

As one of a handful of UK police officers trained by the SAS in deep-cover surveillance, David Corbett infiltrated the toughest communities, living among junkies, prostitutes, murderers and firearm dealers, in order to gather evidence that would lead to dozens of convictions. Trained in urban and rural surveillance by the Scottish Crime Squad, he invented a fictional past for himself and put his life on the line. One false move and his cover could have been blown.

Both Sides of the Fence reveals Corbett's gripping story of life in the perilous world of the undercover police, before he was betrayed by the force that sent him out there in the first place.

THE FILTH
The Explosive Inside Story of Scotland Yard's Top Undercover Cop

Duncan MacLaughlin with William Hall

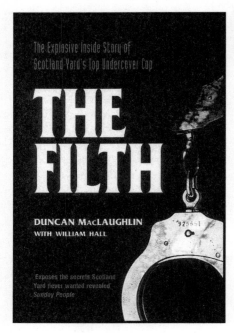

ISBN 1 84018 669 0
October
£7.99 (paperback)
198 x 129mm
256pp

For the first time ever, a senior detective and undercover agent in the Drug Squad and Regional Crime Squad – Britain's equivalent of the FBI – reveals the stark truth about life in the force. SAS-trained for special missions, Duncan MacLaughlin was an expert in surveillance and undercover work that could have got him killed. The dangerous tightrope he walked included cases involving master criminal Kenneth Noye, kidnap victim Julie Dart and the slaying of PC Keith Blakelock. Told with black humour and fascinating investigative detail, MacLaughlin's story is a riveting insight into the world of serious crime.

William Hall is a celebrated writer, broadcaster, film critic and showbusiness journalist. His work includes *Raising Caine*, the critically acclaimed biography of Michael Caine.

'Exposes the secrets Scotland Yard never wanted revealed'
Sunday People